W9-BLP-480

ANNUAL EDITIONS

Technologies, Social Media, and Society 13/14

Nineteenth Edition

EDITOR

Daniel Mittleman, PhD.
DePaul University, College of Computing and Digital Media

Daniel Mittleman is an Associate Professor in the College of Computing and Digital Media at DePaul University. He teaches coursework in virtual collaboration, user-focused web design, and social impact of technology. Dr. Mittleman's research is in collaboration engineering, focusing on the design of team processes, software, and physical environment to support virtual work. His work experience includes several years providing IT systems support at Ticketmaster Corporation, as well as consulting projects with several Fortune 500 corporations and federal government agencies.

McGraw Hill
Connect Learn Succeed™

The McGraw·Hill Companies

Connect
Learn
Succeed™

ANNUAL EDITIONS: TECHNOLOGIES, SOCIAL MEDIA, AND SOCIETY,
NINETEENTH EDITION

Published by McGraw-Hill, a business unit of The McGraw-Hill Companies, Inc., 1221 Avenue
of the Americas, New York, NY 10020. Copyright © 2014 by The McGraw-Hill Companies, Inc.
All rights reserved. Printed in the United States of America. Previous edition(s) © 2013, 2012, and
2011. No part of this publication may be reproduced or distributed in any form or by any means,
or stored in a database or retrieval system, without the prior written consent of The McGraw-
Hill Companies, Inc., including, but not limited to, in any network or other electronic storage or
transmission, or broadcast for distance learning.

Some ancillaries, including electronic and print components, may not be available to customers
outside the United States.

This book is printed on acid-free paper.

Annual Editions® is a registered trademark of the McGraw-Hill Companies, Inc.
Annual Editions is published by the **Contemporary Learning Series** group within the
McGraw-Hill Higher Education division.

1 2 3 4 5 6 7 8 9 0 QDB/QDB 1 0 9 8 7 6 5 4 3

ISBN: 978-0-07-352877-9
MHID: 0-07-352877-3
ISSN: 1094-2629 (print)
ISSN: 2159-1024 (online)

Acquisitions Editor: *Joan L. McNamara*
Marketing Director: *Adam Kloza*
Marketing Manager: *Nathan Edwards*
Senior Developmental Editor: *Dave Welsh*
Senior Project Manager: *Joyce Watters*
Buyer: *Nichole Birkenholz*
Cover Designer: *Studio Montage, St. Louis, MO*
Content Licensing Specialist: *Beth Thole*
Media Project Manager: *Sridevi Palani*

Compositor: Laserwords Private Limited
Cover Image Credits: Purestock/SuperStock (inset), McGraw-Hill Companies, Inc. Mark Dierker,
photographer (background)

www.mhhe.com

Editors/Academic Advisory Board

Members of the Academic Advisory Board are instrumental in the final selection of articles for each edition of ANNUAL EDITIONS. Their review of articles for content, level, and appropriateness provides critical direction to the editors and staff. We think that you will find their careful consideration well reflected in this volume.

ANNUAL EDITIONS: Technologies, Social Media, and Society 13/14
19th Edition

EDITOR

Daniel Mittleman
DePaul University, College of Computing and Digital Media

ACADEMIC ADVISORY BOARD MEMBERS

Ghassan Alkadi
Southeastern Louisiana University

David Allen
Temple University

James Barnard
Embry-Riddle Aeronautical University–Worldwide

Peggy Batchelor
Furman University

Beverly Bohn
Park University

Maria I. Bryant
College of Southern Maryland

Cliff Cockerham
School of Community Health and Public Services at Whites Creek

Arthur I. Cyr
Carthage College

Peter A. Danielson
University of British Columbia

Michael J. Day
Northern Illinois University

Therese DonGiovanni O'Neil
Indiana University of Pennsylvania

Kenneth Fidel
DePaul University

Laura Finnerty Paul
Skidmore College

Norman Garrett
Eastern Illinois University

David C. Gibbs
University of Wisconsin–Stevens Point

Kenton Graviss
Indiana University–Southeast

Keith Harman
Oklahoma Baptist University

Dava James
Marshalltown Community College

Malynnda A. Johnson
Carroll University

Patricia A. Joseph
Slippery Rock University

John Karayan
Woodbury University

Donna Kastner
California State University–Fullerton

Edward Kisailus
Canisius College

Eugene J. Kozminski
Aquinas College

Christine Kukla
North Central College

Richard A. Lejk
University of North Carolina–Charlotte

Xiangdong Li
NYC College of Technology

David Little
High Point University

Michael Martel
Ohio University

Marc D. Miller
University of New Hampshire

Ottis L. Murray
University of North Carolina, Pembroke

Gail Niklason
Weber State College

Morris Pondfield
Towson University

Scott Rader
University of St. Thomas, Opus College of Business

Ramona R. Santa Maria
Buffalo State College (SUNY)

Thomas Schunk
SUNY Orange County

Keith Stearns
University of Wisconsin–Eau Claire

Ronald Thomas
Embry Riddle Aeronautical University–Daytona Beach

Edwin Tjoe
St. John's University

Zeynep Tufekci
University of Maryland, Baltimore County

Lawrence E. Turner
Southwestern Adventist University

Lih-Ching Chen Wang
Cleveland State University

Caroline Shaffer Westerhof
California National University

Fred Westfall
Troy University

Rene Weston-Eborn
Weber State College

Nathan White
McKendree University

Preface

In publishing ANNUAL EDITIONS we recognize the enormous role played by the magazines, newspapers, and journals of the public press in providing current, first-rate educational information in a broad spectrum of interest areas. Many of these articles are appropriate for students, researchers, and professionals seeking accurate, current material to help bridge the gap between principles and theories and the real world. These articles, however, become more useful for study when those of lasting value are carefully collected, organized, indexed, and reproduced in a low-cost format, which provides easy and permanent access when the material is needed. That is the role played by ANNUAL EDITIONS.

A Note to the Reader

In vetting articles for *Technologies, Social Media, and Society* from the sea of contenders, I have tried to continue in the tradition of the previous editors. The writers are journalists, computer scientists, lawyers, economists, policy analysts, and academics, the kinds of professions you would expect to find represented in a collection on the social implications of computing. They write for newspapers, business and general circulation magazines, academic journals, professional publications, and more and more for websites. Their writing is mostly free from both the unintelligible jargon and the breathless enthusiasm that prevents people from forming clear ideas about computing and social media policy. This is by design, of course, and I hope that after reading the selections you agree.

Annual Editions: Technologies, Social Media, and Society is organized around important dimensions of society rather than of computing. This book's major themes are the economy, community, politics considered broadly, and the balance of the risk and reward of new technology. The introduction begins the conversation with an article by the late Neil Postman that provides us with a five point model that can be used to frame a conversation about most every article that follows.

The Units are organized to lead us through several of the critical issues of our day. You may notice that many of these issues (outsourcing, telecommuting, causes of unemployment, women in the workplace, intellectual property, freedom of speech, as examples) only tangentially seem to be technology or social media issues. This too is by design and serves as evidence for how intertwined technology policy has become with other social and economic policy decisions in the world today.

We are living during a very exciting time, probably comparable to the twenty-five or so years that followed the invention of Guttenberg's printing press. The principal modes for communication and collaboration in our society are changing faster than we know how to make public policy or evolve culture to deal with it. As such, business models, property rules, international treaty rules, and a myriad of other economic and social norms are experiencing evolution and revolution, often with unanticipated or controversial outcomes. At the same time, these technological advances are empowering masses of people around the world who just a generation ago had little or no access to real opportunity. And technological advances are making available incredible new gains in medicine and productivity.

A word of caution. Each article has been selected because it is topical, interesting, and (insofar as the form permits) nicely written. To say that an article is interesting or well-written, however, does not mean that it is right. This is as true of both the facts presented in each article and the point of view of the author. I hope you will approach these articles as you might a good discussion among friends. You may not agree with all opinions, but you will come away nudged in one direction or another by reasoned arguments, holding a richer, more informed view of important issues.

This book includes several features I hope will be helpful to students and professionals. A topic guide lists each key issue and the articles that explore that issue. I have included study questions after each article. Though some of the questions can be answered from within the article, many more invite further investigation, in essence, your own contributions. The articles I've gathered for this volume along with the questions that follow are intended to get the discussion flowing, not to provide definitive answers to anything.

We want *Annual Editions: Technologies, Social Media, and Society* to help you participate more fully in some of the most important discussions of the time: those about the promises and risks engendered by new developments in information technology and social media.

A Note to Instructors

McGraw-Hill hosts a *faculty only* website at http://iteach-socialmedia.com. While adoption of this book is expressly not required for site membership (and we encourage those of you simply reviewing this book to join), you will find the site organized to fit the Unit structure of this Annual Editions reader with materials more current than a book publication schedule permits, additional thought questions for your students, and insights others have gleaned from teaching with this material. We hope these materials, support, and conversation will enhance your classroom planning and delivery.

We invite you to provide feedback to the editor (at danny@cdm.depaul.edu) and to the editorial team at McGraw-Hill. We invite suggestions and recommendations of new articles for inclusion in next year's edition of this reader. In addition, I encourage all adopting instructors to drop me a note as I would love to know who is using this reader and what I might do to make your teaching a more enjoyable and productive effort.

A Note of Transition

This is my first year as editor of *Annual Editions: Technologies, Social Media, and Society,* assuming the reins from Paul De Palma who expertly edited this reader for nine years. While I used *Technologies, Social Media, and Society* in my own courses many times over the past decade, it was not until I read the material with an editor's eye that I fully appreciated the care and detail Paul put into this series. In this year of transition you will find that many of his words remain interspersed among mine on these pages. It is with a debt of gratitude for the head start—and tall shoes—he has left me that I take on this endeavor.

Daniel Mittleman,
Editor

The Annual Editions Series

VOLUMES AVAILABLE

Adolescent Psychology

Aging

American Foreign Policy

American Government

Anthropology

Archaeology

Assessment and Evaluation

Business Ethics

Child Growth and Development

Comparative Politics

Criminal Justice

Developing World

Drugs, Society, and Behavior

Dying, Death, and Bereavement

Early Childhood Education

Economics

Educating Children with Exceptionalities

Education

Educational Psychology

Entrepreneurship

Environment

The Family

Gender

Geography

Global Issues

Health

Homeland Security

Human Development

Human Resources

Human Sexualities

International Business

Management

Marketing

Mass Media

Microbiology

Multicultural Education

Nursing

Nutrition

Physical Anthropology

Psychology

Race and Ethnic Relations

Social Problems

Sociology

State and Local Government

Sustainability

Technologies, Social Media, and Society

United States History, Volume 1

United States History, Volume 2

Urban Society

Violence and Terrorism

Western Civilization, Volume 1

World History, Volume 1

World History, Volume 2

World Politics

Contents

UNIT 1
Introduction

UNIT 2
The Economy

The concepts in bold italics are developed in the article. For further expansion, please refer to the Topic Guide.

UNIT 3
Work and the Workplace

UNIT 4
Social Media and Participation

The concepts in bold italics are developed in the article. For further expansion, please refer to the Topic Guide.

UNIT 5
Privacy and Security

UNIT 6
Public Policy and Law

The concepts in bold italics are developed in the article. For further expansion, please refer to the Topic Guide.

UNIT 7
International Issues and Perspectives

UNIT 8
Projecting the Future

The concepts in bold italics are developed in the article. For further expansion, please refer to the Topic Guide.

The concepts in bold italics are developed in the article. For further expansion, please refer to the Topic Guide.

Correlation Guide

The *Annual Editions* series provides students with convenient, inexpensive access to current, carefully selected articles from the public press. **Annual Editions: Technologies, Social Media, and Society 13/14** is an easy-to-use reader that presents articles on important topics such as *the economy, the workplace, social participation,* and many more. For more information on *Annual Editions* and other *McGraw-Hill Contemporary Learning Series* titles, visit www.mhhe.com/cls

This convenient guide matches the units in **Annual Editions: Technologies, Social Media, and Society 13/14** with the corresponding chapters in three of our best-selling McGraw-Hill Computer Science textbooks by Haag/Cummings and Baltzan.

Annual Editions: Technologies, Social Media, and Society 13/14	Management Information Systems for the Information Age, 9/e by Haag/Cummings	Business-Driven Technology, 5/e by Baltzan	M: Information Systems, 2/e by Baltzan
Unit 1: Introduction	**Chapter 1:** The Information Age in Which You Live: Changing the Face of Business	**Chapter 1:** Business-Driven Technology	**Chapter 1:** Information Systems in Business
Unit 2: The Economy	**Chapter 1:** The Information Age in Which You Live: Changing the Face of Business **Chapter 2:** Major Business Initiatives: Gaining Competitive Advantage with IT **Chapter 5:** Electronic Commerce: Strategies for the New Economy	**Chapter 1:** Business-Driven Technology **Chapter 2:** Identifying Competitive Advantages **Chapter 14:** E-Business	**Chapter 2:** Decision and Processes: Value-Driven Business **Chapter 3:** Ebusiness: Electronic Business Value **Chapter 8:** Enterprise Applications: Business Communications
Unit 3: Work and the Workplace	**Chapter 2:** Major Business Initiatives: Gaining Competitive Advantage with IT **Chapter 4:** Analytics, Decision Support, and Artificial Intelligence: Brainpower for Your Business	**Chapter 9:** Enabling the Organization—Decision Making **Chapter 10:** Extending the Organization—Supply Chain Management **Chapter 11:** Building a Customer-Centric Organization—Customer Relationship Management **Chapter 12:** Integrating the Organization from End-to-End—Enterprise Resource Planning	**Chapter 6:** Data: Business Intelligence **Chapter 9:** Systems Development and Project Management: Corporate Responsibility
Unit 4: Social Media and Participation	**Chapter 9:** Emerging Trends and Technologies: Business, People, and Technology Tomorrow	**Chapter 14:** E-Business	**Chapter 4:** Ethics and Information Security: MIS Business Concerns
Unit 5: Privacy and Security			**Chapter 4:** Ethics and Information Security: MIS Business Concerns
Unit 6: Public Policy and Law	**Chapter 8:** Protecting People and Information: Threats and Safeguards	**Chapter 7:** Storing Organizational Information—Databases	**Chapter 4:** Ethics and Information Security: MIS Business Concerns
Unit 7: International Issues and Perspectives			
Unit 8: Projecting the Future	**Chapter 9:** Emerging Trends and Technologies: Business, People, and Technology Tomorrow		

Topic Guide

This topic guide suggests how the selections in this book relate to the subjects covered in your course. You may want to use the topics listed on these pages to search the Web more easily.

   On the following pages a number of websites have been gathered specifically for this book. They are arranged to reflect the units of this Annual Editions reader. You can link to these sites by going to www.mhhe.com/cls

All the articles that relate to each topic are listed below the bold-faced term.

Internet References

The following Internet sites have been selected to support the articles found in this reader. These sites were available at the time of publication. However, because websites often change their structure and content, the information listed may no longer be available. We invite you to visit www.mhhe.com/cls for easy access to these sites.

Annual Editions: Technologies, Social Media, and Society 13/14

General Sources

Berkman Center for Internet & Society
http://cyber.law.harvard.edu/

Harvard-based Center whose mission is to explore and understand cyberspace; to study its development, dynamics, norms, and standards; and to assess the need or lack thereof for laws and sanctions.

Internet and American Life
www.pewinternet.org

Provides "reports exploring the impact of the Internet on families, communities, work and home, daily life, education, health care, and civic and political life."

Livelink Intranet Guided Tour
www.opentext.com

Livelink Intranet helps companies to manage and control documents, business processes, and projects more effectively. Take this tour to see how. www.youtube.com/results?search_query=medieval+helpdesk&aq=f This clever YouTube video, called *Medieval Help Desk,* makes the point that writing and books are technologies.

UNIT 1: Introduction

Beyond the Information Revolution
www.theatlantic.com/magazine/archive/1999/10/beyond-the-information-revolution/4658

Peter Drucker has written a three-part article, available at this site, that uses history to gauge the significance of e-commerce—"a totally unexpected development"—to throw light on the future of, in his words, "the knowledge worker."

The Internet in a Cup
www.economist.com/node/2281736

Essay comparing the advent of coffee houses to today's social networking communities. Standage also wrote an excellent short book called The Victorian Internet.

Short History of the Internet
http://ei.cs.vt.edu/~wwwbtb/book/chap1/index.html

Shahrooz Feizabadi presents the history of the World Wide Web as well as the history of several ideas and underlying technologies from which the World Wide Web emerged.

The 17th Century Paper Social Network
www.theatlantic.com/technology/archive/2012/07/the-17th-century-paper-social-network/260346/

Article comparing the 17th century use of small shared paper notes to Twitter today.

UNIT 2: The Economy

E-Commerce Times
www.ecommercetimes.com

E-Commerce Times is a gateway to a wealth of current information and resources concerning e-commerce.

Fight Spam on the Internet
http://spam.abuse.net

This is an anti-spam site that has been in operation since 1996. Its purpose is to promote responsible net commerce, in part, by fighting spam. Up-to-date news about spam can be found on the home page.

MacroWikinomics
www.macrowikinomics.com

Current site of Don Tapscott, author of Wikinomics

Smart Card Group
www.smartcard.co.uk

This website bills itself as "the definitive website for Smart Card Technology." At this site you can download Dr. David B. Everett's definitive "Introduction to Smart Cards."

Smart Cards: A Primer
www.smartcardbasics.com/overview.html

This site describes the smart card, its applications, and its value in e-commerce.

UNIT 3: Work and the Workplace

American Telecommuting Association
www.yourata.com/telecommuting

What is good about telecommuting is examined at this site that also offers information regarding concepts, experiences, and the future of telecommuting.

Computers in the Workplace
www.cpsr.org/issues/industry

"Computers in the Workplace (initiated by the CPSR/Palo Alto chapter) became a national level project in 1988. The Participatory Design conferences have explored workplace issues since the conference's inception in 1992."

Computer Supported Cooperative Work
http://cscw.acm.org

Annual conference of people who develop virtual communication and collaboration software and study its impacts on how we work.

Internet References

STEP ON IT! Pedals: Repetitive Strain Injury
www.bilbo.com/rsi2.html

Data on carpal tunnel syndrome are presented here with links to alternative approaches to the computer keyboard and links to related information.

What about Computers in the Workplace?
http://law.freeadvice.com/intellectual_ property/computer_law/computers_workplace.htm

This site, which is the leading legal site for consumers and small businesses, provides general legal information to help people understand their legal rights in 100 legal topics—including the answer to the question "Can my boss watch what I'm doing?"

UNIT 4: Social Media and Participation

Alliance for Childhood: Computers and Children
http://drupal6.allianceforchildhood.org/computer_ position_statement

How are computers affecting the intellectual growth of children? Here is one opinion provided by the Alliance for Childhood.

The Core Rules of Netiquette
www.albion.com/netiquette/corerules.html

Excerpted from Virginia Shea's book *Netiquette,* this is a classic work in the field of online communication.

SocioSite: Networks, Groups, and Social Interaction
www.sociosite.net

This site provides sociological and psychological resources and research regarding the effect of computers on social interaction.

Snopes.Com
www.snopes.com

This site is definitive Internet reference source for urban legends, folklore, myths, rumors, and misinformation.

WordPress
www.wordpress.com

Place where you can build your own hosted blog or social media site for no money and minimal training.

UNIT 5: Privacy and Security

Center for Democracy and Technology
www.cdt.org

These pages are maintained for discussion and information about data privacy and security, encryption, and the need for policy reform. The site discusses pending legislation, Department of Commerce Export Regulations, and other initiatives.

Cyber Warfare
http://en.wikipedia.org/wiki/Cyberwarfare

Wikipedia's up-to-the-minute account of the risks of cyber warfare. The site includes many interesting links in the short history of cyber warfare, 1982 to the present.

A Declaration of Cyber-War
www.vanityfair.com/culture/features/2011/04/stuxnet-201104

Excellent long article detailing the Stuxnet attack for those who become fascinated by the attack.

Electronic Frontier Foundation
www.eff.org

EFF is the preeminent advocacy organization for user and consumer rights on the Internet.

Electronic Privacy Information Center (EPIC)
http://epic.org

EPIC is a private research organization that was established to focus public attention on emerging civil liberties issues and to protect privacy, the First Amendment, and constitutional values. This site contains news, resources, policy archives, and a search mechanism.

Survive Spyware
http://reviews.cnet.com/4520-3688_7-6456087-1.html

Internet spying is a huge problem. Advertisers, Web designers, and even the government are using the Net to spy on you. CNET.com provides information about spyware and detecting spying eyes that will help you eliminate the threat.

UNIT 6: Public Policy and Law

BitLaw
www.bitlaw.com

BitLaw is a comprehensive Internet resource on technology and intellectual property law.

Did You Say "Intellectual Property"? It's a Seductive Mirage
www.gnu.org/philosophy/not-ipr.html

Opinionated, but very useful, short primer about intellectual property by Richard Stallman.

Trans-Pacific Partnership (Pro and Con Sites)
Office of the United States Trade Representative (pro)

www.ustr.gov/tpp

EFF: Trans Pacific Partnership Agreement (con)

www.eff.org/issues/tpp

Sites advocating each side of this controversial treaty proposal.

United States Copyright Office: Resources
www.copyright.gov/resces.html

Internet resource links about copyright.

United States Patent and Trademark Office
www.uspto.gov

This is the official home page of the United States Patent and Trademark Office. Use this site to search patents and trademarks, apply for patents, and more.

World Intellectual Property Organization
www.wipo.org

Visit the World Intellectual Property Organization website to find information and issues pertaining to virtual and intellectual property.

UNIT 7: International Issues and Perspectives

Global Censorship ChokePoints
https://globalchokepoints.org/

Global Chokepoints is an online resource created to document and monitor global proposals that threaten free speech and privacy on the Internet.

OpenNet Initiative
http://opennet.net/

The OpenNet Initiative investigates, exposes and analyzes Internet censorship practices in a credible and non-partisan fashion.

Internet References

Oxford Internet Institute
www.oii.ox.ac.uk

Oxford University in England offers an international perspective on the social implications of the Internet, complete with interesting links and webcasts.

Wikileaks
http://wikileaks.org/

Wikileaks is an online archive where government and corporate whistleblowers can safely publish materials they believe beneficial to the public if publicly available. Some in the US have urged the government to declare Wikileaks a terrorist organization. Wikileaks has also been nominated for the Nobel Peace Prize and has won many other awards.

UNIT 8: Projecting the Future

Freakonomics
www.freakonomicsradio.com/hour-long-special-the-folly-of-prediction.html

A market-based explanation for why so many people, despite so many mistakes, continue to try to predict the future.

IBM Watson: Ushering in a New Era of Computing
www.ibm.com/watson

Site with current news and information about the IBM Watson computer and its application to real world problems.

Institute for Ethics & Emerging Technologies
www.ieet.org

Organization seeking to contribute to the understanding of the impact of emerging technologies on individuals and societies.

Institute for the Future
www.iftf.org

The IFTF has been systematically studying the predicting the future for 40 years.

International Society for Augmentative and Alternative Communication
www.isaac-online.org

The ISAAC works to improve the lives of children and adults who use augmentative and alternative communication technologies.

World Future Society
www.wfs.org

Organization for people interested in how social and technological developments are shaping the future.

UNIT 1
Introduction

Unit Selections

1. **Five Things We Need to Know about Technological Change,** Neil Postman
2. **The Social Century: 100 Years of Talking, Watching, Reading and Writing in America,** Derek Thompson
3. **It's a Flat World, After All,** Thomas L. Friedman

Learning Outcomes

After reading this Unit, you will be able to:

- Understand what is meant by "technology."

- Understand what is meant by technological change.

- Be able to argue for and against the idea that "all technological change is a trade-off."

- Be able to argue for and against the idea that "technological change is not additive; it is ecological."

- Understand how technology is playing a role in the globalization of our economy.

- Identify 10 forces that are "flattening the world."

- Be able to identify events and forces that are "flattening the world."

- Be able to define "offshoring" and understand the dynamic it plays in our economy.

- Be able to argue for and against the idea that the flattening of the world will have a profound impact on the United States and the next generation of Americans.

Student Website
www.mhhe.com/cls

Internet References

Beyond the Information Revolution
www.theatlantic.com/magazine/archive/1999/10/beyond-the-information-revolution/4658

The Internet in a Cup
www.economist.com/node/2281736

Short History of the Internet
http://ei.cs.vt.edu/~wwwbtb/book/chap1/index.html

The 17th Century Paper Social Network
www.theatlantic.com/technology/archive/2012/07/the-17th-century-paper-social-network/260346/

Unit 1 of this book presents to you three readings to introduce you to concepts that underlie the remaining units. Each of the readings serves a distinct purpose, and after each you are invited to explore additional readings outside of this book if the topic sparks your interest.

Until recently, most people studying the sociology of science and technology considered technological advances to be value-neutral. A given technology, it was supposed, carries no values of its own. The ethics of a technology depends on what is done with it. Atomic power, they argued, is value neutral. Whether atomic power is used to help mankind or destroy mankind is a decision in the domain of the politicians. The job of the scientist is to advance knowledge, not to contemplate about the use of that knowledge. The job of the engineer is to build new technologies, not to contemplate about the impact of those technologies. A vestige of this thinking is still with us. When people say "Guns don't kill people. People kill people," they are asserting that technology somehow stands outside—separate—of societal decisions about its use.

More recently, scientists have become more aware of the social implications of their work. We see this among climate scientists who have begun to advocate to politicians to do something about global warming. While politicians bicker about the causes, effects, and perhaps the existence of global warming, among the academic climate science community virtually 100 percent of the scientists agree the data shows global warming is happening; about 97 percent agree it is due, at least in part, to man-made causes.[1] These scientists recognize that advances in human technologies over the past have had widespread systemic impacts.

But how might they explore or explain the relationships among the many candidate primary, secondary, and tertiary impacts? And how might we anticipate future systemic tangential impacts from current or proposed new technologies? Further, how might we evaluate the trade-offs—both good and bad—among those possible impacts?

Neil Postman, in the first article "Five Things We Need to Know about Technological Change," provides us with a framework—a set of ideas to consider—for evaluating technological change. Postman argues that the invention of new technology is a trade-off. For everything new affordance we get, we lose something old.

Consider the automobile: a wonderful invention a little over a century ago that enabled us to travel faster and farther than we previously could by horse. The invention of the automobile, though, meant the end of horse-drawn carriages. That trade off, perhaps, was positive. It certainly changed man's relationship to the horse. It created new fields of work; and it contributed to the end of other fields of work.

Postman suggests that embedded in every new technology is one or more powerful abstract ideas. Without the automobile, we would not have suburbs as we currently know them. We would not have strip plazas, shopping malls, chain restaurants, and a culture where the suburbs of most every city look uncomfortably similar. We would not have gas stations on every other corner and, consequently, we might not have the diplomatic and military interest over Middle East oil that has grown over much of the last century. These are very powerful and encompassing

© Comstock/PunchStock

ideas with significant social and political ramifications. And, arguably, they are directly tied to mass adoption of combustion engine automobiles a century ago.

Postman's examples show this systemic multiplier of technological impact exists not just for the automobile, but for every technological change.

Computing, as we know it today, has evolved quickly. Early commercial computers of the 1950s filled the space of a large room, required their own air conditioning plants, and were so expensive only the government and the largest corporations could own one. Today, the computer power of a Kindle™ vastly surpasses those computers by several orders of magnitude. But the explosion of recent technological growth is not limited to computers. It includes all communication technology as well as most every other realm of science and industry.

Derek Thompson, in "The Social Century: 100 Years of Talking, Watching, Reading, and Writing in America," evaluates data presented in a McKinsey Global Institute study of social networks that visually shows changes in the technologies Americans have used over the past 100 years to communicate. This short essay, actually a blog post—and the idea that a blog post merits inclusion in this Reader is noteworthy in itself, is included for several reasons.

- One, it demonstrates how much additional insight can be gained by not only reading the data in a study, but by contemplating relationships among the data and postulating new relationships and causal models. It suggests that developing the habit of questioning and manipulating data is a useful endeavor of intellectual exploration.

- Two, it demonstrates how the visual presentation of data can enable additional insight to the meaning and implications of that data; and that choices in how the data is presented can inhibit insight into other relationships. How different might Thompson's analysis have been if the McKinsey study presented not the average time per day spent using each technology, but the percentage of Americans who used each technology by year?

- Three, it suggests that a historical analysis of how technologies have been adopted—and the societal changes that occurred along with or because of that adoption—might inform us as to how new advances in technology could impact us tomorrow. Toward this last point, three additional outside readings are suggested at the end of Thompson's essay. One reading explores how European scholars in the 1670s traded short paper notes back and forth in a manner that took on modern day characteristics of blogging or Twitter. Another reading compares 17th century coffeehouses to modern social networks.[2] And a third reading discusses the first generation of telephone use by business. Each of these historical analogs adds richness and insight to our current day observations of computer and mobile communication technology use.

As Postman suggests, access to the Internet and to a wide array of recently developed wireless technologies, the marketing of new mobile devices by Apple and others, and the development of a wide array of server-based software technologies we loosely refer to as Web2.0 and Cloud Computing cannot be viewed as technology advances alone. Rather, they are all enablers for a far greater social change we are currently in the midst of. Just as the printing press, the telegraph, and the telephone all effected change to work life and the economy far greater than might have been imagined ahead of time, so too are the implications of our modern communication technology advances.

Thomas Friedman, in 2005, wrote *The World Is Flat,* a seminal book about these technology driven global systemic changes. Our third reading is an essay that condenses the arguments made in his book and asks the question: if technology is enabling enormous global social change, how does this impact me? And, what can I do so I won't be left behind?

This Friedman essay is the first reading I have been assigning in my own *Social Issues of Technology* courses since 2005. I assign it first as I believe that makes it more likely my students will actually read it—and that it might motivate them to read more of the remaining essays than they would otherwise read. Those who do read it often report back to me that it was the most important essay they read during their four years of college. For these reasons it is included here to close the Introduction.

I've placed it third in this collection so that Friedman is read with Postman's five ideas fresh in the reader's mind and so that it is read within the historical context suggested by the thought exercises stemming from Thompson's essay. All three of these readings contribute important pieces to the context of this entire collection. But it is the Friedman essay that, hopefully, answers the questions: Why should I care about any of this? What's in it for me?

Notes

1. William R. L. Anderegg, James W. Prall, Jacob Harold, and Stephen H. Schneider, "Expert credibility in climate change," *Proceedings of the National Academy of Sciences of the United States of America,* PNAS June 21, 2010. Retrieved from http://www.pnas.org/content/early/2010/06/04/1003187107.full.pdf+html

2. This author, Tom Standage, has also written a brilliant short book, *The Victorian Internet,* comparing the use and societal implications of the telegraph to our modern day experience of use and implications of the Internet.

Five Things We Need to Know about Technological Change

NEIL POSTMAN

Good morning your Eminences and Excellencies, ladies, and gentlemen.

The theme of this conference, "The New Technologies and the Human Person: Communicating the Faith in the New Millennium," suggests, of course, that you are concerned about what might happen to faith in the new millennium, as well you should be. In addition to our computers, which are close to having a nervous breakdown in anticipation of the year 2000, there is a great deal of frantic talk about the 21st century and how it will pose for us unique problems of which we know very little but for which, nonetheless, we are supposed to carefully prepare. Everyone seems to worry about this—business people, politicians, educators, as well as theologians.

The human dilemma is as it has always been, and it is a delusion to believe that the technological changes of our era have rendered irrelevant the wisdom of the ages and the sages.

At the risk of sounding patronizing, may I try to put everyone's mind at ease? I doubt that the 21st century will pose for us problems that are more stunning, disorienting or complex than those we faced in this century, or the 19th, 18th, 17th, or for that matter, many of the centuries before that. But for those who are excessively nervous about the new millennium, I can provide, right at the start, some good advice about how to confront it. The advice comes from people whom we can trust, and whose thoughtfulness, it's safe to say, exceeds that of President Clinton, Newt Gingrich, or even Bill Gates. Here is what Henry David Thoreau told us: "All our inventions are but improved means to an unimproved end." Here is what Goethe told us: "One should, each day, try to hear a little song, read a good poem, see a fine picture, and, if possible, speak a few reasonable words." Socrates told us: "The unexamined life is not worth living." Rabbi Hillel told us: "What is hateful to thee, do not do to another." And here is the prophet Micah: "What does the Lord require of thee but to do justly, to love mercy and to walk humbly with thy God." And

I could say, if we had the time, (although you know it well enough) what Jesus, Isaiah, Mohammad, Spinoza, and Shakespeare told us. It is all the same: There is no escaping from ourselves. The human dilemma is as it has always been, and it is a delusion to believe that the technological changes of our era have rendered irrelevant the wisdom of the ages and the sages.

. . . all technological change is a trade-off. . . . a Faustian bargain.

Nonetheless, having said this, I know perfectly well that because we do live in a technological age, we have some special problems that Jesus, Hillel, Socrates, and Micah did not and could not speak of. I do not have the wisdom to say what we ought to do about such problems, and so my contribution must confine itself to some things we need to know in order to address the problems. I call my talk *Five Things We Need to Know About Technological Change*. I base these ideas on my thirty years of studying the history of technological change but I do not think these are academic or esoteric ideas. They are the sort of things everyone who is concerned with cultural stability and balance should know and I offer them to you in the hope that you will find them useful in thinking about the effects of technology on religious faith.

First Idea

The first idea is that all technological change is a trade-off. I like to call it a Faustian bargain. Technology giveth and technology taketh away. This means that for every advantage a new technology offers, there is always a corresponding disadvantage. The disadvantage may exceed in importance the advantage, or the advantage may well be worth the cost. Now, this may seem to be a rather obvious idea, but you would be surprised at how many people believe that new technologies are unmixed blessings. You need only think of the enthusiasms with which most people approach their understanding of computers. Ask anyone who knows something about computers to talk about them, and you will find that they will, unabashedly and relentlessly, extol the wonders of computers. You will also find that in most cases they will completely neglect to mention any of the liabilities of computers. This is a dangerous imbalance, since the greater the wonders of a technology, the greater will be its negative consequences.

Think of the automobile, which for all of its obvious advantages, has poisoned our air, choked our cities, and degraded the beauty of our natural landscape. Or you might reflect on the paradox of medical technology which brings wondrous cures but is, at the same time, a demonstrable cause of certain diseases and disabilities, and has played a significant role in reducing the diagnostic skills of physicians. It is also well to recall that for all of the intellectual and social benefits provided by the printing press, its costs were equally monumental. The printing press gave the Western world prose, but it made poetry into an exotic and elitist form of communication. It gave us inductive science, but it reduced religious sensibility to a form of fanciful superstition. Printing gave us the modern conception of nationwide, but in so doing turned patriotism into a sordid if not lethal emotion. We might even say that the printing of the Bible in vernacular languages introduced the impression that God was an Englishman or a German or a Frenchman—that is to say, printing reduced God to the dimensions of a local potentate.

Perhaps the best way I can express this idea is to say that the question, "What will a new technology do?" is no more important than the question, "What will a new technology undo?" Indeed, the latter question is more important, precisely because it is asked so infrequently. One might say, then, that a sophisticated perspective on technological change includes one's being skeptical of Utopian and Messianic visions drawn by those who have no sense of history or of the precarious balances on which culture depends. In fact, if it were up to me, I would forbid anyone from talking about the new information technologies unless the person can demonstrate that he or she knows something about the social and psychic effects of the alphabet, the mechanical clock, the printing press, and telegraphy. In other words, knows something about the costs of great technologies.

Idea Number One, then, is that culture always pays a price for technology.

Second Idea

This leads to the second idea, which is that the advantages and disadvantages of new technologies are never distributed evenly among the population. This means that every new technology benefits some and harms others. There are even some who are not affected at all. Consider again the case of the printing press in the 16th century, of which Martin Luther said it was "God's highest and extremest act of grace, whereby the business of the gospel is driven forward." By placing the word of God on every Christian's kitchen table, the mass-produced book undermined the authority of the church hierarchy, and hastened the breakup of the Holy Roman See. The Protestants of that time cheered this development. The Catholics were enraged and distraught. Since I am a Jew, had I lived at that time, I probably wouldn't have given a damn one way or another, since it would make no difference whether a pogrom was inspired by Martin Luther or Pope Leo X. Some gain, some lose, a few remain as they were.

Let us take as another example, television, although here I should add at once that in the case of television there are

very few indeed who are not affected in one way or another. In America, where television has taken hold more deeply than anywhere else, there are many people who find it a blessing, not least those who have achieved high-paying, gratifying careers in television as executives, technicians, directors, newscasters and entertainers. On the other hand, and in the long run, television may bring an end to the careers of school teachers since school was an invention of the printing press and must stand or fall on the issue of how much importance the printed word will have in the future. There is no chance, of course, that television will go away but school teachers who are enthusiastic about its presence always call to my mind an image of some turn-of-the-century blacksmith who not only is singing the praises of the automobile but who also believes that his business will be enhanced by it. We know now that his business was not enhanced by it; it was rendered obsolete by it, as perhaps an intelligent blacksmith would have known.

The questions, then, that are never far from the mind of a person who is knowledgeable about technological change are these: Who specifically benefits from the development of a new technology? Which groups, what type of person, what kind of industry will be favored? And, of course, which groups of people will thereby be harmed?

. . . there are always winners and losers in technological change.

These questions should certainly be on our minds when we think about computer technology. There is no doubt that the computer has been and will continue to be advantageous to large-scale organizations like the military or airline companies or banks or tax collecting institutions. And it is equally clear that the computer is now indispensable to high-level researchers in physics and other natural sciences. But to what extent has computer technology been an advantage to the masses of people? To steel workers, vegetable store owners, automobile mechanics, musicians, bakers, bricklayers, dentists, yes, theologians, and most of the rest into whose lives the computer now intrudes? These people have had their private matters made more accessible to powerful institutions. They are more easily tracked and controlled; they are subjected to more examinations, and are increasingly mystified by the decisions made about them. They are more than ever reduced to mere numerical objects. They are being buried by junk mail. They are easy targets for advertising agencies and political institutions.

In a word, these people are losers in the great computer revolution. The winners, which include among others computer companies, multi-national corporations and the nation state, will, of course, encourage the losers to be enthusiastic about computer technology. That is the way of winners, and so in the beginning they told the losers that with personal computers the average person can balance a checkbook more neatly, keep better track of recipes, and make more logical shopping lists. Then they told them that computers will make it possible to vote at home, shop at home, get all the entertainment they wish at home, and thus make community life unnecessary. And now, of course, the winners speak constantly of the Age of Information, always implying that the more information we have, the better we will be in solving significant problems—not only personal ones but large-scale social problems, as well. But how true is this? If there are children starving in the world—and there are—it is not because of insufficient information. We have known for a long time how to produce enough food to feed every child on the planet. How is it that we let so many of them starve? If there is violence on our streets, it is not because we have insufficient information. If women are abused, if divorce and pornography and mental illness are increasing, none of it has anything to do with insufficient information. I dare say it is because something else is missing, and I don't think I have to tell this audience what it is. Who knows? This age of information may turn out to be a curse if we are blinded by it so that we cannot see truly where our problems lie. That is why it is always necessary for us to ask of those who speak enthusiastically of computer technology, why do you do this? What interests do you represent? To whom are you hoping to give power? From whom will you be withholding power?

I do not mean to attribute unsavory, let alone sinister motives to anyone. I say only that since technology favors some people and harms others, these are questions that must always be asked. And so, that there are always winners and losers in technological change is the second idea.

Third Idea

Here is the third. Embedded in every technology there is a powerful idea, sometimes two or three powerful ideas. These ideas are often hidden from our view because they are of a somewhat abstract nature. But this should not be taken to mean that they do not have practical consequences.

The third idea is the sum and substance of what Marshall McLuhan meant when he coined the famous sentence, "The medium is the message."

Perhaps you are familiar with the old adage that says: To a man with a hammer, everything looks like a nail. We may extend that truism: To a person with a pencil, everything looks like a sentence. To a person with a TV camera, everything looks like an image. To a person with a computer, everything looks like data. I do not think we need to take these aphorisms literally. But what they call to our attention is that every technology has a prejudice. Like language itself, it predisposes us to favor and value certain perspectives and accomplishments. In a culture without writing, human memory is of the greatest importance, as are the proverbs, sayings and songs which contain the accumulated oral wisdom of centuries. That is why Solomon was thought to be the wisest of men. In Kings I we are told he knew 3,000 proverbs. But in a culture with writing, such feats of memory are considered a waste of time, and proverbs are merely irrelevant fancies. The writing person favors logical organization and systematic analysis, not proverbs. The telegraphic person values speed, not introspection. The television person values

immediacy, not history. And computer people, what shall we say of them? Perhaps we can say that the computer person values information, not knowledge, certainly not wisdom. Indeed, in the computer age, the concept of wisdom may vanish altogether.

The consequences of technological change are always vast, often unpredictable and largely irreversible.

The third idea, then, is that every technology has a philosophy which is given expression in how the technology makes people use their minds, in what it makes us do with our bodies, in how it codifies the world, in which of our senses it amplifies, in which of our emotional and intellectual tendencies it disregards. This idea is the sum and substance of what the great Catholic prophet, Marshall McLuhan meant when he coined the famous sentence, "The medium is the message."

Fourth Idea

Here is the fourth idea: Technological change is not additive; it is ecological. I can explain this best by an analogy. What happens if we place a drop of red dye into a beaker of clear water? Do we have clear water plus a spot of red dye? Obviously not. We have a new coloration to every molecule of water. That is what I mean by ecological change. A new medium does not add something; it changes everything. In the year 1500, after the printing press was invented, you did not have old Europe plus the printing press. You had a different Europe. After television, America was not America plus television. Television gave a new coloration to every political campaign, to every home, to every school, to every church, to every industry, and so on.

That is why we must be cautious about technological innovation. The consequences of technological change are always vast, often unpredictable and largely irreversible. That is also why we must be suspicious of capitalists. Capitalists are by definition not only personal risk takers but, more to the point, cultural risk takers. The most creative and daring of them hope to exploit new technologies to the fullest, and do not much care what traditions are overthrown in the process or whether or not a culture is prepared to function without such traditions. Capitalists are, in a word, radicals. In America, our most significant radicals have always been capitalists—men like Bell, Edison, Ford, Carnegie, Sarnoff, Goldwyn. These men obliterated the 19th century, and created the 20th, which is why it is a mystery to me that capitalists are thought to be conservative. Perhaps it is because they are inclined to wear dark suits and grey ties.

I trust you understand that in saying all this, I am making no argument for socialism. I say only that capitalists need to be carefully watched and disciplined. To be sure, they talk of family, marriage, piety, and honor but if allowed to exploit new technology to its fullest economic potential, they may undo the institutions that make such ideas possible. And here I might just give two examples of this point, taken from the American encounter with technology. The first concerns education. Who, we may ask, has had the greatest impact on American education in this century? If you are thinking of John Dewey or any other education philosopher, I must say you are quite wrong. The greatest impact has been made by quiet men in grey suits in a suburb of New York City called Princeton, New Jersey. There, they developed and promoted the technology known as the standardized test, such as IQ tests, the SATs and the GREs. Their tests redefined what we mean by learning, and have resulted in our reorganizing the curriculum to accommodate the tests.

A second example concerns our politics. It is clear by now that the people who have had the most radical effect on American politics in our time are not political ideologues or student protesters with long hair and copies of Karl Marx under their arms. The radicals who have changed the nature of politics in America are entrepreneurs in dark suits and grey ties who manage the large television industry in America. They did not mean to turn political discourse into a form of entertainment. They did not mean to make it impossible for an overweight person to run for high political office. They did not mean to reduce political campaigning to a 30-second TV commercial. All they were trying to do is to make television into a vast and unsleeping money machine. That they destroyed substantive political discourse in the process does not concern them.

Fifth Idea

I come now to the fifth and final idea, which is that media tend to become mythic. I use this word in the sense in which it was used by the French literary critic, Roland Barthes. He used the word "myth" to refer to a common tendency to think of our technological creations as if they were God-given, as if they were a part of the natural order of things. I have on occasion asked my students if they know when the alphabet was invented. The question astonishes them. It is as if I asked them when clouds and trees were invented. The alphabet, they believe, was not something that was invented. It just is. It is this way with many products of human culture but with none more consistently than technology. Cars, planes, TV, movies, newspapers—they have achieved mythic status because they are perceived as gifts of nature, not as artifacts produced in a specific political and historical context.

When a technology become mythic, it is always dangerous because it is then accepted as it is, and is therefore not easily susceptible to modification or control. If you should propose to the average American that television broadcasting should not begin until 5 P.M. and should cease at 11 P.M., or propose that there should be no television commercials, he will think the idea ridiculous. But not because he disagrees with your cultural agenda. He will think it ridiculous because he assumes you are proposing that something in nature be changed; as if you are suggesting that the sun should rise at 10 A.M. instead of at 6.

The best way to view technology is as a strange intruder.

Whenever I think about the capacity of technology to become mythic, I call to mind the remark made by Pope John Paul II. He said, "Science can purify religion from error and superstition. Religion can purify science from idolatry and false absolutes."

What I am saying is that our enthusiasm for technology can turn into a form of idolatry and our belief in its beneficence can be a false absolute. The best way to view technology is as a strange intruder, to remember that technology is not part of God's plan but a product of human creativity and hubris, and that its capacity for good or evil rests entirely on human awareness of what it does for us and to us.

Conclusion

And so, these are my five ideas about technological change. First, that we always pay a price for technology; the greater the technology, the greater the price. Second, that there are always winners and losers, and that the winners always try to persuade the losers that they are really winners. Third, that there is embedded in every great technology an epistemological, political or social prejudice. Sometimes that bias is greatly to our advantage. Sometimes it is not. The printing press annihilated the oral tradition; telegraphy annihilated space; television has humiliated the word; the computer, perhaps, will degrade community life. And so on. Fourth, technological change is not additive; it is ecological, which means, it changes everything and is, therefore too important to be left entirely in the hands of Bill Gates. And fifth, technology tends to become mythic; that is, perceived as part of the natural order of things, and therefore tends to control more of our lives than is good for us.

If we had more time, I could supply some additional important things about technological change but I will stand by these for the moment, and will close with this thought. In the past, we experienced technological change in the manner of sleepwalkers. Our unspoken slogan has been "technology über alles," and we have been willing to shape our lives to fit the requirements of technology, not the requirements of culture. This is a form of stupidity, especially in an age of vast technological change. We need to proceed with our eyes wide open so that we may use technology rather than be used by it.

Critical Thinking

1. All U.S. schoolchildren learn that the first message Samuel F. B. Morse transmitted over his newly invented telegraph were the words, "What hath God wrought." What they probably do not learn is that Morse was quoting from the poem of Balaam in the Book of Numbers, chapter 23. Read the text of this poem.

2. The overview to this unit presents two ways to understand technical and scientific discoveries. In which camp is Morse? Richard Lewontin, a Harvard geneticist, says ("The Politics of Science," *The New York Review of Books,* May 9, 2002) that "The state of American science and its relation to the American state are the product of war." What does he mean?

From *Address to New Tech 98 Conference*, March 27, 1998. Copyright © 1998 by Neil Postman. Reprinted by permission.

The Social Century: 100 Years of Talking, Watching, Reading and Writing in America

DEREK THOMPSON

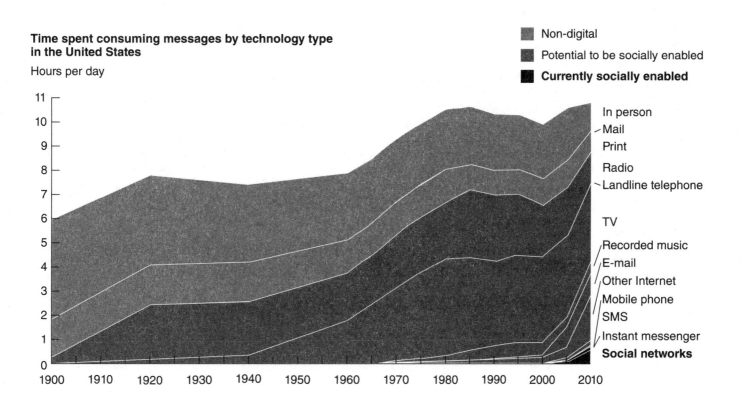

Time spent consuming messages by technology type in the United States

Hours per day

Legend:
- Non-digital
- Potential to be socially enabled
- **Currently socially enabled**

In person
Mail
Print
Radio
Landline telephone
TV
Recorded music
E-mail
Other Internet
Mobile phone
SMS
Instant messenger
Social networks

In 1900, communicating was simple. You could talk to somebody. You could write a letter. You could read ink, printed on paper. That was it, really. If you owned a telephone, you were the 1%.

In 1950, four in ten households owned a telephone or radio. Otherwise, the instruments of making and consuming information hadn't much changed. Talking to people and reading pages made up almost all of the rest of the typical family's communications diet. If you owned a television, you were the 9%.

In 2012, we've lived through a Cambrian explosion of communications technology. If you want to make or consume information, you can do it on Facebook, on Tumblr, on Twitter, on Pinterest, on Foursquare, in texts, on mobile phones, on land-line phones, on VOIP phones, on TV, on iPads, with head phones, with speakers, on the radio, in print, in the mail, and—especially in the case of a Gchat and Twitter black out—you are still permitted to speak into a real-live human's face, directly.

The graph at the top of this post, from a McKinsey Global Institute paper on social networks, is a 110-year history of talking, watching, reading, and writing. It's a fun graph to sort of gaze into and take in, but here are three things I found particularly interesting:

1. In the late 1970s, Americans spent as much time watching TV and listening to radio (6 hours) as they did talking to people and reading in 1900. That's pretty remarkable as a statement of TV and radio's ability to capture and sustain attention.

2. The graph has a harder time showing simultaneous communications consumption. When I watch TV, I'm often on my phone. When I'm listening to the radio, sometimes I'm also IMing. As more communications tools developed that engaged only one of our senses, or (like TV, and unlike reading) that required a very low level of attention, it allowed for easy simultaneous use of communications tech.

3. It's interesting how new technologies expand the amount of time we spend communicating rather than replace each other within a finite band of talking/watching/reading/writing. The adoption of the land-line phone, for example, doesn't seem to have replaced in-person conversation. It simply added about 2 hours to the typical person's communications diet. Moving from farms (where 40% of workers were employed in 1900) to factories and then finally to cubicles has dramatically expanded the time we can spend (indeed, must spend) keeping in touch with people and information.

Critical Thinking

1. In 2013, Americans spend about nine hours a day engaged in electronic communication. In 1913, it was about 90 minutes on average, most of that being listening to radio. What do you think people did with the other 7.5 hours a day they had available? Do you think, in the over all, people communicated as much a century ago as they do today? How do you think the quality of their communication might have differed a century ago?

2. Thompson makes three observations about the graph. What additional and different observations can you make?

3. What do you think the profile of an average American's communication patterns will be in 2023, a decade in the future?

4. Take a look at the full McKinsey Global Institute study Thompson pulled this graph from. It is at www.mckinsey.com/insights/mgi/research/technology_and_innovation/the_social_economy.

DEREK THOMPSON—Derek Thompson is a senior editor at The Atlantic, where he oversees business coverage for the website.

From *The Atlantic*, July 26, 2012. Copyright © 2012 by The Atlantic Media Co. Reprinted by permission of Tribune Media Services. www.theatlantic.com

It's a Flat World, After All

Thomas L. Friedman

In 1492 Christopher Columbus set sail for India, going west. He had the Nina, the Pinta and the Santa Maria. He never did find India, but he called the people he met "Indians" and came home and reported to his king and queen: "The world is round." I set off for India 512 years later. I knew just which direction I was going. I went east. I had Lufthansa business class, and I came home and reported only to my wife and only in a whisper: "The world is flat."

And therein lies a tale of technology and geoeconomics that is fundamentally reshaping our lives—much, much more quickly than many people realize. It all happened while we were sleeping, or rather while we were focused on 9/11, the dot-com bust and Enron—which even prompted some to wonder whether globalization was over. Actually, just the opposite was true, which is why it's time to wake up and prepare ourselves for this flat world, because others already are, and there is no time to waste.

I wish I could say I saw it all coming. Alas, I encountered the flattening of the world quite by accident. It was in late February of last year, and I was visiting the Indian high-tech capital, Bangalore, working on a documentary for the Discovery Times channel about outsourcing. In short order, I interviewed Indian entrepreneurs who wanted to prepare my taxes from Bangalore, read my X-rays from Bangalore, trace my lost luggage from Bangalore and write my new software from Bangalore. The longer I was there, the more upset I became—upset at the realization that while I had been off covering the 9/11 wars, globalization had entered a whole new phase, and I had missed it. I guess the eureka moment came on a visit to the campus of Infosys Technologies, one of the crown jewels of the Indian outsourcing and software industry. Nandan Nilekani, the Infosys C.E.O., was showing me his global video-conference room, pointing with pride to a wall-size flat-screen TV, which he said was the biggest in Asia. Infosys, he explained, could hold a virtual meeting of the key players from its entire global supply chain for any project at any time on that supersize screen. So its American designers could be on the screen speaking with their Indian software writers and their Asian manufacturers all at once. That's what globalization is all about today, Nilekani said. Above the screen there were eight clocks that pretty well summed up the Infosys workday: 24/7/365. The clocks were labeled U.S. West, U.S. East, G.M.T., India, Singapore, Hong Kong, Japan, Australia.

"Outsourcing is just one dimension of a much more fundamental thing happening today in the world," Nilekani explained. "What happened over the last years is that there was a massive investment in technology, especially in the bubble era, when hundreds of millions of dollars were invested in putting broadband connectivity around the world, undersea cables, all those things." At the same time, he added, computers became cheaper and dispersed all over the world, and there was an explosion of e-mail software, search engines like Google and proprietary software that can chop up any piece of work and send one part to Boston, one part to Bangalore and one part to Beijing, making it easy for anyone to do remote development. When all of these things suddenly came together around 2000, Nilekani said, they "created a platform where intellectual work, intellectual capital, could be delivered from anywhere. It could be disaggregated, delivered, distributed, produced and put back together again—and this gave a whole new degree of freedom to the way we do work, especially work of an intellectual nature. And what you are seeing in Bangalore today is really the culmination of all these things coming together."

At one point, summing up the implications of all this, Nilekani uttered a phrase that rang in my ear. He said to me, "Tom, the playing field is being leveled." He meant that countries like India were now able to compete equally for global knowledge work as never before—and that America had better get ready for this. As I left the Infosys campus that evening and bounced along the potholed road back to Bangalore, I kept chewing on that phrase: "The playing field is being leveled."

"What Nandan is saying," I thought, "is that the playing field is being flattened. Flattened? Flattened? My God, he's telling me the world is flat!"

Here I was in Bangalore—more than 500 years after Columbus sailed over the horizon, looking for a shorter route to India using the rudimentary navigational technologies of his day, and returned safely to prove definitively that the world was round—and one of India's smartest engineers, trained at his country's top technical institute and backed by the most modern technologies of his day, was telling me that the world was flat, as flat as that screen on which he can host a meeting of his whole global supply chain. Even more interesting, he was citing this development as a new milestone in human progress and a great opportunity for India and the world—the fact that we had made our world flat!

This has been building for a long time. Globalization 1.0 (1492 to 1800) shrank the world from a size large to a size medium, and the dynamic force in that era was countries globalizing for resources and imperial conquest. Globalization 2.0 (1800 to 2000) shrank the world from a size medium to a size small, and it was spearheaded by companies globalizing for markets and labor. Globalization 3.0 (which started around 2000) is shrinking the world from a size small to a size tiny and flattening the playing field at the same time. And while the dynamic force in Globalization 1.0 was countries globalizing and the dynamic force in Globalization 2.0 was companies globalizing, the dynamic force in Globalization 3.0—the thing that gives it its unique character—is individuals and small groups globalizing. Individuals must, and can, now ask: where do I fit into the global competition and opportunities of the day, and how can I, on my own, collaborate with others globally? But Globalization 3.0 not only differs from the previous eras in how it is shrinking and flattening the world and in how it is empowering individuals. It is also different in that Globalization 1.0 and 2.0 were driven primarily by European and American companies and countries. But going forward, this will be less and less true. Globalization 3.0 is not only going to be driven more by individuals but also by a much more diverse—non-Western, nonwhite—group of individuals. In Globalization 3.0, you are going to see every color of the human rainbow take part.

"Today, the most profound thing to me is the fact that a 14-year-old in Romania or Bangalore or the Soviet Union or Vietnam has all the information, all the tools, all the software easily available to apply knowledge however they want," said Marc Andreessen, a co-founder of Netscape and creator of the first commercial Internet browser. "That is why I am sure the next Napster is going to come out of left field. As bioscience becomes more computational and less about wet labs and as all the genomic data becomes easily available on the Internet, at some point you will be able to design vaccines on your laptop."

Andreessen is touching on the most exciting part of Globalization 3.0 and the flattening of the world: the fact that we are now in the process of connecting all the knowledge pools in the world together. We've tasted some of the downsides of that in the way that Osama bin Laden has connected terrorist knowledge pools together through his Qaeda network, not to mention the work of teenage hackers spinning off more and more lethal computer viruses that affect us all. But the upside is that by connecting all these knowledge pools we are on the cusp of an incredible new era of innovation, an era that will be driven from left field and right field, from West and East and from North and South. Only 30 years ago, if you had a choice of being born a B student in Boston or a genius in Bangalore or Beijing, you probably would have chosen Boston, because a genius in Beijing or Bangalore could not really take advantage of his or her talent. They could not plug and play globally. Not anymore. Not when the world is flat, and anyone with smarts, access to Google and a cheap wireless laptop can join the innovation fray.

When the world is flat, you can innovate without having to emigrate. This is going to get interesting. We are about to see creative destruction on steroids.

How did the world get flattened, and how did it happen so fast?

It was a result of 10 events and forces that all came together during the 1990's and converged right around the year 2000. Let me go through them briefly. The first event was 11/9. That's right—not 9/11, but 11/9. Nov. 9, 1989, is the day the Berlin Wall came down, which was critically important because it allowed us to think of the world as a single space. "The Berlin Wall was not only a symbol of keeping people inside Germany; it was a way of preventing a kind of global view of our future," the Nobel Prize-winning economist Amartya Sen said. And the wall went down just as the windows went up—the breakthrough Microsoft Windows 3.0 operating system, which helped to flatten the playing field even more by creating a global computer interface, shipped six months after the wall fell.

The second key date was 8/9. Aug. 9, 1995, is the day Netscape went public, which did two important things. First, it brought the Internet alive by giving us the browser to display images and data stored on Web sites. Second, the Netscape stock offering triggered the dot-com boom, which triggered the dot-com bubble, which triggered the massive overinvestment of billions of dollars in fiber-optic telecommunications cable. That overinvestment, by companies like Global Crossing, resulted in the willy-nilly creation of a global undersea-underground fiber network, which in turn drove down the cost of transmitting voices, data and images to practically zero, which in turn accidentally made Boston, Bangalore and Beijing next-door neighbors overnight. In sum, what the Netscape revolution did was bring people-to-people connectivity to a whole new level. Suddenly more people could connect with more other people from more different places in more different ways than ever before.

No country accidentally benefited more from the Netscape moment than India. "India had no resources and no infrastructure," said Dinakar Singh, one of the most respected hedge-fund managers on Wall Street, whose parents earned doctoral degrees in biochemistry from the University of Delhi before emigrating to America. "It produced people with quality and by quantity. But many of them rotted on the docks of India like vegetables. Only a relative few could get on ships and get out. Not anymore, because we built this ocean crosser, called fiber-optic cable. For decades you had to leave India to be a professional. Now you can plug into the world from India. You don't have to go to Yale and go to work for Goldman Sachs." India could never have afforded to pay for the bandwidth to connect brainy India with high-tech America, so American shareholders paid for it. Yes, crazy overinvestment can be good. The overinvestment in railroads turned out to be a great boon for the American economy. "But the railroad overinvestment was confined to your own country and so, too, were the benefits," Singh said. In the case of the digital railroads, "it was the foreigners who benefited." India got a free ride.

The first time this became apparent was when thousands of Indian engineers were enlisted to fix the Y2K—the year 2000—computer bugs for companies from all over the world. (Y2K should be a national holiday in India. Call it "Indian Interdependence Day," says Michael Mandelbaum, a foreign-policy analyst at Johns Hopkins.) The fact that the Y2K work could be outsourced to Indians was made possible by the first two flatteners, along with a third, which I call "workflow." Workflow is shorthand for all the software applications, standards and electronic transmission pipes, like middleware, that connected all those computers and fiber-optic cable. To put it another way, if the Netscape moment connected people to people like never before, what the workflow revolution did was connect applications to applications so that people all over the world could work together in manipulating and shaping words, data and images on computers like never before.

Indeed, this breakthrough in people-to-people and application-to-application connectivity produced, in short order, six more flatteners—six new ways in which individuals and companies could collaborate on work and share knowledge. One was "outsourcing." When my software applications could connect seamlessly with all of your applications, it meant that all kinds of work—from accounting to software-writing—could be digitized, disaggregated and shifted to any place in the world where it could be done better and cheaper. The second was "offshoring." I send my whole factory from Canton, Ohio, to Canton, China. The third was "open-sourcing." I write the next operating system, Linux, using engineers collaborating together online and working for free. The fourth was "insourcing." I let a company like UPS come inside my company and take over my whole logistics operation—everything from filling my orders online to delivering my goods to repairing them for customers when they break. (People have no idea what UPS really does today. You'd be amazed!). The fifth was "supply-chaining." This is Wal-Mart's specialty. I create a global supply chain down to the last atom of efficiency so that if I sell an item in Arkansas, another is immediately made in China. (If Wal-Mart were a country, it would be China's eighth-largest trading partner.) The last new form of collaboration I call "informing"—this is Google, Yahoo and MSN Search, which now allow anyone to collaborate with, and mine, unlimited data all by themselves.

So the first three flatteners created the new platform for collaboration, and the next six are the new forms of collaboration that flattened the world even more. The 10th flattener I call "the steroids," and these are wireless access and voice over Internet protocol (VoIP). What the steroids do is turbocharge all these new forms of collaboration, so you can now do any one of them, from anywhere, with any device.

The world got flat when all 10 of these flatteners converged around the year 2000. This created a global, Web-enabled playing field that allows for multiple forms of collaboration on research and work in real time, without regard to geography, distance or, in the near future, even language. "It is the creation of this platform, with these unique attributes, that is the truly important sustainable breakthrough that made what you call the flattening of the world possible," said Craig Mundie, the chief technical officer of Microsoft.

No, not everyone has access yet to this platform, but it is open now to more people in more places on more days in more ways than anything like it in history. Wherever you look today—whether it is the world of journalism, with bloggers bringing down Dan Rather; the world of software, with the Linux code writers working in online forums for free to challenge Microsoft; or the world of business, where Indian and Chinese innovators are competing against and working with some of the most advanced Western multinationals—hierarchies are being flattened and value is being created less and less within vertical silos and more and more through horizontal collaboration within companies, between companies and among individuals.

Do you recall "the IT revolution" that the business press has been pushing for the last 20 years? Sorry to tell you this, but that was just the prologue. The last 20 years were about forging, sharpening and distributing all the new tools to collaborate and connect. Now the real information revolution is about to begin as all the complementarities among these collaborative tools start to converge. One of those who first called this moment by its real name was Carly Fiorina, the former Hewlett-Packard C.E.O., who in 2004 began to declare in her public speeches that the dot-com boom and bust were just "the end of the beginning." The last 25 years in technology, Fiorina said, have just been "the warm-up act." Now we are going into the main event, she said, "and by the main event, I mean an era in which technology will truly transform every aspect of business, of government, of society, of life."

As if this flattening wasn't enough, another convergence coincidentally occurred during the 1990's that was equally important. Some three billion people who were out of the game walked, and often ran, onto the playing field. I am talking about the people of China, India, Russia, Eastern Europe, Latin America and Central Asia. Their economies and political systems all opened up during the course of the 1990's so that their people were increasingly free to join the free market. And when did these three billion people converge with the new playing field and the new business processes? Right when it was being flattened, right when millions of them could compete and collaborate more equally, more horizontally and with cheaper and more readily available tools. Indeed, thanks to the flattening of the world, many of these new entrants didn't even have to leave home to participate. Thanks to the 10 flatteners, the playing field came to them!

It is this convergence—of new players, on a new playing field, developing new processes for horizontal collaboration—that I believe is the most important force shaping global economics and politics in the early 21st century. Sure, not all three billion can collaborate and compete. In fact, for most people the world is not yet flat at all. But even if we're talking about only 10%, that's 300 million people—about twice the size of the American work force. And be advised: the Indians and Chinese are not racing us to the bottom. They are racing us to the top. What China's leaders really want is that the next generation of underwear and airplane wings not just be "made in China" but also be "designed in China." And that is where things are heading. So in 30 years we will have gone from "sold in China" to "made in China" to "designed in China" to "dreamed up in China"—or from China as collaborator with the worldwide manufacturers on nothing to China as a low-cost, high-quality, hyperefficient collaborator with worldwide manufacturers on everything. Ditto India. Said Craig Barrett, the C.E.O. of Intel, "You don't bring three billion people into the world economy overnight without huge consequences, especially from three societies"—like India, China and Russia—"with rich educational heritages."

That is why there is nothing that guarantees that Americans or Western Europeans will continue leading the way. These new players are stepping onto the playing field legacy free, meaning that many of them were so far behind that they can leap right into the new technologies without having to worry about all the sunken costs of old systems. It means that they can move very fast to adopt new, state-of-the-art technologies, which is why there are already more cellphones in use in China today than there are people in America.

If you want to appreciate the sort of challenge we are facing, let me share with you two conversations. One was with some of the Microsoft officials who were involved in setting up Microsoft's research center in Beijing, Microsoft Research Asia, which opened in 1998—after Microsoft sent teams to Chinese universities to administer I.Q. tests in order to recruit the best brains from China's 1.3 billion people. Out of the 2,000 top Chinese engineering and science students tested, Microsoft hired 20. They have a saying at Microsoft about their Asia center, which captures the intensity of competition it takes to win a job there and explains why it is already the most productive research team at Microsoft: "Remember, in China, when you are one in a million, there are 1,300 other people just like you."

The other is a conversation I had with Rajesh Rao, a young Indian entrepreneur who started an electronic-game company from Bangalore, which today owns the rights to Charlie Chaplin's image for mobile computer games. "We can't relax," Rao said. "I think in the case of the United States that is what happened a bit. Please look at me: I am from India. We have been at a very different level before in terms of technology and business. But once we saw we had an infrastructure that made the world a small place, we promptly tried to make the best use of it. We saw there were so many things we could do. We went ahead, and today what we are seeing is a result of that. There is no time to rest. That is gone. There are dozens of people who are doing the same thing you are doing, and they are trying to do it better. It is like water in a tray: you shake it, and it will find the path of least resistance. That is what is going to happen to so many jobs—they will go to that corner of the world where there is the least resistance and the most opportunity. If there is a skilled person in Timbuktu, he will get work if he knows how to access the rest of the world, which is quite easy today. You can make a Web site and have an e-mail address and you are up and running. And if you are able to demonstrate your work, using the same infrastructure, and if people are comfortable giving work to you and if you are diligent and clean in your transactions, then you are in business."

Instead of complaining about outsourcing, Rao said, Americans and Western Europeans would "be better off thinking about how you can raise your bar and raise yourselves into doing something better. Americans have consistently led in innovation over the last century. Americans whining—we have never seen that before."

Rao is right. And it is time we got focused. As a person who grew up during the cold war, I'll always remember driving down the highway and listening to the radio, when suddenly the music would stop and a grim-voiced announcer would come on the air and say: "This is a test. This station is conducting a test of the Emergency Broadcast System." And then there would be a 20-second high-pitched siren sound. Fortunately, we never had to live through a moment in the cold war when the announcer came on and said, "This is a not a test."

That, however, is exactly what I want to say here: "This is not a test."

The long-term opportunities and challenges that the flattening of the world puts before the United States are profound. Therefore, our ability to get by doing things the way we've been doing them—which is to say not always enriching our secret sauce—will not suffice any more. "For a country as wealthy we are, it is amazing how little we are doing to enhance our natural competitiveness," says Dinakar Singh, the Indian-American hedge-fund manager. "We are in a world that has a system that now allows convergence among many billions of people, and we had better step back and figure out what it means. It would be a nice coincidence if all the things that were true before were still true now, but there are quite a few things you actually need to do differently. You need to have a much more thoughtful national discussion."

If this moment has any parallel in recent American history, it is the height of the cold war, around 1957, when the Soviet Union leapt ahead of America in the space race by putting up the Sputnik satellite. The main challenge then came from those who wanted to put up walls; the main challenge to America today comes from the fact that all the walls are being taken down and many other people can now compete and collaborate with us much more directly. The main challenge in that world was from those practicing extreme Communism, namely Russia, China and North Korea. The main challenge to America today is from those practicing extreme capitalism, namely China, India and South Korea. The main objective in that era was building a strong state, and the main objective in this era is building strong individuals.

Meeting the challenges of flatism requires as comprehensive, energetic and focused a response as did meeting the challenge of Communism. It requires a president who can summon the nation to work harder, get smarter, attract more young women and men to science and engineering and build the broadband infrastructure, portable pensions and health care that will help every American become more employable in an age in which no one can guarantee you lifetime employment.

We have been slow to rise to the challenge of flatism, in contrast to Communism, maybe because flatism doesn't involve ICBM missiles aimed at our cities. Indeed, the hot line, which used to connect the Kremlin with the White House, has been replaced by the help line, which connects everyone in America to call centers in Bangalore. While the other end of the hot line might have had Leonid Brezhnev threatening nuclear war, the other end of the help line just has a soft voice eager to help you sort out your AOL bill or collaborate with you on a new piece of software. No, that voice has none of the menace of Nikita

Khrushchev pounding a shoe on the table at the United Nations, and it has none of the sinister snarl of the bad guys in "From Russia with Love." No, that voice on the help line just has a friendly Indian lilt that masks any sense of threat or challenge. It simply says: "Hello, my name is Rajiv. Can I help you?"

No, Rajiv, actually you can't. When it comes to responding to the challenges of the flat world, there is no help line we can call. We have to dig into ourselves. We in America have all the basic economic and educational tools to do that. But we have not been improving those tools as much as we should. That is why we are in what Shirley Ann Jackson, the 2004 president of the American Association for the Advancement of Science and president of Rensselaer Polytechnic Institute, calls a "quiet crisis"—one that is slowly eating away at America's scientific and engineering base.

"If left unchecked," said Jackson, the first African-American woman to earn a Ph.D. in physics from M.I.T., "this could challenge our pre-eminence and capacity to innovate." And it is our ability to constantly innovate new products, services and companies that has been the source of America's horn of plenty and steadily widening middle class for the last two centuries. This quiet crisis is a product of three gaps now plaguing American society. The first is an "ambition gap." Compared with the young, energetic Indians and Chinese, too many Americans have gotten too lazy. As David Rothkopf, a former official in the Clinton Commerce Department, puts it, "The real entitlement we need to get rid of is our sense of entitlement." Second, we have a serious numbers gap building. We are not producing enough engineers and scientists. We used to make up for that by importing them from India and China, but in a flat world, where people can now stay home and compete with us, and in a post-9/11 world, where we are insanely keeping out many of the first-round intellectual draft choices in the world for exaggerated security reasons, we can no longer cover the gap. That's a key reason companies are looking abroad. The numbers are not here. And finally we are developing an education gap. Here is the dirty little secret that no C.E.O. wants to tell you: they are not just outsourcing to save on salary. They are doing it because they can often get better-skilled and more productive people than their American workers.

These are some of the reasons that Bill Gates, the Microsoft chairman, warned the governors' conference in a Feb. 26 speech that American high-school education is "obsolete." As Gates put it: "When I compare our high schools to what I see when I'm traveling abroad, I am terrified for our work force of tomorrow. In math and science, our fourth graders are among the top

students in the world. By eighth grade, they're in the middle of the pack. By 12th grade, United States students are scoring near the bottom of all industrialized nations. . . . The percentage of a population with a college degree is important, but so are sheer numbers. In 2001, India graduated almost a million more students from college than the United States did. China graduates twice as many students with bachelor's degrees as the United States, and they have six times as many graduates majoring in engineering. In the international competition to have the biggest and best supply of knowledge workers, America is falling behind."

We need to get going immediately. It takes 15 years to train a good engineer, because, ladies and gentlemen, this really is rocket science. So parents, throw away the Game Boy, turn off the television and get your kids to work. There is no sugar-coating this: in a flat world, every individual is going to have to run a little faster if he or she wants to advance his or her standard of living. When I was growing up, my parents used to say to me, "Tom, finish your dinner—people in China are starving." But after sailing to the edges of the flat world for a year, I am now telling my own daughters, "Girls, finish your homework—people in China and India are starving for your jobs."

I repeat, this is not a test. This is the beginning of a crisis that won't remain quiet for long. And as the Stanford economist Paul Romer so rightly says, "A crisis is a terrible thing to waste."

Critical Thinking

1. What differentiates Globalization 3.0 from Globalization 2.0? Did the whole world arrive at 3.0 at the same time? Is the whole world at 3.0 now?

2. What does Friedman mean when he says, "When the world is flat, you can innovate without having to emigrate"?

3. Did IT really fuel the productivity surge of the 1990s, or were other factors at work?

4. Friedman wrote this article in 2005. Has his view of the world been validated in the years since? What fundamental events since 2005 have led to additional flattening, or have taken his vision in a different direction?

5. Where do you see Friedman's "flattening" trend headed over the next decade?

6. What are the implications of "It's a Flat World, After All" for your education, and your life in general?

Thomas L. Friedman is the author of *The World Is Flat: A Brief History of the Twenty-First Century*, from which this article is adapted.

As seen in *The New York Times*, April 3, 2005, adapted from THE WORLD IS FLAT: A Brief History of the 21st Century (Farrar Straus & Giroux 2005). Copyright © 2005, 2006, 2007 by Thomas L. Friedman. Reprinted by permission of Farrar Straus and Giroux, LLC.

UNIT 2
The Economy

Unit Selections

Learning Outcomes

After reading this Unit, you will be able to:

- Be able to explain the assertion in Gleick's article that "Google's business is not search but advertising," and how it came to be that way.

- Understand the basic concept of PageRank as a search engine algorithm.

- Know something of booms and busts in the computer industry and how Facebook fits into the mix.

- Understand the role of digital money in our economy.

- Be able to discuss some possible futures for digital money.

- Understand how and why Google, Facebook, and other sites collect demographic and behavioral data.

- Understand how social networking data can be monetized at both the personal and aggregate level.

Student Website

www.mhhe.com/cls

Internet References

E-Commerce Times
    www.ecommercetimes.com
Fight Spam on the Internet
    http://spam.abuse.net
MacroWikinomics
    www.macrowikinomics.com/
Smart Card Group
    www.smartcard.co.uk
Smart Cards: A Primer
    www.smartcardbasics.com/overview.html

Most of us by the time we reach college (or in Western Civ. during freshman year) learn that the history of economics can be divided into several eras: agricultural age; industrial age; and information age. Each age is characterized by a key scarce resource; accumulation of that resource is the basis for wealth. In an agricultural economy, the basis for wealth is arable land. While land alone won't provide wealth—one needs access to labor and tools to work the land—it is the scarce and core necessary enabler for the creation of wealth.

In the industrial age (late 18th to the late 20th century), land became less important. Wealth was created by building factories to produce quantities of items for sale. But factories were expensive to build, and raw materials were required to make finished goods. The scarce resource that drove wealth in this economy was capital: money or credit to acquire buildings, equipment, and materials.

The information age (mid 20th century to perhaps the beginning of the 21st century) was brought about by mass adoption of computing technologies. It became possible to accumulate vast wealth by building software tools and databases to access and organize information better than others. The scarce resource that drove this economy was information, and the knowledge to use it effectively.

Several commentators have suggested that the information age was short lived; that we are moving into a new age already. But few have captured just what differentiates this new age from the information age. Clearly information is no longer a scarce resource. All of us can google most any information we need. Most of us are bombarded with way too much information on a daily basis in the form of e-mail, text messages, tweets, and Facebook status updates. Few of us are able to find the time to consume more than a small fraction of the information we would find interesting or useful. So, if information is no longer scarce, what is it that is scarce?

[Stop for a moment and think about this before reading on.]

James Gleick, in "How Google Dominates Us" gives us a clue. What Google provides to us is information, yes. But we find that same information elsewhere. Several search engines exist; Wikipedia and other online archives contain a wealth of data; there are a growing number of question and answer websites (such as Ask.com and Quora.com) available to us. If Google—or anyone else—wanted to charge us for this information, we wouldn't pay given its ubiquity: we could find it elsewhere for free.

With all of this free information available, with the constant barrage of blog posts, e-mail, text, chat, and social networking messages coming at us, the scarce resource of this economic age is our own attention resource. We do not have the ability to absorb, filter, and prioritize all of the useful and interesting information fired at each of us. What Google does better than anyone else, through a variety of loosely integrated products, is to help us make sense of all of this.

Google's search engine prioritizes results of our searches guessing at which pages will be most useful. Google's Gmail filters our incoming e-mail messages guessing at which ones are important. Google Maps helps us navigate the physical

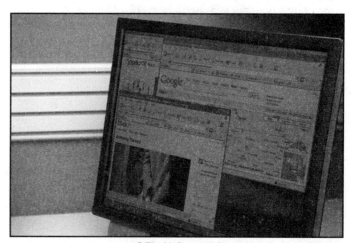

© The McGraw-Hill Companies, Inc./John Flournoy

world—and makes shopping recommendations if we request them. Google Docs, Pixlr and YouTube (all Google products) help us organize multi-media resources in the cloud. In each case, the tool provides information, but more importantly, it organizes, filters, and prioritizes to permit us to consume information using less attention resources.

While the label has not yet caught on, Gleick might well be calling our current era the Attention Age. Gleick notes that Google defines its mission as "to organize the world's information." In this sense, Google appears to be trying to build links among all data—everything, everywhere—to enable you to find what you need (or let Google suggest what you need) simply by asking.

If Google's *raison d'etre* (reason for being) is to possess and organize all data, then Facebook's *raison d'etre* is to possess and organize all data (and people) relationships. This is a subtle difference, but it speaks to what each company wants to know about you, and to how they use and present the information they collect.

As you read Tom Simonite's profile "What Facebook Knows," consider how Facebook's collection and use of data is similar to and different from Google's approach. Consider what Google, through data collected from its family of products, is able to know about each of us compared to what Facebook, through understanding our behaviors on its site and application realm—as well as the behaviors of our Facebook friends, is able to know about each of us.

If your response to learning the extent to which Google and Facebook are able to capture and aggregate our information is to decide "then I just won't share my information with them," consider what Helen Knight found in "The Decision Lens" when she went out shopping but forgot her smartphone at home. Her typical pattern of consulting decision support sites via her mobile device was unavailable and Knight found the experience of shopping without these tools to be overwhelming.

Knight had come to rely on ubiquitously available software to support her own filtering and prioritization of information for her regular daily tasks. That is to say: Google, NetFlix, and other platforms were supporting her limited attention resources. And she had scarcely come to understand how much they were doing so, until she found herself without them.

Knight asks the questions: "What are the implications of delegating everyday choices? If we are not doing the deciding, who or what is? And should we be concerned, or might removing some choice from our lives actually make us happier?"

Several themes emerge from these first three readings. Among them are: the vast power that arises from aggregating so much individual information about human behaviors and relationships; the dependence we are developing on these products and tools to support our everyday human activities; and the commercial monetary value that can created by supporting our limited attention resources. It follows then that integrating commercial transactions into a rich data repository such as Google's or Facebook's will provide significantly more useful information that can be further monetized.

What are the major financial firms planning as they consider their place in this attention age economy? In the last reading of this Unit: Beyond Credit Cards, Jessica Leber interviews Dan Schulman, the head of the Enterprise Growth division at American Express.

How Google Dominates Us

JAMES GLEICK

Tweets Alain de Botton, philosopher, author, and now online aphorist:

The logical conclusion of our relationship to computers: expectantly to type "what is the meaning of my life" into Google.

You can do this, of course. Type "what is th" and faster than you can find the *e* Google is sending choices back at you: what is the *cloud?* what is the *mean?* what is the *american dream?* what is the *illuminati?* Google is trying to read your mind. Only it's not your mind. It's the World Brain. And whatever that is, we know that a twelve-year-old company based in Mountain View, California, is wired into it like no one else.

Google is where we go for answers. People used to go elsewhere or, more likely, stagger along not knowing. Nowadays you can't have a long dinner-table argument about who won the Oscar for that Neil Simon movie where she plays an actress who doesn't win an Oscar; at any moment someone will pull out a pocket device and Google it. If you need the art-history meaning of "picturesque," you could find it in *The Book of Answers,* compiled two decades ago by the New York Public Library's reference desk, but you won't. Part of Google's mission is to make the books of answers redundant (and the reference librarians, too). "A hamadryad is a wood-nymph, also a poisonous snake in India, and an Abyssinian baboon," says the narrator of John Banville's 2009 novel, *The Infinities.* "It takes a god to know a thing like that." Not anymore.

The business of finding facts has been an important gear in the workings of human knowledge, and the technology has just been upgraded from rubber band to nuclear reactor. No wonder there's some confusion about Google's exact role in that— along with increasing fear about its power and its intentions.

Most of the time Google does not actually *have* the answers. When people say, "I looked it up on Google," they are committing a solecism. When they try to erase their embarrassing personal histories "on Google," they are barking up the wrong tree. It is seldom right to say that anything is true "according to Google." Google is the oracle of redirection. Go there for "hamadryad," and it points you to Wikipedia. Or the Free Online Dictionary. Or the Official Hamadryad Web Site (it's a rock band, too, wouldn't you know). Google defines its mission as "to organize the world's information," not to possess it or accumulate it. Then again, a substantial portion of the world's printed books have now been copied onto the company's servers, where they share space with millions of hours of video and detailed multilevel imagery of the entire globe, from satellites and from its squadrons of roving street-level cameras. Not to mention the great and growing trove of information Google possesses regarding the interests and behavior of, approximately, everyone.

When I say Google "possesses" all this information, that's not the same as owning it. What it means to own information is very much in flux.

In barely a decade Google has made itself a global brand bigger than Coca-Cola or GE; it has created more wealth faster than any company in history; it dominates the information economy. How did that happen? It happened more or less in plain sight. Google has many secrets but the main ingredients of its success have not been secret at all, and the business story has already provided grist for dozens of books. Steven Levy's new account, *In the Plex,* is the most authoritative to date and in many ways the most entertaining. Levy has covered personal computing for almost thirty years, for *Newsweek* and *Wired* and in six previous books, and has visited Google's headquarters periodically since 1999, talking with its founders, Larry Page and Sergey Brin, and, as much as has been possible for a journalist, observing the company from the inside. He has been able to record some provocative, if slightly self-conscious, conversations like this one in 2004 about their hopes for Google:

"It will be included in people's brains," said Page. "When you think about something and don't really know much about it, you will automatically get information."

"That's true," said Brin. "Ultimately I view Google as a way to augment your brain with the knowledge of the world. Right now you go into your computer and type a phrase, but you can imagine that it could be easier in the future, that you can have just devices you talk into, or you can have computers that pay attention to what's going on around them. . . ."

. . . Page said, "Eventually you'll have the implant, where if you think about a fact, it will just tell you the answer."

In 2004, Google was still a private company, five years old, already worth $25 billion, and handling about 85 percent of Internet searches. Its single greatest innovation was the algorithm called PageRank, developed by Page and Brin when they were Stanford graduate students running their research project from a computer in a dorm room. The problem was that most Internet searches produced useless lists of low-quality results.

The solution was a simple idea: to harvest the implicit knowledge already embodied in the architecture of the World Wide Web, organically evolving.

The essence of the Web is the linking of individual "pages" on websites, one to another. Every link represents a recommendation—a vote of interest, if not quality. So the algorithm assigns every page a rank, depending on how many other pages link to it. Furthermore, all links are not valued equally. A recommendation is worth more when it comes from a page that has a high rank itself. The math isn't trivial—PageRank is a probability distribution, and the calculation is recursive, each page's rank depending on the ranks of pages that depend . . . and so on. Page and Brin patented PageRank and published the details even before starting the company they called Google.

Most people have already forgotten how dark and unsignposted the Internet once was. A user in 1996, when the Web comprised hundreds of thousands of "sites" with millions of "pages," did not expect to be able to search for "Olympics" and automatically find the official site of the Atlanta games. That was too hard a problem. And what was a search supposed to produce for a word like "university"? AltaVista, then the leading search engine, offered up a seemingly unordered list of academic institutions, topped by the Oregon Center for Optics.

Levy recounts a conversation between Page and an AltaVista engineer, who explained that the scoring system would rank a page higher if "university" appeared multiple times in the headline. Alta Vista seemed untroubled that the Oregon center did not qualify as a major university. A conventional way to rank universities would be to consult experts and assess measures of quality: graduate rates, retention rates, test scores. The Google approach was to trust the Web and its numerous links, for better and for worse.

PageRank is one of those ideas that seem obvious after the fact. But the business of Internet search, young as it was, had fallen into some rigid orthodoxies. The main task of a search engine seemed to be the compiling of an index. People naturally thought of existing technologies for organizing the world's information, and these were found in encyclopedias and dictionaries. They could see that alphabetical order was about to become less important, but they were slow to appreciate how dynamic and ungraspable their target, the Internet, really was. Even after Page and Brin flipped on the light switch, most companies continued to wear blindfolds.

The Internet had entered its first explosive phase, boom and then bust for many ambitious startups, and one thing everyone knew was that the way to make money was to attract and retain users. The buzzword was "portal"—the user's point of entry, like Excite, Go.com, and Yahoo—and portals could not make money by rushing customers into the rest of the Internet. "Stickiness," as Levy says, "was the most desired metric in websites at the time." Portals did not want their search functions to be *too good.* That sounds stupid, but then again how did Google intend to make money when it charged users nothing? Its user interface at first was plain, minimalist, and emphatically free of advertising—nothing but a box for the user to type a query, followed by two buttons, one to produce a list of results and one with the famously brash tag "I'm feeling lucky."

The Google founders, Larry and Sergey, did everything their own way. Even in the unbuttoned culture of Silicon Valley they stood out from the start as originals, "Montessori kids" (per Levy), unconcerned with standards and proprieties, favoring big red gym balls over office chairs, deprecating organization charts and formal titles, showing up for business meetings in roller-blade gear. It is clear from all these books that they believed their own hype; they believed with moral fervor in the primacy and power of information. (Sergey and Larry did not invent the company's famous motto—"Don't be evil"—but they embraced it, and now they may as well own it.)

As they saw it from the first, their mission encompassed not just the Internet but all the world's books and images, too. When Google created a free e-mail service—Gmail—its competitors were Microsoft, which offered users two megabytes of storage of their past and current e-mail, and Yahoo, which offered four megabytes. Google could have trumped that with six or eight; instead it provided 1,000—a *giga*byte. It doubled that a year later and promised "to keep giving people more space forever."

They have been relentless in driving computer science forward. Google Translate has achieved more in machine translation than the rest of the world's artificial intelligence experts combined. Google's new mind-reading type-ahead feature, Google Instant, has "to date" (boasts the 2010 annual report) "saved our users over 100 billion keystrokes and counting." (If you are seeking information about the Gobi Desert, for example, you receive results well before you type the word "desert.")

Somewhere along the line they gave people the impression that they didn't care for advertising—that they scarcely had a business plan at all. In fact it's clear that advertising was fundamental to their plan all along. They did scorn conventional marketing, however; their attitude seemed to be that Google would market itself. As, indeed, it did. Google was a verb and a meme. "The media seized on Google as a marker of a new form of behavior," writes Levy.

Endless articles rhapsodized about how people would Google their blind dates to get an advance dossier or how they would type in ingredients on hand to Google a recipe or use a telephone number to Google a reverse lookup. Columnists shared their self-deprecating tales of Googling themselves. . . . A contestant on the TV show *Who Wants to Be a Millionaire?* arranged with his brother to tap Google during the Phone-a-Friend lifeline. . . . And a fifty-two-year-old man suffering chest pains Googled "heart attack symptoms" and confirmed that he was suffering a coronary thrombosis.

Google's first marketing hire lasted a matter of months in 1999; his experience included Miller Beer and Tropicana and his proposal involved focus groups and television commercials. When Doug Edwards interviewed for a job as marketing manager later that year, he understood that the key word was "viral." Edwards lasted quite a bit longer, and now he's the first Google insider to have published his memoir of the experience. He was, as he says proudly in his subtitle to *I'm Feeling Lucky,* Google employee number 59. He provides two other indicators of how early that was: so early that he nabbed the e-mail address doug@google.com; and so early that Google's entire server hardware lived in a rented "cage."

Less than six hundred square feet, it felt like a shotgun shack blighting a neighborhood of gated mansions. Every square inch was crammed with racks bristling with stripped-down CPUs [central processing units]. There were twenty-one racks and more than fifteen hundred machines, each sprouting cables like Play-Doh pushed through a spaghetti press. Where other cages were right-angled and inorganic, Google's swarmed with life, a giant termite mound dense with frenetic activity and intersecting curves.

Levy got a glimpse of Google's data storage a bit later and remarked, "If you could imagine a male college freshman made of gigabytes, this would be his dorm."

Not anymore. Google owns and operates a constellation of giant server farms spread around the globe—huge windowless structures, resembling aircraft hangars or power plants, some with cooling towers. The server farms stockpile the exabytes of information and operate an array of staggeringly clever technology. This is Google's share of the cloud (that notional place where our data live) and it is the lion's share.

How thoroughly and how radically Google has already transformed the information economy has not been well understood. The merchandise of the information economy is not information; it is attention. These commodities have an inverse relationship. When information is cheap, attention becomes expensive. Attention is what we, the users, give to Google, and our attention is what Google sells—concentrated, focused, and crystallized.

Google's business is not search but advertising. More than 96 percent of its $29 billion in revenue last year came directly from advertising, and most of the rest came from advertising-related services. Google makes more from advertising than all the nation's newspapers combined. It's worth understanding precisely how this works. Levy chronicles the development of the advertising engine: a "fantastic achievement in building a money machine from the virtual smoke and mirrors of the Internet." In *The Googlization of Everything (and Why We Should Worry)*, a book that can be read as a sober and admonitory companion, Siva Vaidhyanathan, a media scholar at the University of Virginia, puts it this way: "We are not Google's customers: we are its product. We—our fancies, fetishes, predilections, and preferences—are what Google sells to advertisers."

The evolution of this unparalleled money machine piled one brilliant innovation atop another, in fast sequence:

1. Early in 2000, Google sold "premium sponsored links": simple text ads assigned to particular search terms. A purveyor of golf balls could have its ad shown to everyone who searched for "golf" or, even better, "golf balls." Other search engines were already doing this. Following tradition, they charged according to how many people saw each ad. Salespeople sold the ads to big accounts, one by one.

2. Late that year, engineers devised an automated self-service system, dubbed AdWords. The opening pitch went, "Have a credit card and 5 minutes? Get your ad on Google today," and suddenly thousands of small businesses were buying their first Internet ads.

3. From a short-lived startup called Go To (by 2003 Google owned it) came two new ideas. One was to charge per click rather than per view. People who click on an ad for golf balls are more likely to buy them than those who simply see an ad on Google's website. The other idea was to let advertisers bid for keywords—such as "golf ball"—against one another in fast online auctions. Pay-per-click auctions opened a cash spigot. A click meant a *successful* ad, and some advertisers were willing to pay more for that than a human salesperson could have known. Plaintiffs' lawyers seeking clients would bid as much as fifty dollars for a single click on the keyword "mesothelioma"—the rare form of cancer caused by asbestos.

4. Google—monitoring its users' behavior so systematically—had instant knowledge of which ads were succeeding and which were not. It could view "click-through rates" as a measure of ad quality. And in determining the winners of auctions, it began to consider not just the money offered but the appeal of the ad: an effective ad, getting lots of clicks, would get better placement.

   Now Google had a system of profitable cycles in place, positive feedback pushing advertisers to make more effective ads and giving them data to help them do it and giving users more satisfaction in clicking on ads, while punishing noise and spam. "The system enforced Google's insistence that advertising shouldn't be a transaction between publisher and advertiser but a three-way relationship that also included the user," writes Levy. Hardly an equal relationship, however. Vaidhyanathan sees it as exploitative: "The Googlization of everything entails the harvesting, copying, aggregating, and ranking of information about and contributions made by each of us."

   By 2003, AdWords Select was serving hundreds of thousands of advertisers and making so much money that Google was deliberating hiding its success from the press and from competitors. But it was only a launching pad for the next brilliancy.

5. So far, ads were appearing on Google's search pages, discreet in size, clearly marked, at the top or down the right side. Now the company expanded its platform outward. The aim was to develop a form of artificial intelligence that could analyze chunks of text—websites, blogs, e-mail, books—and match them with keywords. With two billion Web pages already in its index and with its close tracking of user behavior, Google had exactly the information needed to tackle this problem. Given a website (or a blog or an e-mail), it could predict which advertisements would be effective.

This was, in the jargon, "content-targeted advertising." Google called its program AdSense. For anyone hoping to—in the jargon—"monetize" their content, it was the Holy Grail. The biggest digital publishers, such as *The New York Times*, quickly signed up for AdSense, letting Google handle growing portions of their advertising business. And so did the smallest publishers, by the millions—so grew the "long tail" of possible advertisers, down to individual bloggers. They signed up because the ads were so powerfully, measurably productive. "Google conquered the advertising world with nothing more than applied mathematics," wrote Chris Anderson, the editor of *Wired*. "It didn't pretend to know anything about the culture and conventions of advertising—it just assumed that better data, with better analytical tools, would win the day. And Google was right." Newspapers and other traditional media have complained from time to time about the arrogation of their content, but it is by absorbing the world's advertising that Google has become their most destructive competitor.

Like all forms of artificial intelligence, targeted advertising has hits and misses. Levy cites a classic miss: a gory *New York Post* story about a body dismembered and stuffed in a garbage bag, accompanied on the *Post* website by a Google ad for plastic bags. Nonetheless, anyone could now add a few lines of code to their website, automatically display Google ads, and start cashing monthly checks, however small. Vast tracts of the Web that had been free of advertising now became Google partners. Today Google's ad canvas is not just the search page but the entire Web, and beyond that, great volumes of e-mail and, potentially, all the world's books.

Search and advertising thus become the matched edges of a sharp sword. The perfect search engine, as Sergey and Larry imagine it, reads your mind and produces the answer you want. The perfect advertising engine does the same: it shows you the ads you want. Anything else wastes your attention, the advertiser's money, and the world's bandwidth. The dream is virtuous advertising, matching up buyers and sellers to the benefit of all. But virtuous advertising in this sense is a contradiction in terms. The advertiser is paying for a slice of our limited attention; our minds would otherwise be elsewhere. If our interests and the advertisers' were perfectly aligned, they would not need to pay. There is no information utopia. Google users are parties to a complex transaction, and if there is one lesson to be drawn from all these books it is that we are not always witting parties.

Seeing ads next to your e-mail (if you use Google's free e-mail service) can provide reminders, sometimes startling, of how much the company knows about your inner self. Even without your e-mail, your search history reveals plenty—as Levy says, "your health problems, your commercial interests, your hobbies, and your dreams." Your response to advertising reveals even more, and with its advertising programs Google began tracking the behavior of individual users from one Internet site to the next. They observe our every click (where they can) and they measure in milliseconds how long it takes us to decide. If they didn't, their results wouldn't be so uncannily effective. They have no rival in the depth and breadth of their data mining. They make statistical models for everything they know, connecting the small scales with the large, from queries and clicks to trends in fashion and season, climate and disease.

It's for your own good—that is Google's cherished belief. If we want the best possible search results, and if we want advertisements suited to our needs and desires, we must let them into our souls.

The Google corporate motto is "Don't be evil." Simple as that is, it requires parsing.

It was first put forward in 2001 by an engineer, Paul Buchheit, at a jawboning session about corporate values. "People laughed," he recalled. "But I said, 'No, *really.*'" (At that time the booming tech world had its elephant-in-the-room, and many Googlers understood "Don't be evil" explicitly to mean "Don't be like Microsoft"; i.e., don't be a ruthless, take-no-prisoners monopolist.)

Often it is misquoted in stronger form: "Do no evil." That would be a harder standard to meet.

Now they're mocked for it, but the Googlers were surely sincere. They believed a corporation should behave ethically, like a person. They brainstormed about their values. Taken at face value, "Don't be evil" has a finer ring than some of the other contenders: "Google will strive to honor all its commitments" or "Play hard but keep the puck down."

"Don't be evil" does not have to mean transparency. None of these books can tell you how many search queries Google fields, how much electricity it consumes, how much storage capacity it owns, how many streets it has photographed, how much e-mail it stores; nor can you Google the answers, because Google values its privacy.

It does not have to mean "Obey all the laws." When Google embarked on its program to digitize copyrighted books and copy them onto its servers, it did so in stealth, deceiving publishers with whom it was developing business relationships. Google knew that the copying bordered on illegal. It considered its intentions honorable and the law outmoded. "I think we knew that there would be a lot of interesting issues," Levy quotes Page as saying, "and the way the laws are structured isn't really sensible."

Who, then, judges what is evil? "Evil is what Sergey says is evil," explained Eric Schmidt, the chief executive officer, in 2002.

As for Sergey: "I feel like I shouldn't impose my beliefs on the world. It's a bad technology practice." But the founders seem sure enough of their own righteousness. ("'Bastards!' Larry would exclaim when a blogger raised concerns about user privacy," recalls Edwards. "'Bastards!' they would say about the press, the politicians, or the befuddled users who couldn't grasp the obvious superiority of the technology behind Google's products.")

Google did some evil in China. It collaborated in censorship. Beginning in 2004, it arranged to tweak and twist its algorithms and filter its results so that the native-language Google.cn would omit results unwelcome to the government. In the most notorious example, "Tiananmen Square" would produce sightseeing guides but not history lessons. Google figured out what to censor by checking China's approved search engine, Baidu, and by accepting the government's supplementary guidance.

Yet it is also true that Google pushed back against the government as much as any other American company. When results were blocked, Google insisted on alerting users with a notice at the bottom of the search page. On balance Google clearly believed (and I think it was right, despite the obvious self-interest) that its presence benefited the people of China by increasing information flow and making clear the violation of transparency. The adventure took a sharp turn in January 2010, after organized hackers, perhaps with government involvement, breached Google's servers and got access to the e-mail accounts of human rights activists. The company shut down Google.cn and now serves China only from Hong Kong—with results censored not by Google but by the government's own ongoing filters.

So is Google evil? The question is out there now; it nags, even as we blithely rely on the company for answers—which now also means maps, translations, street views, calendars, video, financial data, and pointers to goods and services. The strong version of the case against Google is laid out starkly in *Search & Destroy,* by a self-described "Google critic" named Scott Cleland. He wields a blunt club; the book might as well been have been titled *Google: Threat or Menace?!* "There is evidence that Google is not all puppy dogs and rainbows," he writes.

Google's corporate mascot is a replica of a Tyrannosaurus Rex skeleton on display outside the corporate headquarters. With its powerful jaws and teeth, T-Rex was a terrifying predator. And check out the B-52 bomber chair in Google Chairman Eric Schmidt's office. The B-52 was a long range bomber designed to deliver nuclear weapons.

Levy is more measured: "Google professed a sense of moral purity . . . but it seemed to have a blind spot regarding the consequences of its own technology on privacy and property rights." On all the evidence Google's founders began with an unusually ethical vision for their unusual company. They believe in information—"universally accessible"—as a force for good in and of itself. They have created and led teams of technologists responsible for a golden decade of genuine innovation. They are visionaries in a time when that word is too cheaply used. Now they are perhaps disinclined to submit to other people's ethical standards, but that may be just a matter of personality. It is well to remember that the modern corporation is an amoral creature by definition, obliged to its shareholder financiers, not to the public interest.

The Federal Trade Commission issued subpoenas in June in an antitrust investigation into Google's search and advertising practices; the European Commission began a similar investigation last year. Governments are responding in part to organized complaints by Google's business competitors, including Microsoft, who charge, among other things, that the company manipulates its search results to favor its friends and punish its enemies. The company has always denied that. Certainly regulators are worried about its general "dominance"—Google seems to be everywhere and seems to know everything and offends against cherished notions of privacy.

The rise of social networking upends the equation again. Users of Facebook choose to reveal—even to flaunt—aspects of their private lives, to at least some part of the public world. Which aspects, and which part? On Facebook the user options are notoriously obscure and subject to change, but most users share with "friends" (the word having been captured and drained

bloodless). On Twitter, every remark can be seen by the whole world, except for the so-called "direct message," which former Representative Anthony Weiner tried and failed to employ. Also, the Library of Congress is archiving all tweets, presumably for eternity, a fact that should enter the awareness of teenagers, if not members of Congress.

Now Google is rolling out its second attempt at a social-networking platform, called Google+. The first attempt, eighteen months ago, was Google Buzz; it was an unusual stumble for the company. By default, it revealed lists of contacts with whom users had been chatting and e-mailing. Privacy advocates raised an alarm and the FTC began an investigation, quickly reaching a settlement in which Google agreed to regular privacy audits for the next twenty years. Google+ gives users finer control over what gets shared with whom. Still, one way or another, everything is shared with the company. All the social networks have access to our information and mean to use it. Are they our friends?

This much is clear: We need to decide what we want from Google. If only we can make up our collective minds. Then we still might not get it.

The company always says users can "opt out" of many of its forms of data collection, which is true, up to a point, for savvy computer users; and the company speaks of privacy in terms of "trade-offs," to which Vaidhyanathan objects:

Privacy is not something that can be counted, divided, or "traded." It is not a substance or collection of data points. It's just a word that we clumsily use to stand in for a wide array of values and practices that influence how we manage our reputations in various contexts. There is no formula for assessing it: I can't give Google three of my privacy points in exchange for 10 percent better service.

This seems right to me, if we add that privacy involves not just managing our reputation but protecting the inner life we may not want to share. In any case, we continue to make precisely the kinds of trades that Vaidhyanathan says are impossible. Do we want to be addressed as individuals or as neurons in the world brain? We get better search results and we see more appropriate advertising when we let Google know who we are. And we save a few keystrokes.

Critical Thinking

1. The author of this article is a well-known science writer. What is his most recent book about?

2. Much is made of Google's PageRank algorithm? What is it?

3. What is the overwhelming source of Google's revenue?

4. Google's model is "Don't be evil." Gleick tells a story about Google.cn. Do you think Google behaved ethically in its encounter with the Chinese government?

5. Type your address into Google Street View. Are you comfortable with what comes up? What if the federal government provided the same service? Would that affect your opinion?

From *The New York Review of Books*, August 18, 2011. Copyright © 2011 by James Gleick.

What Facebook Knows

The company's social scientists are hunting for insights about human behavior. What they find could give Facebook new ways to cash in on our data—and remake our view of society.

Tom Simonite

Cameron Marlow calls himself Facebook's "in-house sociologist." He and his team can analyze essentially all the information the site gathers.

Few Privacy Regulations Inhibit Facebook

Laws haven't kept up with the company's ability to mine its users' data.

If Facebook were a country, a conceit that founder Mark Zuckerberg has entertained in public, its 900 million members would make it the third largest in the world.

It would far outstrip any regime past or present in how intimately it records the lives of its citizens. Private conversations, family photos, and records of road trips, births, marriages, and deaths all stream into the company's servers and lodge there. Facebook has collected the most extensive data set ever assembled on human social behavior. Some of your personal information is probably part of it.

And yet, even as Facebook has embedded itself into modern life, it hasn't actually done that much with what it knows about us. Now that the company has gone public, the pressure to develop new sources of profit is likely to force it to do more with its hoard of information. That stash of data looms like an oversize shadow over what today is a modest online advertising business, worrying privacy-conscious Web users and rivals such as Google. Everyone has a feeling that this unprecedented resource will yield something big, but nobody knows quite what.

Even as Facebook has embedded itself into modern life, it hasn't done that much with what it knows about us. Its stash of data looms like an oversize shadow. Everyone has a feeling that this resource will yield something big, but nobody knows quite what.

Heading Facebook's effort to figure out what can be learned from all our data is Cameron Marlow, a tall 35-year-old who until recently sat a few feet away from Zuckerberg. The group Marlow runs has escaped the public attention that dogs Facebook's founders and the more headline-grabbing features of its business. Known internally as the Data Science Team, it is a kind of Bell Labs for the social-networking age. The group has 12 researchers—but is expected to double in size this year. They apply math, programming skills, and social science to mine our data for insights that they hope will advance Facebook's business and social science at large. Whereas other analysts at the company focus on information related to specific online activities, Marlow's team can swim in practically the entire ocean of personal data that Facebook maintains. Of all the people at Facebook, perhaps even including the company's leaders, these researchers have the best chance of discovering what can really be learned when so much personal information is compiled in one place.

Facebook has all this information because it has found ingenious ways to collect data as people socialize. Users fill out profiles with their age, gender, and e-mail address; some people also give additional details, such as their relationship status and mobile-phone number. A redesign last fall introduced profile pages in the form of time lines that invite people to add historical information such as places they have lived and worked. Messages and photos shared on the site are often tagged with a precise location, and in the last two years Facebook has begun to track activity elsewhere on the Internet, using an addictive invention called the "Like" button. It appears on apps and websites outside Facebook and allows people to indicate with a click that they are interested in a brand, product, or piece of digital content. Since last fall, Facebook has also been able to collect data on users' online lives beyond its borders automatically: in certain apps or websites, when users listen to a song or read a news article, the information is passed along to Facebook, even if no one clicks "Like." Within the feature's first five months, Facebook catalogued more than five billion instances of people listening to songs online. Combine that kind of information with a map of the social connections Facebook's users make on the site, and you have an incredibly rich record of their lives and interactions.

"This is the first time the world has seen this scale and quality of data about human communication," Marlow says with a characteristically serious gaze before breaking into a smile at the thought of what he can do with the data. For one thing, Marlow is confident that exploring this resource will revolutionize the scientific understanding of why people behave as they do. His team can also help Facebook influence our social behavior for its own benefit and that of its advertisers. This work may even help Facebook invent entirely new ways to make money.

Contagious Information

Marlow eschews the collegiate programmer style of Zuckerberg and many others at Facebook, wearing a dress shirt with his jeans rather than a hoodie or T-shirt. Meeting me shortly before the company's initial public offering in May, in a conference room adorned with a six-foot caricature of his boss's dog spray-painted on its glass wall, he comes across more like a young professor than a student. He might have become one had he not realized early in his career that Web companies would yield the juiciest data about human interactions.

In 2001, undertaking a PhD at MIT's Media Lab, Marlow created a site called Blogdex that automatically listed the most "contagious" information spreading on weblogs. Although it was just a research project, it soon became so popular that Marlow's servers crashed. Launched just as blogs were exploding into the popular consciousness and becoming so numerous that Web users felt overwhelmed with information, it prefigured later aggregator sites such as Digg and Reddit. But Marlow didn't build it just to help Web users track what was popular online. Blogdex was intended as a scientific instrument to uncover the social networks forming on the Web and study how they spread ideas. Marlow went on to Yahoo's research labs to study online socializing for two years. In 2007 he joined Facebook, which he considers the world's most powerful instrument for studying human society. "For the first time," Marlow says, "we have a microscope that not only lets us examine social behavior at a very fine level that we've never been able to see before but allows us to run experiments that millions of users are exposed to."

Marlow's team works with managers across Facebook to find patterns that they might make use of. For instance, they study how a new feature spreads among the social network's users. They have helped Facebook identify users you may know but haven't "friended," and recognize those you may want to designate mere "acquaintances" in order to make their updates less prominent. Yet the group is an odd fit inside a company where software engineers are rock stars who live by the mantra "Move fast and break things." Lunch with the data team has the feel of a grad-student gathering at a top school; the typical member of the group joined fresh from a PhD or junior academic position and prefers to talk about advancing social science than about Facebook as a product or company. Several members of the team have training in sociology or social psychology, while others began in computer science and started using it to study human behavior. They are free to use some of their time, and Facebook's data, to probe the basic patterns and motivations of human behavior and to publish the results in academic journals—much as Bell Labs researchers advanced both AT&T's technologies and the study of fundamental physics.

It may seem strange that an eight-year-old company without a proven business model bothers to support a team with such an academic bent, but Marlow says it makes sense. "The biggest challenges Facebook has to solve are the same challenges that social science has," he says. Those challenges include understanding why some ideas or fashions spread from a few individuals to become universal and others don't, or to what extent a person's future actions are a product of past communication with friends. Publishing results and collaborating with university researchers will lead to findings that help Facebook improve its products, he adds.

Eytan Bakshy experimented with the way Facebook users shared links so that his group could study whether the site functions like an echo chamber.

For one example of how Facebook can serve as a proxy for examining society at large, consider a recent study of the notion that any person on the globe is just six degrees of separation from any other. The best-known real-world study, in 1967, involved a few hundred people trying to send postcards to a particular Boston stockholder. Facebook's version, conducted in collaboration with researchers from the University of Milan, involved the entire social network as of May 2011, which amounted to more than 10% of the world's population. Analyzing the 69 billion friend connections among those 721 million people showed that the world is smaller than we thought: four intermediary friends are usually enough to introduce anyone to a random stranger. "When considering another person in the world, a friend of your friend knows a friend of their friend, on average," the technical paper pithily concluded. That result may not extend to everyone on the planet, but there's good reason to believe that it and other findings from the Data Science Team are true to life outside Facebook. Last year the Pew Research Center's Internet & American Life Project found that 93% of Facebook friends had met in person. One of Marlow's researchers has developed a way to calculate a country's "gross national happiness" from its Facebook activity by logging the occurrence of words and phrases that signal positive or negative emotion. Gross national happiness fluctuates in a way that suggests the measure is accurate: it jumps during holidays and dips when popular public figures die. After a major earthquake in Chile in February 2010, the country's score plummeted and took many months to return to normal. That event seemed to make the country as a whole more sympathetic when Japan suffered its own big earthquake and subsequent tsunami in March 2011; while Chile's gross national happiness dipped, the figure didn't waver in any other countries tracked (Japan wasn't among them). Adam Kramer, who created the index, says he intended it to show that Facebook's data could provide cheap and accurate ways to track social trends—methods that could be useful to economists and other researchers.

Other work published by the group has more obvious utility for Facebook's basic strategy, which involves encouraging us to make the site central to our lives and then using what it learns to sell ads. An early study looked at what types of updates from friends encourage newcomers to the network to add their own contributions. Right before Valentine's Day this year a blog post from the Data Science Team listed the songs most popular with people who had recently signaled on Facebook that they had entered or left a relationship. It was a hint of the type of correlation that could help Facebook make useful predictions about users' behavior—knowledge that could help it make better guesses about which ads you might be more or less open to at any given time. Perhaps people who have just left a relationship might be interested in an album of ballads, or perhaps no company should associate its brand with the flood of emotion attending the death of a friend. The most valuable online ads today are those displayed alongside certain Web searches, because the searchers are expressing precisely what they want. This is one reason why Google's revenue is 10 times Facebook's. But Facebook might eventually be able to guess what people want or don't want even before they realize it.

Recently the Data Science Team has begun to use its unique position to experiment with the way Facebook works, tweaking the site—the way scientists might prod an ant's nest—to see how users react. Eytan Bakshy, who joined Facebook last year after collaborating with Marlow as a PhD student at the University of Michigan, wanted to learn whether our actions on Facebook are mainly influenced by those of our close friends, who are likely to have similar tastes. That would shed light on the theory that our Facebook friends create an "echo chamber" that amplifies news and opinions we have already heard about. So he messed with how Facebook operated for a quarter of a billion users. Over a seven-week period, the 76 million links that those users shared with each other were logged. Then, on 219 million randomly chosen occasions, Facebook prevented someone from seeing a link shared by a friend. Hiding links this way created a control group so that Bakshy could assess how often people end up promoting the same links because they have similar information sources and interests.

He found that our close friends strongly sway which information we share, but overall their impact is dwarfed by the collective influence of numerous more distant contacts—what sociologists call "weak ties." It is our diverse collection of weak ties that most powerfully determines what information we're exposed to.

That study provides strong evidence against the idea that social networking creates harmful "filter bubbles," to use activist Eli Pariser's term for the effects of tuning the information we receive to match our expectations. But the study also reveals the power Facebook has. "If [Facebook's] News Feed is the thing that everyone sees and it controls how information is disseminated, it's controlling how information is revealed to society, and it's something we need to pay very close attention to," Marlow says. He points out that his team helps Facebook understand what it is doing to society and publishes its findings to fulfill a public duty to transparency. Another recent study, which investigated which types of Facebook activity cause people to feel a greater sense of support from their friends, falls into the same category.

Facebook is not above using its platform to tweak users' behavior, as it did by nudging them to register as organ donors.

Unlike academic social scientists, Facebook's employees have a short path from an idea to an experiment on hundreds of millions of people.

But Marlow speaks as an employee of a company that will prosper largely by catering to advertisers who want to control the flow of information between its users. And indeed, Bakshy is working with managers outside the Data Science Team to extract advertising-related findings from the results of experiments on social influence. "Advertisers and brands are a part of this network as well, so giving them some insight into how people are sharing the content they are producing is a very core part of the business model," says Marlow.

Facebook told prospective investors before its IPO that people are 50% more likely to remember ads on the site if they're visibly endorsed by a friend. Figuring out how influence works could make ads even more memorable or help Facebook find ways to induce more people to share or click on its ads.

Social Engineering

Marlow says his team wants to divine the rules of online social life to understand what's going on inside Facebook, not to develop ways to manipulate it. "Our goal is not to change the pattern of communication in society," he says. "Our goal is to understand it so we can adapt our platform to give people the experience that they want." But some of his team's work and the attitudes of Facebook's leaders show that the company is not above using its platform to tweak users' behavior. Unlike academic social scientists, Facebook's employees have a short path from an idea to an experiment on hundreds of millions of people.

In April, influenced in part by conversations over dinner with his med-student girlfriend (now his wife), Zuckerberg decided that he should use social influence within Facebook to increase organ donor registrations. Users were given an opportunity to click a box on their Timeline pages to signal that they were registered donors, which triggered a notification to their friends. The new feature started a cascade of social pressure, and organ donor enrollment increased by a factor of 23 across 44 states.

Marlow's team is in the process of publishing results from the last U.S. midterm election that show another striking example of Facebook's potential to direct its users' influence on one another. Since 2008, the company has offered a way for users to signal that they have voted; Facebook promotes that to their friends with a note to say that they should be sure to vote, too. Marlow says that in the 2010 election his group matched voter registration logs with the data to see which of the Facebook users who got nudges actually went to the polls. (He stresses that the researchers worked with cryptographically "anonymized" data and could not match specific users with their voting records.)

Sameet Agarwal figures out ways for Facebook to manage its enormous trove of data—giving the company a unique and valuable level of expertise.

This is just the beginning. By learning more about how small changes on Facebook can alter users' behavior outside the site, the company eventually "could allow others to make use of Facebook in the same way," says Marlow. If the American Heart Association wanted to encourage healthy eating, for example, it might be able to refer to a playbook of Facebook social engineering. "We want to be a platform that others can use to initiate change," he says.

Advertisers, too, would be eager to know in greater detail what could make a campaign on Facebook affect people's actions in the outside world, even though they realize there are limits to how firmly human beings can be steered. "It's not clear to me that social science will ever be an engineering science in a way that building bridges is," says Duncan Watts, who works on computational social science at Microsoft's recently opened New York research lab and previously worked alongside Marlow at Yahoo's labs. "Nevertheless, if you have enough data, you can make predictions that are better than simply random guessing, and that's really lucrative."

Doubling Data

Like other social-Web companies, such as Twitter, Facebook has never attained the reputation for technical innovation enjoyed by such Internet pioneers as Google. If Silicon Valley were a high school, the search company would be the quiet math genius who didn't excel socially but invented something indispensable. Facebook would be the annoying kid who started a club with such social momentum that people had to join whether they wanted to or not. In reality, Facebook employs hordes of talented software engineers (many poached from Google and other math-genius companies) to build and maintain its irresistible club. The technology built to support the Data Science Team's efforts is particularly innovative. The scale at which Facebook operates has led it to invent hardware and software that are the envy of other companies trying to adapt to the world of "big data."

In a kind of passing of the technological baton, Facebook built its data storage system by expanding the power of open-source software called Hadoop, which was inspired by work at Google and built at Yahoo. Hadoop can tame seemingly impossible computational tasks—like working on all the data Facebook's users have entrusted to it—by spreading them across many machines inside a data center. But Hadoop wasn't built with data science in mind, and using it for that purpose requires specialized, unwieldy programming. Facebook's engineers solved that problem with the invention of Hive, open-source software that's now independent of Facebook and used by many other companies. Hive acts as a translation service, making it possible to query vast Hadoop data stores using relatively simple code. To cut down on computational demands, it can request random samples of an entire data set, a feature that's invaluable for companies swamped by data. Much of Facebook's data resides in one Hadoop store more than 100 petabytes (a million gigabytes) in size, says Sameet Agarwal, a director of engineering at Facebook who works on data infrastructure, and the quantity is growing exponentially. "Over the last few years we have more than doubled in size every year," he says. That means his team must constantly build more efficient systems.

One potential use of Facebook's data storehouse would be to sell insights mined from it. Such information could be the basis for any kind of business. Assuming Facebook can do this without upsetting users and regulators, it could be lucrative.

All this has given Facebook a unique level of expertise, says Jeff Hammerbacher, Marlow's predecessor at Facebook, who initiated the company's effort to develop its own data storage and analysis technology. (He left Facebook in 2008 to found Cloudera, which develops Hadoop-based systems to manage large collections of data.) Most large businesses have paid established software companies such as Oracle a lot of money for data analysis and storage. But now, big companies are trying to understand how Facebook handles its enormous information trove on open-source systems, says Hammerbacher. "I recently spent the day at Fidelity helping them understand how the 'data scientist' role at Facebook was conceived . . . and I've had the same discussion at countless other firms," he says.

As executives in every industry try to exploit the opportunities in "big data," the intense interest in Facebook's data technology suggests that its ad business may be just an offshoot of something much more valuable. The tools and techniques the company has developed to handle large volumes of information could become a product in their own right.

Mining for Gold

Facebook needs new sources of income to meet investors' expectations. Even after its disappointing IPO, it has a staggeringly high price-to-earnings ratio that can't be justified by the barrage of cheap ads the site now displays. Facebook's new campus in Menlo Park, California, previously inhabited by Sun Microsystems, makes that pressure tangible. The company's 3,500 employees rattle around in enough space for 6,600. I walked past expanses of empty desks in one building; another, next door, was completely uninhabited. A vacant lot waited nearby, presumably until someone invents a use of our data that will justify the expense of developing the space.

One potential use would be simply to sell insights mined from the information. DJ Patil, data scientist in residence with the venture capital firm Greylock Partners and previously leader of LinkedIn's data science team, believes Facebook could take inspiration from Gil Elbaz, the inventor of Google's AdSense ad business, which provides over a quarter of Google's revenue. He has moved on from advertising and now runs a fast-growing startup, Factual, that charges businesses to access large, carefully curated collections of data ranging from restaurant locations to celebrity body-mass indexes, which the company collects from free public sources and by buying private data sets. Factual cleans up data and makes the result available over the Internet as an on-demand knowledge store to be tapped by software, not humans. Customers use it to fill in the gaps in their own data and make smarter apps or services; for example, Facebook itself uses Factual for information about business locations. Patil points out that Facebook could become a data source in its own right, selling access to information compiled from the actions of its users. Such information, he says, could be the basis for almost any kind of business, such as online dating or charts of popular music. Assuming Facebook can take this step without upsetting users and regulators, it could be lucrative. An online store wishing to target its promotions, for example, could pay to use Facebook as a source of knowledge about which brands are most popular in which places, or how the popularity of certain products changes through the year.

Hammerbacher agrees that Facebook could sell its data science and points to its currently free Insights service for advertisers and website owners, which shows how their content is being shared on Facebook. That could become much more useful to businesses if Facebook added data obtained when its "Like" button tracks activity all over the Web, or demographic data or information about what people read on the site. There's precedent for offering such analytics for a fee: at the end of 2011 Google started charging $150,000 annually for a premium version of a service that analyzes a business's Web traffic.

Back at Facebook, Marlow isn't the one who makes decisions about what the company charges for, even if his work will shape them. Whatever happens, he says, the primary goal of his team is to support the well-being of the people who provide Facebook with their data, using it to make the service smarter. Along the way, he says, he and his colleagues will advance humanity's understanding of itself. That echoes Zuckerberg's often doubted but seemingly genuine belief that Facebook's job is to improve how the world communicates. Just don't ask yet exactly what that will entail. "It's hard to predict where we'll go, because we're at the very early stages of this science," says Marlow. "The number of potential things that we could ask of Facebook's data is enormous."

Critical Thinking

1. The article states that the manager in charge of mining all the personal data Facebook collect believes it will revolutionize the scientific understanding of why people behave as they do. Do you think this will be a good or bad thing for the average Facebook user? For society in general?

2. If we had a better understanding of why people behave as they do, what could we do with such knowledge?

3. Simonite writes, "Facebook might eventually be able to guess what people want or don't want even before they realize it." If so, how might this impact sales and marketing? Homeland security? Personal relationships?

4. Facebook was able to increase organ donations by a factor of 23 simply by permitting people to check a box saying they were organ donors and sharing that information with friends. Is Facebook's ability to manipulate behavior on this scale a good or bad thing? Why?

Tom Simonite is *Technology Review's* senior IT editor.

From *Technology Review*, July/August 2012. Copyright © 2012 by MIT Press. Reprinted by permission via Copyright Clearance Center.

The Decision Lens

Your phone and web browser are making choices for you, whether you want them to or not, says Helen Knight.

HELEN KNIGHT

I first realised I had a problem inside the department store. I was meant to be choosing a gift for my niece. My bored 2-year-old had begun pulling the items off the shelves, in a desperate bid for entertainment. That was because I had been standing still, just staring at a display of colourful children's toys, for well over 10 minutes.

The problem was that I had left my smartphone at home. Usually when I can't make a decision, I whip out my phone and ask Google or one of my apps for advice or reviews. Without it, I was paralysed by choice.

I now continually turn to apps and websites for recommendations about what to buy, what to eat and where to go. Life's big decisions remain my own, but many of my everyday choices are essentially delegated. As well as regularly turning to search engines for advice, I use apps like MapMyRun to set a jogging route, for instance, and iTunes to select the music to listen to while I run. I let Google News tell me what stories I should read, and have Netflix pick which movies to watch.

I'm not alone. For example, more than one-third of turn to the internet on their smartphones for guidance just before they make a buying decision. Smartphones and tablets have become more than simple communication devices: they are very often the source of the information we use to decide how to navigate the world.

Although there is nothing wrong with being constantly plugged in and informed, this habit inevitably means that our subtly influenced without us even realising. You might not have elected to cede control of your choices, but if you spend any time online, it is almost certain that you are unwittingly doing so already. And in the next few years, we could hand over even more autonomy. Our portable devices are poised to become intelligent "personal assistants"—perhaps even capable of acting independently on our behalf in work, entertainment and relationships.

So what are the implications of delegating everyday choices? If we are not doing the deciding, who or what is? And should we be concerned, or might removing some choice from our lives actually make us happier?

We all have free will, and it would be ridiculous to argue that turning to an iPhone for advice could take that away. Still, we can only make informed choices on the basis of the information available. A lot of the time, that information comes from a product review usually written by a person. But increasingly, much of the information and recommendations we get from the internet have already been filtered and personalised by "recommender" algorithms. These bits of computer code use our previous preferences, and those of people with similar tastes, to present a view of the world that is different to that of our neighbour's.

For example, websites like Amazon and Netflix continually recommend items targeted at you, and many smartphone apps now do the same. One app, called Alfred, uses your past choices to suggest nearby restaurants you'd like, and is dubbed "your personal robot". These algorithms are already highly influential. Around 60 per cent of all movies rented from Netflix are based on the recommendations of the site's algorithm, says the company.

Since 2009, Google has worked in a similar way, personalising the results provided by its web searches for each individual, largely based on their past activity using the search engine. Social network feeds are also personalised: the status updates and photos that appear on your Facebook news feed have been edited by an algorithm based on factors such as how it rates the strength of your friendships (see "Got friendly world syndrome?").

By carrying our tastes, previous choices and background around with us as we visit each corner of the internet, we are enabling companies to make decisions on our behalf about what we see when we are there—which in turn will influence our subsequent choices.

For an illustration of how, consider this example from Eli Pariser, author of the 2011 book The Filter Bubble. Imagine two people entering the search term "BP" immediately after the company's Gulf of Mexico oil spill. One, a liberal, is presented with news stories about the environmental effect of the spill, while the other is given stock tips about the company. If they are both investors trying to decide whether to buy BP shares, they could come to quite different conclusions.

Even the adverts we see online are personalised, which can affect the range of choices we think are available. As Pariser points out in The Filter Bubble: "Students who go to Ivy League colleges see targeted advertisements for jobs that students at state schools are never even aware of."

Most of the time all this personalisation is helpful—especially for battling the modern malady of information overload. Take Netflix. "Its users have some version of the entire library of film in front of them," says Kevin Slavin, a New York-based entrepreneur who has raised concerns about the influence of algorithms. "How are they supposed to make a decision about that?"

But at the same time, algorithms are far from perfect at forecasting complex human desires, Slavin says. They break down our tastes and behaviour into categories they can understand—so that because I like Jane Austen novels, I am also likely to watch Downton Abbey, for instance. In reality, we are much less predictable. Some people might, like me, find it unsettling that all this personalisation is happening without fanfare. Few of us are even aware that it is going on, says Dean Eckles at Stanford University in California, who studies the social influence of interactive technologies. "It is basically invisible to people," he says.

So how concerned should we be? To tackle that question, we need to look at where this technology trend is headed. After all, the current wave of personalisation is just the beginning, says Justin Donaldson, president of machine-learning company BigML, based in Corvallis, Oregon. He and his colleagues argue that we are on the verge of a new wave of systems that can act directly on our behalf, instead of just suggesting options (AI Magazine, vol 32, p 19).

The increasing use of recommender systems on smartphones is giving them access to a rich source of data about our everyday lives. My smartphone, for example, knows not only what search terms I enter into Google and who my friends are on Facebook, but what my GPS coordinates are at any given moment. It also has access to my calendar, emails and daily notifications.

Donaldson predicts that, using this information, smartphones will soon be able to act like personal assistants, if not old-fashioned butlers. "Butlers knew of all of the quirks, tastes and vices of their employers," he says. "Their task was to promote, suggest or arrange the most appropriate attire, meal or social function."

For a hint of what is to come, says Donaldson, look at Siri on the latest iteration of the iPhone. Billed as a "virtual assistant", Siri is equipped with the artificial intelligence to understand voice commands such as "find me an Italian restaurant", and can use the web or apps to search for nearby eateries. According to Apple, Siri also learns about you over time, using information from your calendar, contacts list, music library and reminders to better understand what you mean. It is not impossible that future versions of programs like Siri could use this information to arrange a night out with friends, plan a business meeting or book a hotel for you.

Soon, your smartphone could even make recommendations and choices based on how you are feeling. Hyun-Jun Kim and Young Sang Choi of the Samsung Advanced Institute of Technology in Yongin, South Korea, are developing a system that uses information about a user's emotional state to shape its recommendations for music or products to fit their mood. Called EmoSens, it uses the phone's sensors to measure signals such as shaking, walking pace and speed of tapping on the screen. It can then conclude that a person is more agitated than usual, for example, and so tailor its recommendations accordingly. For example, if you are looking to book a restaurant, it might propose comfort food if you are in a bad mood. The pair presented EmoSens at a conference on recommender systems in Chicago last October.

Do we want algorithms studying our behaviour and acting on our behalf in this way? How can we be sure that a virtual assistant won't store our information and sell it to marketing companies, for example, or subtly favour particular brands?

There will always be companies taking advantage of any technology when personal details about our lives are involved. Some people may not like that, but the benefits should outweigh the risks, argues Donaldson. And just because recommender systems today tend to work on behalf of companies that want to sell something, that doesn't mean the next generation would do the same, he says.

In principle, tomorrow's virtual assistants could work solely in our best interests, not a company's. So, for example, it might intervene to stop you buying a novel from Amazon, by suggesting you borrow it from a Facebook friend who it knows bought it last month. "These things can genuinely improve our quality of life," says Donaldson. "Our generation just needs to understand where the boundaries are, and how we can protect ourselves."

Culture Shaper

Still, there are wider implications to consider if we collectively delegate more and more of our decision-making to algorithms. The recommender systems used to personalise our entertainment choices could even start to shape culture itself.

It is not impossible that plays and films would make more money if their authors wrote them to satisfy an algorithm's idea of what people with particular tastes like to watch. If that sounds unlikely, consider that many online journalists already write news and headlines in a style that ensures Google's algorithms place their stories higher in the search results. They are not just writing for their human readers; they are writing for algorithms too.

Another issue also gives pause: if we all have the world personalised for us, what experiences do we end up missing out on? We are often rewarded for spontaneous choices. Think of all the movies you have enjoyed because you took a risk, or meals you liked at restaurants you simply stumbled upon. It would be a shame if the world lost some of its serendipity.

On the other hand, we may all end up happier if we had fewer decisions to make each day. Psychologists know that our ability to make good decisions deteriorates after an extended period of making choices—even little ones like what products to buy in a supermarket—in what is called "decision fatigue." And various studies have shown that people with restricted choice—or none at all—often feel happier with a given outcome than those with more freedom (Organizational Behavior and Human Decision Processes, DOI: 10.1016/j.obhdp.2010.03.002).

In one experiment by Simona Botti of the London Business School and Sheena Iyengar of Columbia University in New York, participants were presented with a meal chosen by a friend or given the freedom to choose their own dish. Often the meal would turn out to be unappetising, but the people who had chosen it themselves enjoyed it much less than those who had it recommended by the friend (Journal of Personality and Social Psychology, vol 87, p 312).

As someone who hates making decisions, this makes sense to me. Put an intelligent personal assistant in a smartphone, and I would consider buying it. But I would certainly feel better about algorithms acting on my behalf if I had greater control and awareness of when they were guiding my choices. Anthony Jameson, head of the Choosability Engineering research group at the German Research Center for Artificial Intelligence in Saarbrücken, argues that software developers should make their recommender systems more transparent. For example, existing search engines and recommender systems could easily display a "slider", from which users could choose how varied they want their recommendations to be, he says.

In the meantime, though, I have resolved to think much more carefully before turning to an algorithm to suggest a product or activity. And that is perhaps one of the better-informed choices I have made this year—even if it does mean I spend more time staring blankly at shelves of toys in department stores.

Too much choice can make for unhappy customers

Got Friendly World Syndrome?

In the 1970s, George Gerbner coined the term "mean world syndrome" to describe the way in which people who watch a lot of violent television shows tend to think the world is more unpleasant than it actually is.

Today, the design of social networking sites like Facebook may be having a similar, but opposite, effect. They seem to make the world seem altogether more fun than reality.

To prevent us becoming overwhelmed with status updates on Facebook, the newsfeed is filtered so that stories receiving more comments or "likes" are given priority. The result is that lively updates, such as holiday snaps or anecdotes from a drunken night out, tend to trump more general news, says Dean Eckles of Stanford University in California.

The aggregate effect of this is that it can make us feel as if everyone else is having a better, more interesting time than us, says Eckles. "What you're not hearing about are the people who spent the night at home reading a book." Eckles calls the effect friendly world syndrome.

In principle, this effect could influence our own behaviour and choices, by making us feel as if we should be getting out more, and spending more money to keep up with our friends, says Eckles. To support that idea, he points to research by Sharad Goel and Dan Goldstein at Yahoo! Research in New York suggesting that our friends' buying behaviour, and in particular the amount they spend, can predict our own consumption patterns.

Critical Thinking

1. Knight was frustrated shopping without her iPhone tools providing her with advice. Do you think we make better shopping decisions with more or less information gathered while shopping?

2. How much personal information are you willing to provide to help a personalized advice website provide you with more information? What decision rules do you use do decide how much information to share?

3. What are the risks to having recommender systems guide your purchase decisions?

4. What are the implications of the Eli Pariser example about doing Internet searches on the term "BP"?

5. If you could empower your virtual assistant (in your smart phone or tablet) to do more for you, what tasks would you permit it to do? What tasks would you not want a computer assistant to do for you?

HELEN KNIGHT is a writer based in London.

From *New Scientist Magazine*, April 14, 2012, pp. 36–39. Copyright © 2012 by Reed Business Information, Ltd, UK. Reprinted by permission via Tribune Media Services.

Beyond Credit Cards: Q&A with Dan Schulman of American Express

American Express built its brand around a material that's going out of style. One word: plastic.

JESSICA LEBER

American Express started out in the 19th century delivering money by horseback. It issued the first widely accepted plastic charge card in 1959, and has more or less stayed the course since.

But an expected global boom in payments made on mobile phones and tablets—their dollar value will surge 76 percent to $86 billion in 2012, Gartner predicts—now leaves the third-largest United States credit card issuer preparing for a future without plastic.

Enter Serve, a prepaid, reloadable spending account Amex launched last March. Serve is partly an Internet service and partly a debit card whose minimalist design is missing the familiar gladiator logo. The target market is clear: the young and less obviously credit-worthy. Not only is the service free, but new customers are being offered a $10 credit to get started.

If it is successful, the card design won't matter. Serve is the New York–based company's first product born for the Web and mobile phones, and it aims to compete directly with PayPal. Both, for example, have added applications that let users send money to friends online via Facebook. Verizon Wireless and Sprint have agreed to put Serve on phones, turning it into a "digital wallet" from which money can be zapped to merchants or anyone else.

More is to come. Since 2010, Dan Schulman, once CEO of Virgin Mobile, has headed Amex's Enterprise Growth division, the unit that runs Serve and is busy orchestrating Amex's entry into mobile commerce. Schulman's war chest is sizable: he has $100 million available to invest in technology companies.

Technology Review business writer Jessica Leber interviewed Schulman to learn how Amex is responding to an environment where wireless carriers, retailers, banks, and Internet companies are all vying for a piece of credit card profits.

TR: **How do you see the nature of money changing?**
Schulman: Approximately 85 percent of transactions across the world today are in cash. But cash will start to become less dominant. The mobile phone is going to rapidly become a form factor in which you'll not just pay for your groceries but, increasingly, you'll find out about the information around your groceries. What's organic, what may not be organic? What are your friends thinking about it? What offers and deals may be around it? The

way you fundamentally pay for it could change. You can pay for it now. You can pay for it later. You can use virtual currencies. You can use loyalty points that you've accrued. So the very nature of how we will pay for things will fundamentally transform.

Why did you launch Serve?
The future of our company is along the dimensions of digital commerce. The launch of Serve was one important step in that direction. Serve will begin to realize its full potential as we begin adding features that move Serve from a payments platform to a true enabler of digital commerce.

What's always been part of the ethos of American Express is we aggregate data and share that with merchants, and show where a retailer might be more effective in their marketing. As everything becomes digitized, a marketer can be much more targeted and much more efficient with their marketing. And consumers, instead of getting spammed with one offer after another, could actually get offers for exactly what they are interested in.

American Express began in the 1850s as a competitor to the United States Postal Service. Is anyone worried credit cards are headed to irrelevancy like paper mail?
If you don't change, and you don't constantly innovate, then any company runs the risk of losing relevance going forward. You can name one company after another, from Kodak to the music companies, that have had to fundamentally change their business model.

We recognize that. It was one of the reasons why my group was formed. My online and mobile teams are based in Silicon Alley in New York. We're operating almost as a startup. If you walked into our office space there, it's radically different than what might come to mind when you think "financial services company." The people we have there are primarily from software companies, wireless companies, user design companies, Amazon, you name it.

The difference is we get to leverage all of the assets of American Express. I do think our brand is perhaps more valuable in a digital age than an analog age. When you think about storing your commerce identity online, that's very different than your social persona. Your social persona that you have on Facebook—it could be real or not real. It's really up to you to define what that is. But your commerce persona—that's your financial information, your brand preferences, your shopping list. It needs to be 100 percent accurate. American Express is one of the brands people trust. There are also very unsexy elements of this business—fraud management, risk management, regulatory compliance. Those are things we understand quite well.

You recently opened an office in China. What's the strategy there?

We just announced we are partnering with a Chinese company, Lianlian. The idea behind that partnership is to take our digital platform, to take Serve, and to license that and embed that in Lianlian's infrastructure.

The vast majority of mobile phones over in China are prepaid. So a Chinese consumer goes to a merchant and gives them cash, and that cash is translated into minutes in their mobile phone. Our partnership plans to enable digital wallets for those merchants, and from that digital wallet, the consumer can allocate a percentage to minutes on their cell phone. Lianlian, with the benefit of Serve's technology, will enable online purchasing, digital payments, and getting offers and deals loaded into their wallet. It can now open to the Chinese consumer the ability to do a wide array of digital activities that they might never have been able to do before.

Near-field communication chips are now coming to phones. These could allow us to pay with just a tap on a terminal. Will this technology catch on?

If you're just using your phone instead of a plastic card, I think that will take quite some time to come about for making payments. It may be this technology finds other uses first—it allows you to unlock your house and not have to worry about your keys anymore.

I think the real breakthrough occurs when you can tap your phone on the doorway of a retailer and selectively expose your commerce identity to that retailer. You tell them, "I'm a first-time customer, or a loyal customer. I've got this shopping list that I'm going after, or I'm brand-loyal to these products. I've got this kind of budget." Then you, as a retailer, can segment to an individual—complete personalization around the offers and deals and information the

consumer may want. So then there's a real reason for you to tap your phone. That's what a lot of us are thinking about now.

Is social networking changing your business?

Social networks are becoming this great form of discovery. What do my friends like? The second thing that they've really started to do is create this whole idea around virtual currencies. These virtual currencies are very real. For a certain demographic, giving a virtual flower versus a real flower is actually very meaningful.

We bought a company called Sometrics, which last year did 3.3 trillion units of virtual currency on their platform. You can buy virtual goods such as gold coins or whatever it may be. That acquisition lets us tap into the massively growing space of online gaming and to develop capabilities to manage virtual currencies, a business that is projected to nearly double by 2014. The acquisition isn't just about gaming, though. It's about getting the capabilities and talent we need to expand the Serve platform into new features and applications.

Critical Thinking

1. Schulman states that cash, currently used for 85 percent of transactions worldwide will become less dominant. Why would this be? What are the implications of cash becoming a less dominant currency of transaction?

2. Shulman states that American Express has always shared aggregated data with merchants to inform their marketing. Do you view this as an appropriate action by American Express? Why?

3. Shulman discusses the ability for a mobile phone to provide a retailer with sufficient information so that the retailer can customize the shopping experience in real time. Do you think this is something most shoppers would want, or would most shoppers avoid providing information to the retailer? Does this become a way for traditional physical stores to compete more effectively with online retailers?

From *Technology Review*, March 7, 2012. Copyright © 2012 by MIT Press. Reprinted by permission via Copyright Clearance Center.

UNIT 3

Work and the Workplace

Unit Selections

Learning Outcomes

After reading this Unit, you will be able to:

- Discuss some of the impacts automation is having on the workplace.

- Understand many of the subtle relationships between productivity, labor, and consumption.

- Enumerate some of the explanations for why women avoid computer science.

- Understand issues telecommuters face.

- Define telepresence and virtual teleconferencing, and be able to describe how each are used to support both telecommuting and virtual teamwork.

- Describe the strengths and weaknesses of Steve Jobs' management style.

- Understand how Apple's iPod/iPhone/iPad technologies were informed more by the movie makers at Pixar than by computer makers at Apple and IBM.

Student Website

www.mhhe.com/cls

Internet References

American Telecommuting Association
www.yourata.com/telecommuting

Computers in the Workplace
www.cpsr.org/issues/industry

Computer Supported Cooperative Work
http://cscw.acm.org

STEP ON IT! Pedals: Repetitive Strain Injury
www.bilbo.com/rsi2.html

What about Computers in the Workplace?
http://law.freeadvice.com/intellectual_ property/computer_law/

As I write this introduction, the United States is heading into the final stretch of a Presidential election where the primary topic of policy debate is jobs. The American workforce has just experienced a recession that triggered a wave of unemployment peaking at about ten percent in 2009 and remaining over eight percent late in 2012. Many subsets of the workforce, such as youth (13.7 percent) and workers with no high school education (12.7 percent) are experiencing unemployment rates much higher than this.[1] We are undergoing a shift in the American workforce that many commentators—Tom Friedman among them—believe is due, in part, to technological change. Readings in this Unit explore three distinct dimensions of change in the workplace: how automation—the technology itself—impacts change; how globalization—the Flat World that has emerged with assistance from technology—impacts change; and demographics—in particular the presence or absence of women in the workforce—impacts change.

Beyond automation and gender, a third major trend affecting the workplace today is globalization. If you are a white collar knowledge worker in America today, you most likely work on one or more teams distributed virtually across department, division, or organizational boundaries. Your teammates may work and live in other cities or other countries. Some may work from home and telecommute. Work participation is mediated by several forms of communication and collaboration technology. While some of these technology skills (working with texting and social networking, for example) come naturally to many twenty-somethings entering the workforce, they may be less natural to managers a generation older. Further, many large companies, as Rachel Emma Silverman describes in "My Life as a Telecommuting Robot", are experimenting with virtual telepresence, social immersion, and robot avatars.

As you read Silverman's description of her sometimes awkward experience piloting her telepresence robot around a remote company office, consider what aspects of presence are important. How important is it to see one's surroundings, to hear, to be able to turn one's head, to be able to ambulate (move about)? And why are any of these affordances important?

Perhaps the real affordances are more subtle. Perhaps one needs to have a private conversation; to whisper. Perhaps one needs to steal a peak of the memo upside down on the desk opposite. Perhaps one needs to read non-verbal body language cues—and provide cues oneself. Perhaps one needs to participate in informal conversation over lunch or at a bar after work. For the dimensions you deem important, which technologies help us to get there? And which technologies, if any, actually impede us from achieving what we need.

Brian Hayes, in "Automation on the Job", explores the paradox of automation in the workplace. On one hand, as we develop better technologies: faster assembly lines; smarter computers; better robots, we should become more productive to produce more goods and services in less time and at less cost. As Hayes points out, economist John Maynard Keynes predicted in 1930 that by today we would only have to work a 15 hour workweek to earn sufficient income to live comfortably. Keynes said our

© Blend Images/Inti St Clair/Getty Images

biggest worry would be how to fill all our leisure time. While he was wrong, it is true that on average we work a shorter week and enjoy a higher standard of living that our ancestors 90 years ago.

Well, this is true for some of us. Because the other side of the paradox of automation is the machines that enable us to be more productive do so by doing the jobs of the least skilled in the workforce. Many of those jobs—such as on auto assembly lines—are now manned by robots. And the people who no longer have these low skilled jobs sometimes find there is no other job available to replace it. In this sense, perhaps automation has contributed to the claim we've heard in this presidential election that the rich and the poor in the United States are growing father apart.

As you read this first article, think about how you—if you were enabled to inform national policy—might address the systemic issues of automation. And as you think about this, reflect back on the five ideas about technological change Postman proposes in Unit 1 to see if those ideas help guide you to a resolution of this paradox.

In "The Lost Steve Jobs Tapes", we listen in to highlights from a decade of interviews after Jobs was booted out from Apple in 1985 until the time he returned and became CEO in 1997. Whether or not you read the recent Steve Jobs biography, whether or not you are an Apple fan-boy (or girl), these interviews are fascinating as they depict the growth of Jobs from a brilliant but mercurial child-like tyrant during his first tenure at Apple, to a much more matured (though still sometimes a mercurial tyrant) during his second tenure. Much of the decade journey in between is not well known to the general public but includes his founding of another computer company, NeXT, with both radical computing and business operation ideas, as well as his founding of Pixar, and his role that drove the making of Toy Story. In many ways, Jobs is as much the father of modern computer animation in the movie business as he is of the iPhone. There are several lessons to be learned about creativity, perserverence, leadership, and management from these interviews—both by watching what Jobs did right as well as watching what he did wrong.

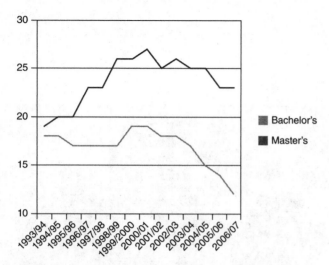

Figure 1   Percentage of Female CS/CE Grads.   Graph from http://blog.jolieodell.com/2010/08/31/women-in-tech-stats/ based on data from http://archive.cra.org/info/taulbee/women.html

The Labor Force Statistics noted above contain interesting interactions between gender and other demographic variables. While youth unemployment (20 to 24 year olds) is at 13.7 percent, men in this age group are at 14.6 percent unemployment while women are only at 12.7 percent. Several hypotheses for this difference might be proposed including differing level of maturity and life experience, differing ratios entering the workforce, or differing occupational preferences. The last hypothesis—that men differ from women in the fields of work they gravitate to and these fields are experiencing different levels of job loss—might explain much of the variance. After all, we see more men who opt to become auto mechanics and more women who opt to become nurses, though there are surely exceptions to the norm in both of these fields.

Finally, the most interesting occupational data comes from observing long term trends. Paul De Palma, in "Women, Mathematics, and Computing", explores a surprising downturn in the ratio of women who opt for computer science degrees since a peak of about 37 percent in 1985 down to about 28 percent by 1994. The table below, updated from the CRA Taulbee Study through 2007[2], shows the trend growing even more severe after in data reported subsequent to De Palma's article.

Two questions arise. One, why is the computing profession experiencing this trend—a trend that differs from other science and engineering professions? What is it about the work or the culture of computer science that is contributing to the downturn in women entering the profession? And two, why should we care? Does it make a difference to society to have less women enter computing fields? Is software, on the whole, different if written by a woman instead of a man?

Notes

1. Labor Force Statistics from the Current Population Survey www.bls.gov/cps/demographics.htm#age July 2012 data, retrieved September 1, 2012.

2. http://archive.cra.org/statistics/ Retreived September 1, 2012.

My Life as a Telecommuting Robot

As more employees work remotely, companies are looking for high-tech ways to hook them in. WSJ's Rachel Emma Silverman experiments with a telepresence robot to zoom around WSJ newsroom and chat with colleagues from her home office in Austin, Texas.

RACHEL EMMA SILVERMAN

I was strolling down the hall to a meeting on a Wednesday afternoon when I suddenly blacked out, coming to a halt. Stopping by a colleague's desk to say hello, I never saw the Nerf ball he aimed at my cranium. Later, when an editor absently patted my head as he passed by, I crashed to the floor.

Thus went my short, eventful life as QB-82, a wheeled, skinny robot that can reach a height of more than six feet. On the QB-82, my face and voice appeared via the robot's 3.5-inch video screen. Using my laptop's arrow keys, I navigated around the Journal's headquarters—becoming a kind of chatty, whirring, stick-figure colleague.

Its maker, Anybots Inc., says such telepresence robots enable far-flung workers to collaborate with peers and log face time at the office—still crucial for getting ahead, recent studies have found.

As a remote worker based for years in Austin, Texas, the idea of being two places at once sounded intriguing. I communicate with my New York-based editors and co-workers via email, phone and occasional Skype chats, but maybe "botting" could be better.

Over several weeks this summer, for a few hours a day, I used the QB to bot into the Wall Street Journal's newsroom from my home office.

Rolling around on a Segway-like wheeled base, with a video screen and camera embedded in my "head," I could see and hear my co-workers, who likewise had a portal into my home office life, complete with cameos from my kids and occasional barks from my dog, Bosco.

The robot made me feel closer to distant colleagues. But is it the future of work?

The workforce is increasingly mobile and spread out, but our jobs require more collaboration than ever before. Sales of "telepresence" and videoconferencing systems, from companies such as Cisco Systems Inc., Polycom Inc. and Logitech International unit LifeSize, were about $3 billion world-wide in 2011, a 34% increase from the $2.2 billion the previous year, according to Infonetics Research, an industry tracker.

Some firms are buying enhanced videoconferencing systems that allow remote workers to join meetings and share notes, data or sketches with ease, imbuing conference calls with Hollywood-style lighting and sound.

Others are installing video screens dubbed "wormholes" or virtual windows, so that far-off teams appear to be working side-by-side. Firms are also installing meeting areas with seating configured in a horseshoe shape so that workers attending via videoconference appear to be sitting in the same room.

Cisco has even experimented with holographic video, which involves three-dimensional representations of meeting participants, but says the technology is still too costly for wide use.

The small number of firms trying out telepresence robots say they spur more personal connections with remote workers. Phil Libin, chief executive of software maker Evernote Corp., uses a QB to check in on his Redwood City, Calif., office when he's away. "I'll roll around and chat with people. It gives you that casual, serendipitous connection," he says.

During my robot days, I interacted with co-workers I'd never met before, as well as others I hadn't talked with in years; each of them was compelled to greet me as I cruised down the hall. I chitchatted at the office coffee bar, a more lively scene than sipping coffee alone in my kitchen.

Digital Bridges

Other technologies for remote office workers:

- Virtual "windows" or "wormholes" that allow faraway teams to appear to be working alongside each other.
- High-definition "telepresence" videoconferencing systems, allowing workers to toggle between images of shared data and their colleagues' faces.
- Telepresence robots that employees can use to move around the office remotely.
- Holographic video, producing 3-D representations of meeting participants, but Cisco Systems says the technology is still too expensive for wide use.

But I also nearly careened into glass walls, got stuck in an elevator, could barely hear the discussions in story meetings and got little other writing or interview work done while botting into the newsroom.

Technical glitches delayed our progress—we cycled through two robots before a third worked reliably, and it required hours of in-house tech support from Willie Bennett, an indefatigable member of our IT staff whose Job-like patience was tested here. (To their credit, Anybots went above and beyond to troubleshoot, even flying a technician to our New York offices from California to investigate an issue.) Bill Murvihill, a business development executive at Anybots, says customers can send faulty robots back for repairs, but given the Journal's deadlines, the company opted to send a technician.

Wherever I went, I needed a constant handler and guide, and the spotty wireless signal often left me stranded—the video window on my laptop in Texas frozen as the Robot Rachel in New York went dead.

When a co-worker attempted to roll me into an area with better connectivity, the robot would thrash around, emitting an alarming, guttural noise that startled all in its vicinity.

Because of technological hurdles and expense, it will be some time before robots are as common in the office as, say, Skype. Anybots has built only 130 of its "QB" robots, and sold about 50 since they were first released in 2010. Current models sell for about $9,700. (Other companies developing telepresence robots include VGo Communications Inc., Xaxxon Technologies, iRobot Corp. and Suitable Technologies.)

Mr. Murvihill says that the Santa Clara, Calif., company is "very much aware of the technical problems" and is planning to have a more reliable robot out before the end of the year. He adds that Anybots had no control over our Wi-Fi coverage and that the robot isn't designed to go into elevators.

The QB was a hit in the office. People connected with Robot Rachel, whose friendly mien was hard to resist, proved by the curious colleagues who left their desks and trailed the rolling bot, Pied Piper-style. I even chatted with the Journal's top editor at the daily morning-news meeting, which never happened before from my desk in Texas.

Research conducted by Cisco, which has experimented with telepresence robots in house, found that employees were, oddly, more honest and open with a human-operated robot than with a human colleague. It's unclear why, says David Hsieh, Cisco's vice president of marketing for video and emerging business.

People may just be more present with a robot, due to the novelty factor. And because the robot "doesn't have the benefit of full body language . . . it results in a higher level of openness," Mr. Hsieh says.

Faith Brady, the receptionist at Mountain View, Calif.-based job-listings site Elance Inc., sees that in her workday. She operates a QB from her home office in Lake Villa, Ill., greeting guests in Silicon Valley and offering them a drink. Because the robot lacks arms, she hops on Skype and asks colleagues to deliver the drink.

"Once [visitors] find out I am in my home office an hour north of Chicago they are amazed," she says.

Still, when my editors and I discussed whether we'd rather invest in a robot or several plane tickets to New York, we'd choose the latter.

I may not be as cute as the QB. And flying across the country is a hassle. But to me at least, person-to-robot can't replace person-to-person—yet.

Critical Thinking

1. Silverman used a robot to virtualize herself in a distant office. As the technology is refined and becomes affordable, do you see this becoming a norm for telecommuters? Why or why not?

2. What are the advantages of a telecommuter to be tied to a mobile robot in a distant office? What are the disadvantages?

3. Silverman makes reference to other virtual workplace technologies such as video-conferencing and tele-presence. Research each of these technologies on the Web and consider the advantages and disadvantages of each compared to virtual robots.

4. About 35 percent of the white collar office workforce telecommutes at least one time a month in the United States, about double from a decade ago.

5. Why do you think we have seen an increase in telecommuting? Why do you think these people choose to telecommute?

6. What recent computing and communication technologies are most important to supporting telecommuting? Which, if any, create barriers to telecommuting?

7. Would you choose to telecommute if you had a choice?

LESLIE KWOH contributed to this article.

From *The Wall Street Journal*, August 8, 2012, pp. B1. Copyright © 2012 by Dow Jones & Company, Inc. Reprinted by permission via Copyright Clearance Center.

Automation on the Job

**Computers were supposed to be labor-saving devices.
How come we're still working so hard?**

Brian Hayes

utomation was a hot topic in the 1950s and
'60s—a subject for congressional hearings, blue-
ribbon panels, newspaper editorials, think-tank
studies, scholarly symposia, documentary films, World's
Fair exhibits, even comic strips and protest songs. There
was interest in the technology itself—everybody wanted
to know about "the factory of the future"—but the editorials and white papers focused mainly on the social and
economic consequences of automation. Nearly everyone
agreed that people would be working less once computers
and other kinds of automatic machinery became widespread. For optimists, this was a promise of liberation:
At last humanity would be freed from constant toil, and
we could all devote our days to more refined pursuits.
But others saw a threat: Millions of people would be
thrown out of work, and desperate masses would roam
the streets.

Looking back from 50 years hence, the controversy
over automation seems a quaint and curious episode. The
dispute was never resolved; it just faded away. The factory of the future did indeed evolve; but at the same time
the future evolved away from the factory, which is no longer such a central institution in the economic scheme of
things, at least in the United States. As predicted, computers guide machine tools and run assembly lines, but
that's a minor part of their role in society. The computer is
far more pervasive in everyday life than even the boldest
technophiles dared to dream back in the days of punch
cards and mainframes.

As for economic consequences, worries about unemployment have certainly not gone away—not with job
losses in the current recession approaching 2 million
workers in the U.S. alone. But recent job losses are commonly attributed to causes other than automation, such
as competition from overseas or a roller-coaster financial
system. In any case, the vision of a world where machines
do all the work and people stand idly by has simply not
come to pass.

The Problem of Leisure

In 1930 the British economist John Maynard Keynes published a short essay titled "Economic Possibilities for Our
Grandchildren." At the time, the economic possibilities
looked pretty grim, but Keynes was implacably cheerful.
By 2030, he predicted, average income would increase by
a factor of between four and eight. This prosperity would
be brought about by gains in productivity: Aided by new
technology, workers would produce more with less effort.

Keynes did not mention *automation*—the word would
not be introduced until some years later—but he did refer
to *technological unemployment,* a term that goes back to
Karl Marx. For Keynes, a drop in the demand for labor
was a problem with an easy solution: Just work less. A
3-hour shift and a 15-hour workweek would become the
norm for the grandchildren of the children of 1930, he
said. This would be a momentous development in human
history. After millennia of struggle, we would have finally
solved "the economic problem": How to get enough to
eat. The new challenge would be the problem of leisure:
How to fill the idle hours.

Decades later, when automation became a contentious
issue, there were other optimists. The conservative economist Yale Brozen wrote in 1963:

> Perhaps the gains of the automation revolution will
> carry us on from a mass democracy to a mass aristoc-
> racy. . . . The common man will become a university-
> educated world traveler with a summer place in the
> country, enjoying such leisure-time activities as
> sailing and concert going.

But others looked at the same prospect and saw a darker picture. Norbert Wiener had made important contributions to the theory of automatic control, but he was wary of its social implications. In *The Human Use of Human Beings* (1950) he wrote:

> Let us remember that the automatic machine . . . is the precise economic equivalent of slave labor. Any labor which competes with slave labor must accept the economic conditions of slave labor. It is perfectly clear that this will produce an unemployment situation, in comparison with which the present recession and even the depression of the thirties will seem a pleasant joke.

A. J. Hayes, a labor leader (and no relation to me), wrote in 1964:

> Automation is not just a new kind of mechanization but a revolutionary force capable of overturning our social order. Whereas mechanization made workers more efficient—and thus more valuable—automation threatens to make them superfluous—and thus without value.

Keynes's "problem of leisure" is also mentioned with much anxiety throughout the literature of the automation era. In a 1962 pamphlet Donald N. Michael wrote:

> These people will work short hours, with much time for the pursuit of leisure activities. . . . Even with a college education, what will they do all their long lives, day after day, four-day weekend after weekend, vacation after vacation . . .?

The opinions I have cited here represent extreme positions, and there were also many milder views. But I think it's fair to say that most early students of automation, including both critics and enthusiasts, believed the new technology would lead us into a world where people worked much less.

Where's My 15-Hour Workweek?

Keynes's forecast of growth in productivity and personal income seemed wildly optimistic in 1930, but in fact he underestimated. The upper bound of his prediction—an eightfold increase over 100 years—works out to an annual growth rate of 2.1 percent. So far, the observed average rate comes to 2.9 percent per year. If that rate is extrapolated to 2030, worldwide income will have increased by a factor of 17 in a century. (These calculations are reported by Fabrizio Zilibotti of the University of Zurich in a recent book reassessing Keynes's 1930 essay.)

Keynes's promise of affluence has already been more than fulfilled—at least for citizens of wealthier nations. It's a remarkable achievement, even if we have not yet truly and permanently "solved the economic problem." If Keynes was right about the accumulation of wealth, however, he missed the mark in predicting time spent on the job. By most estimates, the average workweek was about 60 hours in 1900, and it had fallen to about 50 hours when Keynes wrote in 1930. There was a further decline to roughly 40 hours per week in the 1950s and '60s, but since then the workweek has changed little, at least in the U.S. Western Europeans work fewer hours, but even there the trend doesn't look like we're headed for a 15-hour week anytime soon.

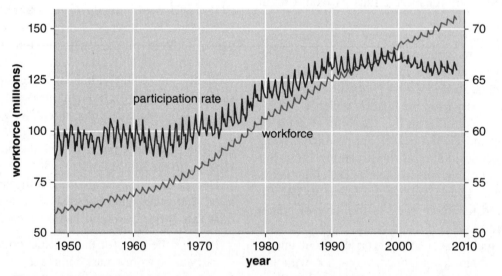

The size of the U.S. labor force has increased steadily throughout the period in which automation has taken hold. The increase is not merely an effect of population growth. The participation rate—the percentage of the adult population that is working or seeking work—has also risen, largely because of women entering the workforce. The data are from the Bureau of Labor Statistics of the U.S. Department of Labor. The saw-tooth fluctuations are seasonal.

Other measures of how hard people are working tell a similar story. The total labor force in the U.S. has increased by a factor of 2.5 since 1950, growing substantially faster than the working-age population. Thus labor-force participation (the percentage of people who hold jobs, among all those who could in principle be working) has risen from 59 percent to 66 percent.

These trends contradict almost all the expectations of early writers on automation, both optimists and pessimists. So far, automation has neither liberated us from the need to work nor deprived us of the opportunity to work. Instead, we're working more than ever.

Economists reflecting on Keynes's essay suggest he erred in supposing that people would willingly trade income for leisure. Instead, the commentators say, people work overtime to buy the new wide-screen TV even if they then have no time to enjoy it. Perhaps so. I would merely add that many who are working long hours (postdocs, say, or parents of young children) do not see their behavior as a product of conscious choice. And they do not think society has "solved the economic problem."

On the Factory Floor

Perhaps the most thoughtful and knowledgeable of the early writers on automation was John Diebold, a consultant and author. It was Diebold who introduced the word *automation* in its broad, modern sense. He clearly understood that there was more to it than reducing labor costs in factories. He foresaw applications to many other kinds of work, including clerical tasks, warehousing and even retailing. Nevertheless, when he chose examples for detailed description, they almost always came from manufacturing.

Automatic control first took hold in continuous-process industries such as oil refining. A closed-loop control mechanism could regulate the temperature of a distilling tower, eliminating the need for a worker to monitor a gauge and adjust valve settings. As such instruments proliferated, a refinery became a depopulated industrial landscape. An entire plant could be run by a few technicians, huddled together in a glass-walled control room. This hands-off mode of operation became the model that other industries strove to emulate.

In the automation literature of the 1950s and '60s, attention focuses mainly on manufacturing, and especially on the machining of metal. A celebrated example was the Ford Motor Company's Cleveland Engine Plant No. 1, built in 1951, where a series of interconnected machines took in raw castings at one end and disgorged finished engine blocks at the other. The various tools within this complex performed several hundred boring and milling operations on each engine, with little manual intervention.

A drawback of the Ford approach to automation was inflexibility. Any change to the product would require an extensive overhaul of the machinery. But this problem was overcome with the introduction of programmable metalworking tools, which eventually became computer-controlled devices.

Other kinds of manufacturing also shifted to automated methods, although the result was not always exactly what had been expected. In the early years, it was easy to imagine a straightforward substitution of machines for labor: Shove aside a worker and install a machine in his or her place. The task to be performed would not change, only the agent performing it. The ultimate expression of this idea was the robot—a one-for-one replacement for the factory worker. But automation has seldom gone this way.

Consider the manufacture of electronic devices. At the outset, this was a labor-intensive process of placing components on a chassis, stringing wires between them and soldering the connections one by one. Attempts to build automatic equipment to perform the same operations proved impractical. Instead, the underlying technology was changed by introducing printed circuit boards, with all the connections laid out in advance. Eventually, machines were developed for automatically placing the parts on the boards and for soldering the connections all at once.

The further evolution of this process takes us to the integrated circuit, a technology that was automated from birth. The manufacture of microprocessor chips could not possibly be carried out as a handicraft business; no sharp-eyed artisan could draw the minuscule circuit patterns on silicon wafers. For many other businesses as well, manual methods are simply unthinkable. Google could not operate by hiring thousands of clerks to read Web pages and type out the answers to queries.

The automation of factories has gone very much according to the script written by Diebold and other early advocates. Computer control is all but universal. Whole sections of automobile assembly plants are now walled off to exclude all workers. A computer screen and a keyboard are the main interface to most factory equipment.

Meanwhile, though, manufacturing as a whole has become a smaller part of the U.S. economy—12 percent of gross domestic product in 2005, down from more than double that in the 1950s. And because of the very success of industrial automation, employment on production lines has fallen even faster than the share of GDP. Thus, for most Americans, the factory automation that was so much the focus of early commentary is all but invisible. Few of us ever get a chance to see it at work.

But automation and computer technology have infiltrated other areas of the economy and daily life—office work, logistics, commerce, finance, household tasks. When you look for the impact of computers on society, barcodes are probably more important than machine tools.

The Do-It-Yourself Economy

In the 1950s, digital computers were exotic, expensive, unapproachable and mysterious. It was far easier to see such a machine becoming the nexus of control in a vast industrial enterprise than to imagine the computer transformed into a household object, comparable to a telephone or a typewriter—or even a toy for the children to play with. Donald Michael wrote:

> Most of our citizens will be unable to understand the cybernated world in which they live. . . . There will be a small, almost separate, society of people in rapport with the advanced computers. . . . Those with the talent for the work probably will have to develop it from childhood and will be trained as intensively as the classical ballerina.

If this attitude of awestruck reverence had persisted, most of the computer's productive potential would have been wasted. Computers became powerful when they became ubiquitous—not inscrutable oracles guarded by a priestly elite but familiar appliances found on every desk. These days, we are all expected to have rapport with computers.

The spread of automation outside of the factory has altered its social and economic impact in some curious ways. In many cases, the net effect of automation is not that machines are doing work that people used to do. Instead we've dispensed with the people who used to be paid to run the machines, and we've learned to run them ourselves. When you withdraw money from the bank via an ATM, buy an airline ticket online, ride an elevator or fill up the gas tank at a self-service pump, you are interacting directly with a machine to carry out a task that once required the intercession of an employee.

The dial telephone is the archetypal example. My grandmother's telephone had no dial; she placed calls by asking a switchboard operator to make the connection. The dial (and the various other mechanisms that have since replaced it) empowers you to set up the communications channel without human assistance. Thus it's not quite accurate to say that the operator has been replaced by a machine. A version of the circuit-switching machine was there all along; the dial merely provided a convenient interface to it.

The process of making travel arrangements has been transformed in a similar way. It was once the custom to telephone a travel agent, who would search an airline database for a suitable flight with seats available. Through the Web, most of us now access that database directly; we even print our own boarding passes. Again, what has

happened here is not exactly the substitution of machines for people; it is a matter of putting the customer in control of the machines.

Other Internet technologies are taking this process one more dizzy step forward. Because many Web sites have published interface specifications, I now have the option of writing a program to access them. Having already removed the travel agent, I can now automate myself out of the loop as well.

The Full-Employment Paradox

Enabling people to place their own phone calls and make their own travel reservations has put whole categories of jobs on the brink of extinction. U.S. telephone companies once employed more than 250,000 telephone operators; the number remaining is a tenth of that, and falling fast. It's the same story for gas-station attendants, elevator operators and dozens of other occupations. And yet we have not seen the great contraction of the workforce that seemed inevitable 50 years ago.

One oft-heard explanation holds that automation brings a net increase in employment by creating jobs for people who design, build and maintain machines. A strong version of this thesis is scarcely plausible. It implies that the total labor requirement per unit of output is higher in the automated process than in the manual one; if that were the case, it would be hard to see the economic incentive for adopting automation. A weaker but likelier version concedes that labor per unit of output declines under automation, but total output increases enough to compensate. Even for this weaker prediction, however, there is no guarantee of such a rosy outcome. The relation may well be supported by historical evidence, but it has no theoretical underpinning in economic principles.

For a theoretical analysis we can turn to Herbert A. Simon, who was both an economist and a computer scientist and would thus seem to be the ideal analyst. In a 1965 essay, Simon noted that economies seek equilibrium, and so "both men and machines can be fully employed regardless of their relative productivity." It's just a matter of adjusting the worker's wage until it balances the cost of machinery. Of course there's no guarantee that the equilibrium wage will be above the subsistence level. But Simon then offered a more complex argument showing that any increase in productivity, whatever the underlying cause, should increase wages as well as the return on capital investment. Do these two results add up to perpetual full employment at a living wage in an automated world? I don't believe they offer any such guarantee, but perhaps the calculations are reassuring nonetheless.

Another kind of economic equilibrium also offers a measure of cheer. The premise is that whatever you earn, you eventually spend. (Or else your heirs spend it for you.) If technological progress makes some commodity cheaper, then the money that used to go that product will have to be spent on something else. The flow of funds toward the alternative sectors will drive up prices there and create new economic opportunities. This mode of reasoning offers an answer to questions such as, "Why has health care become so expensive in recent years?" The answer is: Because everything else has gotten so cheap.

I can't say that any of these formulations puts my mind at ease. On the other hand, I do have faith in the resilience of people and societies. The demographic history of agriculture offers a precedent that is both sobering and reassuring. It's not too much of an exaggeration to say that before 1800 everyone in North America was a farmer, and now no one is. In other words, productivity gains in agriculture put an entire population out of work. This was a wrenching experience for those forced to leave the farm, but the fact remains that they survived and found other ways of life. The occupational shifts caused by computers and automation cannot possibly match the magnitude of that great upheaval.

The Future of the Future

What comes next in the march of progress? Have we reached the end point in the evolution of computerized society?

Since I have poked fun at the predictions of an earlier generation, it's only fair that I put some of my own silly notions on the record, giving some future pundit a chance to mock me in turn. I think the main folly of my predecessors was not being reckless enough. I'll probably make the same mistake myself. So here are three insufficiently outrageous predictions.

1. We'll automate medicine. I don't mean robot surgeons, although they're in the works too. What I have in mind is Internet-enabled, do-it-yourself diagnostics. Google is already the primary-care physician for many of us; that role can be expanded in various directions. Furthermore, as mentioned above, medical care is where the money is going, and so that's where investment in cost-saving technologies has the most leverage.

2. We'll automate driving. The car that drives itself is a perennial on lists of future marvels, mentioned by a number of the automation prophets of the 50s and 60s. A fully autonomous vehicle, able to navigate ordinary streets and roads, is not much closer now than it was then, but a combination of smarter cars and smarter roads could be made to work. Building those roads would require a major infrastructure project, which might help make up for all the disemployed truckers and taxi drivers. I admit to a certain boyish fascination with the idea of a car that drops me at the office and then goes to fetch the dry cleaning and fill up its own gas tank.

3. We'll automate warfare. I take no pleasure in this one, but I see no escaping it either. The most horrific weapons of the 20th century had the redeeming quality that they are difficult and expensive to build, and this has limited their proliferation. When it comes to the most fashionable weapons of the present day—pilotless aircraft, cruise missiles, precision-guided munitions—the key technology is available on the shelf at Radio Shack.

What about trades closer to my own vital interests? Will science be automated? Technology already has a central role in many areas of research; for example, genome sequences could not be read by traditional lab-bench methods. Replacing the scientist will presumably be a little harder that replacing the lab technician, but when a machine exhibits enough curiosity and tenacity, I think we'll just have to welcome it as a companion in zealous research.

And if the scientist is elbowed aside by an automaton, then surely the science writer can't hold out either. I'm ready for my 15-hour workweek.

Bibliography

Buckingham, Walter S. 1961. *Automation: Its Impact on Business and People.* New York: Harper and Row.

Cortada, James W. 2004. *The Digital Hand: How Computers Changed the Work of American Manufacturing, Transportation, and Retail Industries.* Oxford: Oxford University Press.

Diebold, John. 1952. *Automation: The Advent of the Automatic Factory.* New York: D. Van Nostrand Company.

Einzig, Paul. 1956. *The Economic Consequences of Automation.* London: Secker and Warburg.

Hayes, A. J. 1964. Automation: A real "H" bomb. In *Jobs, Men, and Machines: Problems of Automation,* ed. Charles Markham, New York: Frederick A. Praeger, pp. 48–57.

Keynes, John Maynard. 1930. Economic possibilities for our grandchildren. Reprinted in *Revisiting Keynes: Economic Possibilities for Our Grandchildren,* ed. Lorenzo Pecchi and Gustavo Piga, Cambridge, Mass.: The MIT Press.

Leontief, Wassily. 1952. Machines and man. *Scientific American* 187(3):150–160.

Lilley, S. 1957. *Automation and Social Progress.* New York: International Publishers.

Michael, Donald N. 1962. *Cybernation: The Silent Conquest.* Santa Barbara, Calif.: Center for the Study of Democratic Institutions.

Pecchi, Lorenzo, and Gustavo Piga. 2008. *Revisiting Keynes: Economic Possibilities for Our Grandchildren.* Cambridge, Mass.: The MIT Press.

Philipson, Morris. 1962. *Automation: Implications for the Future.* New York: Vintage Books.

Pollock, Frederick. 1957. *Automation: A Study of Its Economic and Social Consequences.* Translated by W. O. Henderson and W. H. Chaloner. New York: Frederick A. Praeger.

Simon, Herbert A. 1965. *The Shape of Automation for Men and Management.* New York: Harper and Row.

Whaples, Robert. 2001. Hours of work in U.S. history. *EH.Net Encyclopedia,* Economic History Association. eh.net/encyclopedia/article/whaples.work.hours.us.

Wiener, Norbert. 1954. *The Human Use of Human Beings: Cybernetics and Society.* New York: Avon Books.

Critical Thinking

1. Who was John Maynard Keynes? His name is associated with a particular way of stimulating a sluggish economy. Use the Internet to find out more about it. Would he be more closely aligned with the modern democratic or republican parties?

2. Hayes says that labor force participation has risen from 59 percent to 66 percent since 1950. That is, more and more of us are working. What change in cultural mores allowed this shift to happen?

3. The decline in manufacturing employment parallels a decline in union membership since the 1950s. Are they related? Use the Internet (and a reference librarian) to try to untangle them.

4. What is the "full-employment paradox"? What are some of the explanations that Hayes offers?

5. Hayes has very little to say about a globalized labor force. Investigate labor productivity in Chinese factories. How has the cost of labor in China affected the incentive to automate?

6. Hayes sometimes writes of technological progress as if it were a force of nature (e.g., "If technological progress makes some commodity cheaper . . ."). Does he slip on Postman's fifth big idea, that is, the tendency to think of technology as a force of its own rather than a specific response to a specific set of circumstances?

From *American Scientist*, January/February 2009. Copyright © 2009 by American Scientist, magazine of Sigma Xi, The Scientific Research Society. Reprinted by permission.

The Lost Steve Jobs Tapes

A treasure trove of unearthed interviews, conducted by the writer who knew him best, reveals how Jobs's ultimate success at Apple can be traced directly to his so-called wilderness years.

BRENT SCHLENDER

If Steve Jobs's life were staged as an opera, it would be a tragedy in three acts. And the titles would go something like this: Act I—The Founding of Apple Computer and the Invention of the PC Industry; Act II—The Wilderness Years; and Act III—A Triumphant Return and Tragic Demise.

The first act would be a piquant comedy about the brashness of genius and the audacity of youth, abruptly turning ominous when our young hero is cast out of his own kingdom. The closing act would plumb the profound irony of a balding and domesticated high-tech rock star coming back to transform Apple far beyond even his own lofty expectations, only to fall mortally ill and then slowly, excruciatingly wither away, even as his original creation miraculously bulks up into the biggest digital dynamo of them all. Both acts are picaresque tales that end with a surge of deep pathos worthy of Shakespeare.

But that second act—The Wilderness Years—would be altogether different in tone and spirit. In fact, the soul of this act would undermine its title, a convenient phrase journalists and biographers use to describe his 1985 to 1996 hiatus from Apple, as if the only meaningful times in Jobs's life were those spent in Cupertino. In fact, this middle period was the most pivotal of his life. And perhaps the happiest. He finally settled down, married, and had a family. He learned the value of patience and the ability to feign it when he lost it. Most important, his work with the two companies he led during that time, NeXT and Pixar, turned him into the kind of man, and leader, who would spur Apple to unimaginable heights upon his return.

Indeed, what at first glance seems like more wandering for the barefoot hippie who dropped out of Reed College to hitchhike around India, is in truth the equivalent of Steve Jobs attending business school. In other words, he grew. By leaps and bounds. In every aspect of his being. With a little massaging, this middle act could even be the plotline for a Pixar movie. It certainly fits the simple mantra John Lasseter ascribes to all the studio's successes, from Toy Story to Up: "It's gotta be about how the main character changes for the better."

I had covered Jobs for Fortune and The Wall Street Journal since 1985, but I didn't come to fully appreciate the importance of these "lost" years until after his death last fall. Rummaging through the storage shed, I discovered some three dozen tapes holding recordings of extended interviews—some lasting as long as three hours—that I'd conducted with him periodically over the past 25 years. (Snippets are scattered throughout this story.) Many I had never replayed—a couple hadn't even been transcribed before now. Some were interrupted by his kids bolting into the kitchen as we talked. During others, he would hit the pause button himself before saying something he feared might come back to bite him. Listening to them again with the benefit of hindsight, the ones that took place during that interregnum jump out as especially enlightening.

The lessons are powerful: Jobs matured as a manager and a boss; learned how to make the most of partnerships; found a way to turn his native stubbornness into a productive perseverance. He became a corporate architect, coming to appreciate the scaffolding of a business just as much as the skeletons of real buildings, which always fascinated him. He mastered the art of negotiation by immersing himself in Hollywood, and learned how to successfully manage creative talent, namely the artists at Pixar. Perhaps most important, he developed an astonishing adaptability that was critical to the hit-after-hit-after-hit climb of Apple's last decade. All this, during a time many remember as his most disappointing.

Eleven years is a big chunk of a lifetime. Especially when one's time on earth is cut short. Moreover, many people—particularly creative types—are often their most prolific during their thirties and early forties. With all the heady success of Apple during Jobs's last 14 years, it's all too easy to dismiss these "lost" years. But in truth, they transformed everything. As I listened again to those hours and hours of tapes, I realized they were, in fact, his most productive.

Steve Jobs did not wander aimlessly into the wilderness after being ousted from Apple in 1985. No happy camper, he was loaded for bear; burning to wreak revenge upon those who had spuriously shoved him into exile, and obsessed with proving to the world that he was no one-trick pony. Within days, he abruptly sold off all but one share of his Apple stock and, flush with a small fortune of about $70 million, set about creating another computer company, this one called NeXT. The startup ostensibly was a vehicle for revolutionizing higher education with powerful, beautiful computers. In reality, it was a bet that one day he would get the better of Apple.

Over all the years Jobs was away from Apple, I can't recall him saying one good thing about the company's brass. Early on, he whined about how CEO John Sculley had "poisoned" the culture of the place. As the years went by, and Apple's fortunes dimmed, Jobs's attacks became more pointed: "Right now it's like the wicked witch in The Wizard of Oz: 'I'm melting. I'm melting,' " he told me in the mid-1990s. "The jig is up. They can't seem to come out with a great computer to save their lives. They need to spend big on industrial design, reintroduce the hipness factor. But no, they hire [Gil] Amelio [as CEO]. It's as if Nike hired the guy that ran Kinney shoes."

At NeXT, Jobs was damn well going to deliver a great computer. He was going to do it with massive resources, raising well over

$100 million from the likes of H. Ross Perot, Japanese printer maker Canon, and Carnegie Mellon University. He was going to do it with an astonishing automated factory in Fremont, California, where every surface and piece of equipment would be painted in specific shades of gray, black, and white. He was going to do it in style, working with a full-time architect to give the corporate headquarters in Redwood City a distinctive, austere aesthetic; NeXT HQ looked much like the interior of one of today's Apple Stores. The centerpiece was a staircase that seemed to float in air.

He was also going to do it with a revolutionary organization, something he dubbed the Open Corporation. "Think of it this way," he explained. "If you look at your own body, your cells are specialized, but every single one of them has the master plan for the whole body. We think our company will be the best possible company if every single person working here understands the whole master plan and can use that as a yardstick to make decisions against. We think a lot of little and medium and big decisions will be made better if all our people know that." It was a bold theory.

If Jobs's time in exile can be seen as an extended trip through business school, the heady start of NeXT represents those early days when a student thinks he knows everything and is in a rush to show that to the world. In fact, Jobs had just about every detail wrong. The Open Corporation was a dismal failure in practice. Its hallmark was that employee salaries were not kept secret; there was even an attempt to impose uniform compensation. It didn't work, of course; all kinds of side deals were cut to satiate key employees.

More concretely, Jobs had the whole business plan wrong. It would be two years before NeXT delivered anything to customers. When the NeXTcube computer finally did arrive, it proved too expensive to ever command a serious market. Ultimately, Jobs was forced to admit that the undeniably beautiful machine he and his engineering team concocted was a flop. He laid off most of the staff and turned the company from hardware to software, first to rewrite NeXT's operating system, called NextSTEP, for Intel-based computers. The company also engineered an ingenious development environment called WebObjects, which eventually became its best-selling program.

Jobs didn't know that WebObjects would later prove instrumental in building the online store for Apple and for iTunes, or that NextSTEP would be his ticket back to Apple. The road for NeXT was always rocky, perhaps appropriate for something that was born out of a desire for revenge. It was a good thing he had something else going on the side.

Of the three companies Jobs helped create, Pixar was the purest corporate and organizational expression of his nature. If NeXT was a travail of spite and malice, Pixar was a labor of love.

The Pixar story began even before Jobs left Apple. In early 1985, Apple fellow Alan Kay called his attention to the computer Graphics Group (GG) skunk works in San Rafael, California, an ill-fitting piece of the filmmaking production puzzle George Lucas had assembled for his Skywalker Ranch studios. It was little more than a team of 25 engineers—including a young "user interface designer" named John Lasseter—who desperately wanted to continue to work together even though Lucas, then embroiled in the costly aftermath of a divorce, was looking to sell.

Jobs's trip to take a look-see left an indelible impression. GG's head geek, Ed Catmull, showed him some short demo films made by Lasseter, who was neither a programmer nor a user interface designer, but a talented animator who had left Disney and been given his faux title by Catmull as a way to convince Lucas to put him on the payroll. The films weren't much to look at, but they were three-dimensional, they were generated by computer rather than hand-drawn, and they displayed the whimsy of a master storyteller.

Fascinated, Jobs tried, unsuccessfully, to persuade Apple's board to buy the group. "These guys were way ahead of us on graphics, way ahead," Jobs remembered. "They were way ahead of anybody. I just knew in my bones that this was going to be very important." After getting bounced from Apple, Jobs went back to Lucas and drove a hard bargain. He paid $5 million for the group's assets and provided another $5 million in working capital for the company, which was christened Pixar. In hindsight, the price was a pittance. But in 1985, nobody would have expected Pixar to one day outstrip NeXT. Certainly not Jobs: He didn't build any fancy digs for his motley crew of animators and engineers, who for years made do with used furniture and dowdy offices.

Once again, what Jobs knew in his bones didn't translate into getting the details right. As with NeXT, Jobs initially intended the company to be a purveyor of high-performance computer hardware, this time for two frightfully niche markets: the special-effects departments of Hollywood studios and medical-imaging specialists. By 1989, however, Pixar had sold only a few hundred of its Pixar Image Computers, faux-granite painted cubes originally stickered at $135,000, that had to be paired with expensive engineering workstations to do anything.

This time, the strategy pivot came from the talent. In 1990, Lasseter and Catmull told Jobs they could make a business of creating computer-animated TV commercials—perhaps one day they could even make, and sell, cartoons! Jobs was smitten with Catmull and Lasseter. They were always teaching him something new. Could they deliver on the ultimate promise of the place, to use computers to create an entirely new kind of animation for the cinema and thus upend the entire business model of animation? Jobs decided to focus on this one disruptive opportunity. It was an instinct he would return to, repeatedly, when he rejoined Apple.

In 1991, he fired much of the Pixar staff, announced the new direction to the survivors, and reorganized so that the studio could pursue one animated project at a time. "I got everybody together," Jobs said, "and I said, 'At our heart, we really are a content company. Let's transition out of everything else. Let's go for it. This is why I bought into Pixar. This is why most of you are here. Let's go for it. It's a higher-risk strategy, but the rewards are gonna be much higher, and it's where our hearts are.'" Then he and CFO Lawrence Levy went to work learning everything they could about the dynamics and economics of the animation business. If they were going to start making cartoons, they were going to do it right.

The shift at Pixar occurred at about the same time as the major turn in Jobs's personal life: the blossoming of his romance with Laurene Powell. In 1991, two years after she met him following an informal lecture at Stanford University's Graduate School of Business, Laurene was his pregnant bride, married by a Buddhist monk at the Ahwahnee Hotel in Yosemite National Park.

Jobs had never seemed like the marrying type and hadn't shown much of a sense of responsibility for Lisa, his first daughter, who was born out of wedlock in 1978. He denied paternity initially, even though he had named an Apple computer after her. Egotistical, narcissistic, and manipulative since childhood, Jobs often behaved like a spoiled brat who was accustomed to getting his way.

His personality didn't change overnight after meeting Laurene, but his selfish ways did begin to moderate, especially after his children, Reed, Erin, and Eve, came into the family in 1991, 1995, and 1998, respectively. As is often the case with new parents, Jobs behaved as if he were the first person in the world to discover and fully appreciate the joys of family life. He literally stayed closer to home, converting a clapboard storefront building catty-corner from the Palo Alto Whole Foods into a satellite office so his commute would be a short bike ride. (He didn't use the office all that much after returning to Apple.)

My bureau was a block up the street, and occasionally I'd see him out for a stroll, usually with someone in tow. He always said he could think better when he walked. During these years, his fame had subsided somewhat, so it wasn't like encountering one of the Beatles at the supermarket. People pretty much left him alone.

I bumped into him on one of those walks when he was alone, and wound up joining him as he shopped for a new bicycle for Laurene's upcoming birthday. This was before you could do your homework on the Internet, but he had done his research, so there wasn't much shopping involved. We were in and out of Palo Alto Bicycles in 10 minutes. "I'd never have Andrea do something like this," he said, referring to his longtime administrative assistant. "I like buying presents for my family myself."

Even after he went back to Apple, there was nothing Jobs liked more than spending time at home. Not that he wasn't a workaholic. We were iChat buddies for several years, so his name would pop up whenever he was working at his computer at home. Almost invariably, he was in front of his Mac until after midnight. We'd occasionally have a video chat, and if it took place early in the evening, I'd often see one of his children in the background looking on.

In hindsight, Jobs's having a real family might have been the best thing to happen to Pixar. He was most effective as a marketer and a business leader when he could think of himself as the primary customer. What would he want from a computer-animated movie, both for himself and for his kids? That was the only market-research question he ever asked. He had always demanded great production values and design for his computer products. He was just as picky about what Pixar produced. Lasseter and Catmull couldn't have asked for a more empathetic benefactor.

Shortly after his decision in 1990 to let Lasseter and Catmull start producing commercials and short films, Jobs pulled a rabbit out of his hat: He negotiated a $26 million marketing distribution deal with Disney that provided enough capital to make a full-length, computer-animated motion picture. Because Disney had been a Pixar customer, licensing its software for managing conventional animators, then-CEO Michael Eisner and his head of animation, Jeffrey Katzenberg, were fully aware that the company's technology was solid and unique, and that Lasseter showed flashes of genius as a new breed of animator.

Jobs was candid about the two Disney execs, telling me that both "make the mistake of not appreciating technology. They just assume that they can throw money at things and fix them. They don't have a clue." Once upon a time, he would have been enraged by the ignorance he perceived. When I asked him what had soured an earlier partnership between IBM and NeXT, he ranted: "The people at the top of IBM knew nothing about computers. Nothing. Nothing. The people at the top of Disney," on the other hand, "know a lot about what a really good film is and what is not."

Even though he believed that Katzenberg and Eisner "had no clue" about how far Pixar could take them—Jobs was convinced that Pixar's technology could revolutionize the business model for animation, which was then primarily a hand-drawn art—he recognized that the partnership had more or less saved the company: "It's the biggest thing I've done for Pixar," he said. So he found a common bond between the companies. "There was a certain amount of fear and trepidation, but what always happened was that making a great movie was the focal point of everybody's concerns. One way to drive fear out of a relationship is to realize that your partner's values are the same as yours, that what you care about is exactly what they care about. In my opinion, that drives fear out and makes for a great partnership, whether it's a corporate partnership or a marriage."

Then he set about designing an organization that could deliver a great movie—and many more. His foray into Hollywood had taught him a great deal. "I started to learn about how films are made. Basically, it's bands of gypsies getting together to make a film. After the film, they disband. The problem with that is we want to build a company, not just make a single movie."

This time, there was no flighty discussion of an "open" corporation. "Incentive structures work," he told me. "So you have to be very careful of what you incent people to do, because various incentive structures create all sorts of consequences that you can't anticipate. Everybody at Pixar is incented to build the company: whether they're working on the film; whether they're working on a potential direct-to-video product; whether they're working on a CD-ROM. Whatever their combination of creative and technical talent may be, we want them incented to make the whole company successful."

There was another compensation detail that reflected how completely Jobs was able to mesh the values of Silicon Valley with Hollywood. Pixar paid its animators just as well as its software geniuses (beginning an escalation in salaries that Katzenberg accelerated later that decade at DreamWorks). "We value them both equally," Jobs said of Pixar's two talent camps. "Some people say we should value one higher than the other, but we value them equally, we pay them equally, they have stock equally. We made that decision very early. Ed Catmull made that decision, actually. We will always do that; that's one of Pixar's core values."

These were the decisions that cemented the company's future success. When Disney surprised Jobs by scheduling Pixar's first movie as its 1995 holiday feature, his team was ready, with a little picture called Toy Story. And Jobs, armed with a renegotiated Disney deal for three pictures, was ready too; Pixar went public 10 days after Toy Story's stunning debut, raising nearly $100 million.

After that, it was as if the company hit the fast-forward button. And for the rest of his life, Jobs enjoyed Pixar as he enjoyed little else. Now was the time to throw away the used furniture and build a proper studio in Emeryville, California. He relished this so much more than the NeXT headquarters—after all, this time he and his team had earned it. The design blended aspects of a Hollywood lot and an old-fashioned brick factory building, perfect for his star animators and programmers, perfect for working with Tom Hanks, Ellen DeGeneres, Owen Wilson, and all the other stars who enjoyed voicing Pixar characters. The custom-made bricks came in 12 shades, and if the colors weren't distributed evenly enough, Jobs would have the bricklayers pull them down and do it again. He would visit the construction site as often as he could as it came together, often clambering around the buildings at night, when no one but the security guards were around.

He also created something called Pixar University for the staff, where his brilliant engineers and clever artists and smart financial people could take classes in all kinds of subjects, to better appreciate what their coworkers did. There were classes in the visual arts, dance, computer programming, foreign languages, drama, mathematics, creative writing, and even accounting. "It is," he once told me, "the coolest place to work in the world."

When Jobs returned to Apple in 1997, one of the first things he did was trim the product line, focusing employees on four clear projects. He liked to explain his strategy while drawing on a whiteboard, like a professor of management.For all the joy that Pixar brought Jobs, it was NeXT that got him back to Apple. After failing to develop new software architecture for the Mac and bungling a joint venture with IBM, Apple was on its deathbed in 1996. NeXT had a powerful, modern operating system and one very persuasive storyteller, who managed to convince CEO Amelio that his stepchild could be Apple's salvation. In late 1996, Jobs sold NeXT to Apple for $400 million, which he used to pay back Perot, Canon, and some other early investors. Within six months, Jobs had mounted a putsch and became Apple's "iCEO," with the i standing for what proved to be a deeply false "interim."

The ensuing tale, the saga of the modern Apple, is simply the story of the man who emerged from that 11-year business school and implemented the lessons he had learned along the way. As was true when he started at Pixar and NeXT, Jobs had many of the details wrong when he first returned to the Apple helm. He imagined that the company's business would always be selling computers. He thought that what was then called the "information highway" would be primarily of interest to businesses. He dismissed the idea that computer networks would carry lots of video.

But some of the tougher years at NeXT and Pixar had taught him how to stretch a company's finances, which helped him ride out his first couple of years back, when Apple was still reliant on a weak jumble of offerings. With newfound discipline, he quickly streamlined the company's product lines. And just as he had at Pixar, he aligned the company behind those projects. In a way that had never been done before at a technology company—but that looked a lot like an animation studio bent on delivering one great movie a year—Jobs created the organizational strength to deliver one hit after another, each an extension of Apple's position as the consumer's digital hub, each as strong as its predecessor. If there's anything that parallels Apple's decade-long string of hits—iMac, PowerBook, iPod, iTunes, iPhone, iPad, to list just the blockbusters—it's Pixar's string of winners, including Toy Story, Monsters, Inc., Finding Nemo, The Incredibles, WALL-E, and Up. These insanely great products could have come only from insanely great companies, and that's what Jobs had learned to build.

Jobs had learned how to treat talent at Pixar; he spoke to me about his colleagues there differently from the way he discussed his NeXT coworkers. When he returned to Apple, he often described his very top management team in the same warm terms, with the occasional notable exception. As he had with animators and programmers at Pixar, he integrated designers and technologists at Apple. He cultivated a team he could count on, including the great designer Jonathan Ive, who is to Apple what Lasseter is to Pixar. "We've done so many hardware products where Jony and I have looked at each other and said, 'We don't know how to make it any better than this, we just don't know how to make it,'" Jobs told me. "But we always do; we realize another way. And then it's not long after the new thing comes out that we look at the older thing and go, 'How can we ever have done that?'"

When I listened to this quote again last month, I was struck by something else in it: the combination of adaptability and intuition that proved so critical to Apple's rise. Jobs may have been impulsive at times, but he was always methodical. This kind of nature suited an autodidact with eclectic tastes, empowering him either to obsess impatiently about a pressing problem that had to be dealt with immediately—much like an engineer—or else to let an idea steep and incubate until he got it right. This is why Jobs was so often right on the big picture, even when he got the details wrong. Open salaries was a dumb detail of the Open Corporation, but its core idea, of a workplace where every single person understands the company's goals, is something that most organizations get wrong and that Apple has gotten so right for well over a decade. If Jobs was initially wrong about Apple getting into phones and handheld devices, he was right on about the big idea of the computer at the center of a whirling digital universe. Hence Apple's ability to deliver a great iTunes store after the iPod, even though it was never planned. Hence the great iPhone, despite Jobs's dismissal of "Swiss Army knife" digital devices.

There was one other big lesson he learned from his Hollywood adventure: People remember stories more than products. "The technology we've been laboring on over the past 20 years becomes part of the sedimentary layer," he told me once. "But when Snow White was re-released [on DVD, in 2001], we were one of the 28 million families that went out and bought a copy of it. This was a film that is 60 years old, and my son was watching it and loving it. I don't think anybody's going to be beating on a Macintosh 60 years from now."

Once he realized he really was going to die, Jobs quietly began to think more seriously about the story of his own life and creations. At his memorial service, Laurene remarked that what struck her most upon really getting to know him was his "fully formed aesthetic sense." He knew exactly what he liked, and he analyzed it until he could tell you precisely why. Jobs always felt that architecture could be a truly lasting expression of one's aesthetic, reaching beyond the limits of one's lifetime. It wasn't incidental, then, that his last public appearance was at a Cupertino City Council meeting to unveil the breathtaking four-story, doughnut-shaped "mother ship" that's nearly a half-mile in diameter and that will one day become Apple's headquarters.

Of course, Jobs wanted his own official story to measure up. So he enlisted Walter Isaacson—creator of a virtual Mount Rushmore of bestselling biographies of Benjamin Franklin, Albert Einstein, and Henry Kissinger—to tell his tale. Like those giants, Jobs is a man whose history will be told many a time, with fresh insights and new reporting. In the retelling, it may well be that the lessons from his "lost" years in the "wilderness" are the ones that will prove most inspiring.

Critical Thinking

1. Steve Jobs in known for being detail oriented to the point of obsession. The story of him micro-managing the color and pattern of bricks for the Pixar headquarters building is but one of many examples. In what ways did this obsession make him a better inventor or CEO? In what ways did this obsession hinder him? What might the ideal balance be?

2. Schlender refers to the 11 years between Jobs' two terms as Apple CEO as his "business school" education. What key lessons did Jobs learn that can be transferred to your own school and work life?

3. Contrast Jobs' behaviors and policies at NeXT from his behaviors and policies at Pixar. Which differences represented Jobs' growth as a manager, and which differences were simply differences in culture between the two industries?

4. How did Jobs' time at Pixar impact the development of the iPod and iPhone?

From *Fast Company*, May 2012, pp. 72–82. Copyright © 2012 by Mansueto Ventures LLC. Reprinted by permission via Copyright Clearance Center.

Women, Mathematics, and Computing[1]

PAUL DE PALMA

Introduction

In 1963, Betty Friedan wrote these gloomy words:

> The problem lay buried, unspoken, for many years in the minds of American women. . . . Each suburban wife struggled with it alone. As she made the beds, shopped for groceries, matched slipcover material, ate peanut butter sandwiches with her children, chauffeured Cub Scouts and Brownies, lay beside her husband at night—she was afraid to ask even of herself the silent question—"Is this all?"

The passage, of course, is from the *The Feminine Mystique* (Friedan, 1983: p. 15). Though, it took another decade for the discontent that Friedan described to solidify into a political movement, even in 1963 women were doing more than making peanut butter sandwiches. They also earned 41% of the bachelor's degrees. By 1995, the number of degrees conferred had nearly tripled. The fraction going to women more than kept pace at almost 55%. Put another way, women's share of bachelor's degrees increased by 25% since Betty Friedan first noticed the isolation of housewives. Consider two more sets of numbers. In 1965, 478 women graduated from medical school. These 478 women accounted for only 6.5% of the new physicians. Law was even less hospitable. Only 404 women, or just 3% of the total, received law degrees in 1965. By 1996, however, almost 39% of medical degrees and 43% of law degrees were going to women (Anderson, 1997).

If so many women are studying medicine and law, why are so few studying computer science? That's a good question, and one that has been getting a lot of attention. A search of an important index of computing literature, the *ACM Digital Portal* (ACM, 2005a), using the key words "women" and "computer," produced 2,223 hits. Of the first 200, most are about the underrepresentation of women in information technology. Judging by the volume of research, what we can do to increase the numbers of women studying computer science remains an open question.

While most investigators fall on one side or the other of the essentialist/social constructivist divide (Trauth, Quesenberry & Morgan, 2005), this article sidesteps the issue

altogether in favor of offering a testable hypothesis: Girls and young women would be drawn to degree programs in computer science in greater numbers if the field were structured with the precision of mathematics. How we arrived at this hypothesis requires a look at the number of women earning degrees in computer science historically and in relation to other apparently similar fields.

Background

In 1997, *The Communications of the ACM* published an article entitled "The Incredible Shrinking Pipeline" (Camp, 1997). The article points out that the fraction of computer science degrees going to women decreased from 1986 to 1994. This bucks the trend of women entering male-dominated professions in increasing numbers. The graph below shows the percent of women earning degrees in various scientific disciplines between 1970–71 and 1994–95 (National Center for Educational Statistics, 1997).

If you did not look at the data over time, you would be justified in concluding that the 13% or so of engineering degrees going to women represents a terrible social injustice. Yet the most striking feature of the degrees conferred in engineering and the physical and life sciences is how closely their curves match that of all degrees conferred to women. Stated another way, the fraction of degrees in engineering

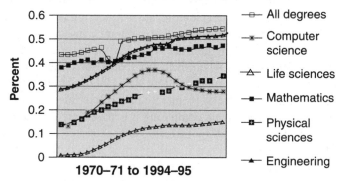

Percent of Women Earning Degrees by Year

Figure 1

and the sciences going to women have increased enormously in a single generation. It has, in fact, outpaced the fraction of all degrees going to women. The curves for engineering and the life sciences both have that nice S shape that economists use to describe product acceptance. When a new kind of product comes to market, acceptance is initially slow. When the price comes down and the technology improves, it accelerates. Acceptance finally flattens out as the market becomes saturated. This appears to be exactly what has happened in engineering. Following the growth of the women's movement in the early 1970s, women slowly began to account for a larger share of degrees conferred. By the early 1980s, the fraction grew more rapidly, and then, by the 1990s, the rate of growth began to slow. A parallel situation has occurred in the life sciences, but at a much higher fraction. Women now earn more than 50% of undergraduate degrees in biology.

Computer science is the anomaly. Rapid growth in the mid-1980s was followed by a sharp decline. The fraction of women graduating in computer science flattens out in the 1990s. What is going on here? A study of German women noticed that the sharp increase in the number of degrees in computer science going to women followed the commercial introduction of the microcomputer in the early 1980s (Oechtering, 1993). This is a crucial observation. In a very few years, computers went from something most people were only vaguely aware of to a consumer product. What the graph does not tell you is that great numbers of men also followed the allure of computing in the early and mid-1980s—numbers that declined by the end of the decade.

Despite many earnest attempts to explain why women do not find computer science as appealing as young men (e.g., Bucciarelli, 1997; Wright, 1994), it is important to point out that computer science is not like the other areas we have been considering. Unlike physics, chemistry, mathematics, and electrical engineering, there is not an agreed-upon body of knowledge that defines the field. An important textbook in artificial intelligence, for instance, has grown three-fold in 10 years. A common programming language used to teach introductory computing barely existed a decade ago. Noam Chomsky has suggested that the maturity of a scientific discipline is inversely proportional to the amount of material that forms its core. By this measure, computer science is far less mature than other scientific and engineering disciplines.

Many studies have shown that girls are consistently less confident about their abilities in mathematics and science than are boys, even when their test scores show them to be more able (e.g., Mittelberg & Lev-Ari, 1999). Other studies attribute the shortage of women to lack of confidence along with the perception that computing is a male domain (Moorman & Johnson, 2003). Unfortunately, computer science, at least as presently constituted, requires a good bit of confidence. The kinds of problems presented to computer science majors tend to be open-ended. Unlike mathematics, the answers are not in the back of the book—even for introductory courses. There is often not a single best way to come up with a solution and, indeed, the solutions themselves, even for trivial problems, have a stunning complexity to them. The tools that students use to solve these problems tend to be vastly more complex than the problems themselves. The reason for this is that the tools were designed for industrial-scale software development. The move over the last decade to object-oriented languages has only exacerbated an existing problem (Hsia, Simpson, Smith, & Cartwright, 2005). A typical lab assignment to write a program in the C++ or Java language will require that the student have a working knowledge of an operating system, a graphical user interface, text editor, debugger and the programming language itself.

One surrogate for complexity is the size of text-books. Kernighan and Ritchie's classic, *The C Programming Language* (1978) is 228 pages long. The first program in the book, the famous "Hello world," appears on page 6. Deitel, Deitel, Lipari, and Yaeger's (2004) *Visual C++ .NET: How to Program,* on the other hand, weighs in at a hefty four pounds and runs to 1,319 pages. Students have to wade through 52 pages before they reach the book's program equivalent to "Hello, world." The key to successful mastery in this environment is the willingness to tinker and the confidence to press forward with a set of tools that one only partially understands. Although we exhort our students to design a solution before they begin to enter it at the keyboard, in fact, the ready availability of computers has encouraged students to develop a trial-and-error attitude to their work. Those students willing to spend night after night at a computer screen acquire the kind of informal knowledge necessary to write successful programs. This is a world that will welcome only very self-assured young women.

Mathematics, Engineering, and Tinkering

Recall Chomsky's observation that the most mature disciplines are the most tightly defined. What discipline can boast the tightness and precision of mathematics? As it happens, many reasonable people have attributed at least some of the shortage of women in science and computing as well as the less-than-positive attitudes toward computers to so-called math anxiety among girls (e.g., Chang, 2002; Jennings & Onwuegbuzie, 2001; Mark, 1993). One study says that "The culture of engineering places particular stress on the importance of mathematical ability. Math is both the most complicated and the purest form of mental activity. It is also the most 'masculine' of subjects" (McIlwee & Robinson, 1992, p. 19, referring to Hacker, 1981). At first glance, the heavier reliance on mathematics might appear to explain why women avoid physics and electrical engineering while embracing biology and oceanography. But this explanation is insufficient for the simple reason that women receive nearly half of the undergraduate degrees in mathematics itself and were receiving almost 40% of them well before the women's movement became a mass phenomenon.

Here, then, is a hypothesis. What if the precision of mathematics is exactly what has appealed to women for so long? And what if the messiness of computing is what has put them off? So far, so good, but we still have to account for electrical engineering and physics. These have a smaller fraction of women than computer science, but are well defined and rely heavily on sophisticated mathematics. What is it about physics and electrical engineering that women find unattractive? The answer is really quite simple. Students drawn to engineering and physics like to tinker with gadgets (e.g., Crawford, Wood, Fowler, & Norell, 1994). That paper describes a grade school curriculum designed to encourage young engineers. It relieves heavily upon "levers, wheels, axles, cams, pulleys, forms of energy to create motion, etc." (p. 173). McIlwee and Robinson (1992) report that 57% of male engineers surveyed chose the field because they like to tinker. Only 16% of women surveyed chose engineering for this reason. It should come as no surprise that the men associated with the microcomputer—Bill Gates, the Paul Allen, Jobs and Wozniak—all got their start as tinkerers. And as all parents know but are hard-pressed to explain, their infant sons are drawn to trucks more readily than their infant daughters (Serbin, Poulin-Dubois, Colburne, Sen, & Eichstedt, 2001).

Microcomputers, a Problem with Computer Science Education

Here we find a convergence with computer science and, finally, an explanation for the steep rise in the number of women in the field following the introduction of the microcomputer and its drop a few years later. The development of the microcomputer changed computing enormously. In 1971, a small number of computer science departments awarded fewer than 2,400 degrees. Most people who worked in the thriving data processing industry had received their training in the military, for-profit vocational schools or on the job. By 1986, that number had jumped to nearly 42,000, including almost 15,000 women. Clearly, the microcomputer played a large part in the growth of the academic discipline of computing. Like the dot-com boom, the growth could not be maintained. If the production of computer science degrees had continued to climb at the rate it climbed between 1975 and 1985, by 2001 every American would have had a Bachelor of Science degree in the field. In fact, the number of degrees awarded began to drop sharply in 1987.

We know why both men and women entered IT in the 1980s. Why did the numbers drop by the late 1980s? We can not really know the answer to this, of course, short of polling those who did not major in computer science during that period; but we can guess. Computer science is hard. What's more, it is not a real profession. There are no licensing barriers to entry, an issue that has been hotly debated in computing literature for at least two decades (ACM, 2005b). Until computing societies agree on licensing and convince state legislatures to go along, students need not earn a degree in computer science to work in the field.

These things are equally true for women, of course, but the tinker factor is an additional burden. Before the mid-1980s and the mass availability of microcomputers, programmers could almost ignore hardware. This article's author wrote programs for a large manufacturer of mainframe computers in the early 1980s without ever having seen the computer he was working on, nor, for that matter, the printer that produced the green bar paper delivered to his cubicle every two hours. There was tinkering going on in those days too, of course. But it was all software tinkering; only computer operators touched the machine. The micro changed all that. Suddenly, those young men who had spent their adolescence installing exotic operating systems and swapping memory chips were in great demand. By adding hardware tinkering to the supposed repertoire of skills necessary to program, the microcomputer reinforced the male-dominated culture of IT (for an account of this very male atmosphere, see De Palma, 2005).

Conclusion

Until the day when baby girls like gadgets as much as baby boys, let us look to mathematics itself to see what we can do about attracting young women to computer science. Well before other fields welcomed women, a significant fraction of degrees in mathematics were going to females. Let us assume that the mathematicians have been on the right track all along. A testable hypothesis presents itself. If we make computer science education more like mathematics education, we will make computer science more appealing to women. Computer science grew out of mathematics. How do we get back to basics?

First, teach girls who like to manipulate symbols how to program. Programming is weaving patterns with logic. If girls can do calculus, they can write programs. Second, try not to stray from logic. If we make computer science education less dependent on complex software tools, we remove some of the barriers between the student and logic. Third, minimize the use of microcomputers. Microcomputers, for all their cleverness, misrepresent computer science, the study of algorithms, as hardware tinkering. Fourth, ask students new to computer science to write many small functions, just as students of mathematics work countless short problems. Since there is something about the precision of mathematics that young women seem to like, let us try to make computing more precise. Later, as their confidence grows, they can take on larger projects. Fifth, regard programming languages as notation. It could well be that for complex systems, modern languages will produce a better product in a shorter time. But students do not produce complex systems. They produce relatively simple systems with extraordinarily complex tools. Choose a notation appropriate to the problem and do not introduce another until students become skilled programmers. Taken together, these suggestions outline a program to test the hypothesis.

Suppose we test the hypothesis and it turns out to have been correct. Suppose that, as a result, we give computing a makeover, and it comes out as clearly defined and as appropriate to the job as mathematics. Now imagine that able young women flock to the field. How might this change computing? To begin, students will no longer confuse half-formed ideas about proprietary products with computer science. Nor will they confuse the ability to plug in Ethernet cards with system design. It might mean that with a critical mass of women holding undergraduate degrees in computing, systems will be designed, not by tinkerers, but by women (and men) for whom the needs of computer users are front and center. Since stories of systems that failed through an over fondness for complexity are legion (De Palma, 2005), the makeover might even reduce the number of jerry-rigged systems. Thus, does social justice converge with the market place—a very happy outcome, indeed.

Note

1. This article grew out of a shorter opinion piece in the "Viewpoint" column of *Communications of the ACM* (De Palma, 2001).

References

ACM (2005a). Search using key words: "Women" and "computer." *The Digital Library*. Retrieved August 23, 2005 from www.acm.org.

ACM (2005b). Search using key words: "license" and "profession." *The Digital Library*. Retrieved August 27, 2005 from www.acm.org.

Anderson, C. (1998). *Fact Book on Higher Education: 1997 edition*. American Council on Education. Phoenix: Oryx Press.

Bucciarelli, L. & Kuhn, S. (1997). Engineering education and engineering practice: improving the fit. In S. R. Barley & J. Orr (Eds.), *Between Craft and Science: Technical Work in U.S. settings* (pp. 210–229). Ithaca, NY: Cornell University Press.

Camp, T. (1997). The incredible shrinking pipeline. *Communications of the ACM, 40*(10), 103–110.

Chang, J. (2002). Women and minorities in the sciences, mathematics, and engineering pipeline. *Eric Clearinghouse for Community Colleges*. Retrieved February 23, 2006, from Eric Digest (ED467855).

Crawford, R., Wood, K., Fowler, M., & Norell, J. (1994, April). An engineering design curriculum for the elementary grades. *Journal of Engineering Education, 83*(2), 172–181.

De Palma, P. (2001). Viewpoint: Why women avoid computer science. *The Communications of the ACM, 44*(6), 27–29.

De Palma, P. (2005). The Software Wars. *The American Scholar, 74*(1), 69–83.

Deitel, H., Deitel, P., Liperi, J., & Yaeger, C. (2003). *Visual C++ .NET: How to Program*. Upper Saddle River, NJ: Pearson Education, Inc.

Friedan, B. (1983). *The feminine mystique*. New York: W.W. Norton & Co.

Hacker, S. (1981). The culture of engineering: Women, workplace and machine. *Women's Studies International Journal Quarterly, 4*, 341–533.

Hsia, J., Simpson, E., Smith, D., & Cartwright, R. (2005). Taming Java for the classroom. Proceedings of the 36th SIGCSE technical symposium on Computer science education. *ACM SIGCSE Bulletin, 37*(1), 327–331.

Kernighan, B., & Ritchie, D. (1978). *The C Programming Language*. Englewood Cliffs: Prentice-Hall.

Mark, J. (1993). *Beyond equal access: Gender equity in learning with computers*. The Eisenhower National Clearinghouse for Mathematics and Science Education. Retrieved August 27, 2005, from www.enc.org/topics/equity/articles.

McIlwee, J. & Robinson, J. G. (1992). *Women in Engineering: Gender, Power and Workplace Culture*. Albany: State University of New York Press.

Mittelberg D. & Lev-Ari, L. (1999). Confidence in mathematics and its consequences: Gender differences among Israeli Jewish and Arab youth. *Gender and Education, 11*(1), 75–92.

Moorman, P., & Johnson, E. (2003). Still a stranger here: Attitudes among secondary school students towards computer science. *Proceedings of the 8th Annual Conference on Innovation and Technology in Computer Science Education*, 193–197.

National Center for Educational Statistics. (1997). *Digest of educational statistics NCES 98–015*. Washington, D.C. U.S. Government Printing Office.

Oechtering, V., & Behnke, R. (1995). Situations and advancement measures in Germany. *Communications of the ACM, 38*(1), 75–82.

Serbin, L., Poulin-Dubois, D., Colburne, K., Sen, M., & Eichstedt, J. (2001). Gender stereotyping in infancy: Visual preferences for and knowledge of gender-stereotyped *toys* in the second year. *International Journal of Behavioral Development, 25*(1), 7–15.

Trauth, E., Quesenberry, J., & Morgan, A. (2004). *Proceedings of the 2004 SIGMIS Conference on Computer Personnel Research, 114–119*. New York: ACM Press.

Wright, R., & Jacobs, J. (1994). Male flight from computer work. *American Sociological Review, 59*, 511–536.

Key Terms

Computer Science: An academic discipline that studies the design and implementation of algorithms. Algorithms are step-by-step procedures for solving well-defined problems. A precise description of a technique for putting words in alphabetical order is an algorithm.

Ethernet Card: Hardware that allows a computer to be attached to a network of computers.

Memory Chip: An informal term for RAM (random access memory) or just plain memory. It is internal to a computer and loses its contents when the power is shut off. Programs must be loaded into RAM to execute.

Microcomputer: Also called a personal computer. The machine on your desk is a microcomputer.

Operating System: The collection of programs that controls all of the computer's hardware and software. Important operating systems are Windows XP and Unix.

Program: A sequence of instructions that tells a computer how to accomplish a well-defined task.

Programming Language: The notational system that a programmer uses to construct a program. This program is transformed by another program, known as a compiler, into the instructions that a computer can execute. Important languages are Java and C++.

Critical Thinking

1. Are you persuaded that computer science would more appealing to women if computer science education were more like mathematics education?

2. There have been many hypotheses about why women find computer science relatively unattractive. Name two mentioned in the article.

3. Do you agree with Noam Chomsky's observation that the maturity of scientific discipline is inversely proportional to the amount of material that forms its core? Is this observation true outside of science? Use the Internet to find out how long it takes to earn a PhD., on average, in a selection of scientific disciplines compared to a selection of disciplines from the social sciences and humanities.

From *Encyclopedia of Gender and Information Technology*, 2006, pp. 1303–1308. Copyright © 2006 by IGI Global. Reprinted by permission.

UNIT 4

Social Media and Participation

Unit Selections

Learning Outcomes

After reading this Unit, you will be able to:

- Have a deeper understand of the role of Twitter in Iran's recent elections.

- Be able to argue both for and against the notion of the Internet as a vehicle for social and political change.

- Have contended with an especially counterintuitive argument: the contributions of the Internet to political change are not as obvious as is usually portrayed.

- Be able to argue for and against the proposition that humans were more studious and attentive before the Internet.

- Be able to articulate how social networking friends are both similar and different from face to face friends.

- Understand the implications of the spread of viral information over social media.

- Understand and be able to articulate the benefits of the development of "serious games" for several facets of our lives.

Student Website

www.mhhe.com/cls

Internet References

Alliance for Childhood: Computers and Children

    http://drupal6.allianceforchildhood.org/computer_ position_statement

The Core Rules of Netiquette

    www.albion.com/netiquette/corerules.html

Snopes.Com

    www.snopes.com

SocioSite: Networks, Groups, and Social Interaction

    www.sociosite.net

WordPress

    www.wordpress.com

Most every American college student knows that the First Amendment to the U.S. Constitution guarantees the right to practice any religion and to exercise free speech. What many may not know are the additional rights specified by the First Amendment are the right to peaceably assemble and the right to petition the government. The founders of the American government recognized that to establish and maintain a free and open society, not only must the ability to speak be protected, but the ability to gather in groups, form associations, and network must also be protected. Without those protections, citizens would not be able to form the critical mass necessary to stand up to the government should doing so become desired or necessary.

The early and astute observer of American culture, Alexis de Tocqueville (1805–1859), had this to say about the proclivity of Americans to form civic associations:

"... Americans make associations to give entertainments, to found seminaries, to build inns, to construct churches, to diffuse books, to send missionaries to the Antipodes; in this manner they found hospitals, prisons, and schools. . . . Nothing, in my opinion, is more deserving of our attention than the intellectual and moral associations of America. . . . In democratic countries the science of association is the mother of science; the progress of all the rest depends upon the progress it has made."[1]

He recognized the relationship between association and democracy. If all men—we're talking about the first half of the 19th century here—are equal before the law, then, to do any civic good requires that these equal, but individually powerless, men band together.

A century and a half later, we have the technical means to communicate almost instantly and effortlessly across great distances. And with that, the bounds of traditional association are being abandoned.

Robert Putnam, in "Bowling Alone," argued that the civil associations de Tocqueville had noticed were breaking down. Americans were not joining the PTA, the Boy Scouts, the local garden club, or bowling leagues in their former numbers. Putnam discovered that although more people bowl than ever, participation in leagues was down by 40 percent since 1980.[2]

But it isn't that people are not associating any more, it is the environment of association that changes by generation enabled by their newest technologies. Watching kids play from neighborhood stoops has given way to afterschool programs and nanny cams. Shopping in locally owned main street stores gave way to the commercial chains and protected space of shopping malls, which in turn are now giving way to Amazon and eBay. Playing little league has given way to massive multiplayer online role playing games (MMPORGs). After school malt shop gatherings (think: Happy Days) have given way to texting, Facebook, and music sharing activities.

But Americans still associate. The question we might ponder while reading the articles in this Unit is: Do modern computer and communication tools assist or detract from our needs to associate?

Another French social observer, Emile Durkheim (1858–1917), argued that a vital society must have members who feel a sense of community. Community is easily evident in pre-industrial

© John Lund/Blend Images LLC

societies where kinship ties, shared religious belief, and custom reinforce group identity and shared values. Not so in modern societies, particularly in the United States, where a mobile population commutes long distances and retreats each evening to the sanctity and seclusion of individual homes. Contemporary visitors to the United States are struck by the cultural cafeteria available to Americans. They find a dizzying array of religions, beliefs, moral and philosophical perspectives, modes of social interaction, entertainment venues and, now, digital gadgets.

One can argue that the new communications technologies permit associations that were never before possible. Nevermind that Facebook now gets over one billion different visitors a month, social network technologies are being used effectively to assemble and to petition governments.

Protests over the rigged 2009 Iranian election were channeled over the Internet. Opposition candidate Mir Hussein Moussavi's Facebook fan group reached 50,000 members during the election aftermath. At the peak of the protests, Twitter mentions "Iran" spiked from a steady flow of about 20,000 per hour to over 221,000 tweets.[3]

Similar increases in social media use were found during the 2011 Arab Spring. Tweets about political change in Egypt rose from about 2,300 to 230,000 a day. The top 23 protest and political commentary YouTube videos were viewed over 5 million times.[4]

Such groundswells of social media use to protest government action has not been limited to the Middle East. In January 2012, a largely grassroots campaign emerged to defeat the related SOPA and PIPA bills before Congress that, if passed, would have significantly increased the government's powers to police the Internet and prosecute copyright violations. Twitter published 2.4 million SOPA related tweets in 16 key hours of the protest; more than 162 million people viewed Wikipedia's protest page; more than 8 million people used Wikipedia's search tool to find their representatives' contact information; and more than 4.5 million people signed Google's anti-SOPA/PIPA petition.[5]

It is with knowledge of this world we begin the Unit with a counterintuitive article, Small Change, by Malcolm Gladwell. A popular writer at "The New Yorker", Gladwell has made a career of writing eloquent pieces that take counterintuitive positions.

Ever since President Obama's masterful marshaling of the new media in the 2008 presidential campaign, writers everywhere have been praising its power to mobilize people for one cause or another. Gladwell argues that real change requires real old-fashioned organizing. Do you agree?

More and more our social lives appear to be spent online. One could lament this or embrace it, teasing all of its implications, especially for commerce. This is the stance taken by Arnold Brown in "Relationships, Community, and Identity in the New Virtual Society." "Clearly," he writes, "the Internet has radically reshaped our social lives over the span of just a couple of decades, luring us into a virtual metaworld where traditional interactions—living, loving, belonging, and separating, as well as finding customers and keeping them—require new protocols." Among those new protocols is just how you are to behave with your digital devices when face-to-face with a real person.

In "R U Friends 4 Real?", Amy Novotney examines what it means to be a social network friend. Do those friendships provide the same kinds and levels of interpersonal support off line friendshps provide? Or are they just a form of virtual neighborhood acquaintanceship? Conversely, might online friendships provide some form value that traditional friendships do not?

Certainly the web of acquaintances many of us acquire online provide us with soapboxes to speak to a larger audience than we might have reached before. Surely the grassroots campaign against SOPA/PIPA would not have taken hold without the millions of Facebook, Reddit, Tumbler, and Twitter posts and comments posted and shared. Of course, the pro-SOPA/PIPA advocates did not see this movement in the same positive light. Their perception, of course, was that the messages being posted were propogandic misinformation. Whatever your personal take is about the validity of SOPA/PIPA, this point of view surfaces the potential for misuse of social networking to spread mistaken information or intentional disinformation.

Consider the controversy of the link between childhood vaccinations and autism. The 1998 Lancet Journal article that triggered the controversy has long ago been retracted by the author; no subsequent scientist has ever found a link between vaccinations and autism, yet a movement resisting vaccination remains with websites, Facebook pages, YouTube videos, and other social media. Katie Moisse, in "The YouTube Cure", examines a similar case of an unproven surgical treatment for MS developing an online community of support, looking at both the potential benefits of widespread sharing of cutting-edge medical information as well as the inherent risks in doing so.

The last article in this unit, Adam L. Penenberg's "Everyone's a Player", changes pace by examining the growing use of online games in most every part of our lives. Even if you are not a gamer—especially if you are not a gamer (and I am not)—you may find this article fascinating as it argues that games are becoming ubiquitous. As you read how games are used for everything from business simulation and product development, to military training, and to testing alternative civic planning scenarios consider, as Postman modeled in Unit 1, the systemic outcomes from applying this new technology. Consider both the upsides and downsides of this broad application of computer games.

Notes

1. Alexis de Tocqueville, *Democracy in America,* Vintage Books, 2000, vol. 2, 114–118.

2. See http://bowlingalone.com/

3. Ben Parr, Mindblowing #IranElection Stats: 221,744 Tweets Per Hour at Peak, *Mashable Social Media,* June 17, 2009. (See http://mashable.com/2009/06/17/iranelection-crisis-numbers/)

4. Philip N. Howard, Aiden Duffy, Deen Freelon, Muzammil Hussain, Will Mari, Marwa Mazaid, Opening Closed Regimes: What Was the Role of Social Media During the Arab Spring?, Prject on Information Technology & Political Islam, Working Paper, January 2011. (Accessed at http://pitpi.org/?p=1051 on October 12, 2012)

5. Ian Paul, Were SOPA/PIPA Protests a Success? The Results Are In, *PC World,* January 19, 2012. (See http://www.pcworld.com/article/248401/were_sopa_pipa_protests_a_success_the_results_are_in.html)

Small Change
Why the Revolution Will Not Be Tweeted

Malcolm Gladwell

Social media can't provide what social change has always required.

At four-thirty in the afternoon on Monday, February 1, 1960, four college students sat down at the lunch counter at the Woolworth's in downtown Greensboro, North Carolina. They were freshmen at North Carolina A. & T., a black college a mile or so away.

"I'd like a cup of coffee, please," one of the four, Ezell Blair, said to the waitress.

"We don't serve Negroes here," she replied.

The Woolworth's lunch counter was a long L-shaped bar that could seat sixty-six people, with a standup snack bar at one end. The seats were for whites. The snack bar was for blacks. Another employee, a black woman who worked at the steam table, approached the students and tried to warn them away. "You're acting stupid, ignorant!" she said. They didn't move. Around five-thirty, the front doors to the store were locked. The four still didn't move. Finally, they left by a side door. Outside, a small crowd had gathered, including a photographer from the Greensboro *Record*. "I'll be back tomorrow with A. & T. College," one of the students said.

By next morning, the protest had grown to twenty-seven men and four women, most from the same dormitory as the original four. The men were dressed in suits and ties. The students had brought their schoolwork, and studied as they sat at the counter. On Wednesday, students from Greensboro's "Negro" secondary school, Dudley High, joined in, and the number of protesters swelled to eighty. By Thursday, the protesters numbered three hundred, including three white women, from the Greensboro campus of the University of North Carolina. By Saturday, the sit-in had reached six hundred. People spilled out onto the street. White teen-agers waved Confederate flags. Someone threw a firecracker. At noon, the A. & T. football team arrived. "Here comes the wrecking crew," one of the white students shouted.

By the following Monday, sit-ins had spread to Winston-Salem, twenty-five miles away, and Durham, fifty miles away. The day after that, students at Fayetteville State Teachers College and at Johnson C. Smith College, in Charlotte, joined in, followed on Wednesday by students at St. Augustine's College and Shaw University, in Raleigh. On Thursday and Friday, the protest crossed state lines, surfacing in Hampton and Portsmouth, Virginia, in Rock Hill, South Carolina, and in Chattanooga, Tennessee. By the end of the month, there were sit-ins throughout the South, as far west as Texas. "I asked every student I met what the first day of the sitdowns had been like on his campus," the political theorist Michael Walzer wrote in *Dissent*. "The answer was always the same: 'It was like a fever. Everyone wanted to go.'" Some seventy thousand students eventually took part. Thousands were arrested and untold thousands more radicalized. These events in the early sixties became a civil-rights war that engulfed the South for the rest of the decade—and it happened without e-mail, texting, Facebook, or Twitter.

The world, we are told, is in the midst of a revolution. The new tools of social media have reinvented social activism. With Facebook and Twitter and the like, the traditional relationship between political authority and popular will has been upended, making it easier for the powerless to collaborate, coördinate, and give voice to their concerns. When ten thousand protesters took to the streets in Moldova in the spring of 2009 to protest against their country's Communist government, the action was dubbed the Twitter Revolution, because of the means by which the demonstrators had been brought together. A few months after that, when student protests rocked Tehran, the State Department took the unusual step of asking Twitter to suspend scheduled maintenance of its Web site, because the Administration didn't want such a critical organizing tool out of service at the height of the demonstrations. "Without Twitter the people of Iran would not have felt empowered and confident to stand up for freedom and democracy," Mark Pfeifle, a former national-security adviser, later wrote, calling for Twitter to be nominated for the Nobel Peace Prize. Where activists were once defined by their causes, they are now defined by their tools. Facebook warriors go online to push for change. "You are the best hope for us all," James K. Glassman, a former senior State Department official, told a crowd of cyber activists at a recent conference sponsored by Facebook, A. T. & T., Howcast, MTV, and Google. Sites like Facebook, Glassman said, "give the U.S. a significant competitive advantage over terrorists. Some time ago, I said that Al Qaeda was 'eating our lunch on the Internet.' That is no longer the case. Al Qaeda is stuck in Web 1.0. The Internet is now about interactivity and conversation."

These are strong, and puzzling, claims. Why does it matter who is eating whose lunch on the Internet? Are people who log on to their Facebook page really the best hope for us all? As for Moldova's so-called Twitter Revolution, Evgeny Morozov, a scholar at Stanford who has been the most persistent of digital evangelism's critics, points out that Twitter had scant internal significance in Moldova, a country where very few Twitter accounts exist. Nor does it seem to have been a revolution, not least because the protests—as Anne Applebaum suggested in the *Washington Post*—may well have been a bit of stagecraft cooked up by the government. (In a country paranoid about Romanian revanchism, the protesters flew a Romanian flag over the Parliament building.) In the Iranian case, meanwhile, the people tweeting about the demonstrations were almost all in the West. "It is time to get Twitter's role in the events in Iran right," Golnaz Esfandiari wrote, this past summer, in *Foreign Policy*. "Simply put: There was no Twitter

Revolution inside Iran." The cadre of prominent bloggers, like Andrew Sullivan, who championed the role of social media in Iran, Esfandiari continued, misunderstood the situation. "Western journalists who couldn't reach—or didn't bother reaching?—people on the ground in Iran simply scrolled through the English-language tweets post with tag #iranelection," she wrote. "Through it all, no one seemed to wonder why people trying to coordinate protests in Iran would be writing in any language other than Farsi."

Some of this grandiosity is to be expected. Innovators tend to be solipsists. They often want to cram every stray fact and experience into their new model. As the historian Robert Darnton has written, "The marvels of communication technology in the present have produced a false consciousness about the past—even a sense that communication has no history, or had nothing of importance to consider before the days of television and the Internet." But there is something else at work here, in the outsized enthusiasm for social media. Fifty years after one of the most extraordinary episodes of social upheaval in American history, we seem to have forgotten what activism is.

Greensboro in the early nineteen-sixties was the kind of place where racial insubordination was routinely met with violence. The four students who first sat down at the lunch counter were terrified. "I suppose if anyone had come up behind me and yelled 'Boo,' I think I would have fallen off my seat," one of them said later. On the first day, the store manager notified the police chief, who immediately sent two officers to the store. On the third day, a gang of white toughs showed up at the lunch counter and stood ostentatiously behind the protesters, ominously muttering epithets such as "burr-head nigger." A local Ku Klux Klan leader made an appearance. On Saturday, as tensions grew, someone called in a bomb threat, and the entire store had to be evacuated.

The dangers were even clearer in the Mississippi Freedom Summer Project of 1964, another of the sentinel campaigns of the civil-rights movement. The Student Nonviolent Coordinating Committee recruited hundreds of Northern, largely white unpaid volunteers to run Freedom Schools, register black voters, and raise civil-rights awareness in the Deep South. "No one should go *anywhere* alone, but certainly not in an automobile and certainly not at night," they were instructed. Within days of arriving in Mississippi, three volunteers—Michael Schwerner, James Chaney, and Andrew Goodman—were kidnapped and killed, and, during the rest of the summer, thirty-seven black churches were set on fire and dozens of safe houses were bombed; volunteers were beaten, shot at, arrested, and trailed by pickup trucks full of armed men. A quarter of those in the program dropped out. Activism that challenges the status quo—that attacks deeply rooted problems—is not for the faint of heart.

What makes people capable of this kind of activism? The Stanford sociologist Doug McAdam compared the Freedom Summer dropouts with the participants who stayed, and discovered that the key difference wasn't, as might be expected, ideological fervor. "*All* of the applicants—participants and withdrawals alike—emerge as highly committed, articulate supporters of the goals and values of the summer program," he concluded. What mattered more was an applicant's degree of personal connection to the civil-rights movement. All the volunteers were required to provide a list of personal contacts—the people they wanted kept apprised of their activities—and participants were far more likely than dropouts to have close friends who were also going to Mississippi. High-risk activism, McAdam concluded, is a "strong-tie" phenomenon.

This pattern shows up again and again. One study of the Red Brigades, the Italian terrorist group of the nineteen-seventies, found that seventy per cent of recruits had at least one good friend already in the organization. The same is true of the men who joined the mujahideen in Afghanistan. Even revolutionary actions that look spontaneous, like the demonstrations in East Germany that led to the fall of the Berlin Wall, are, at core, strong-tie phenomena. The opposition movement in East Germany consisted of several hundred groups, each with roughly a dozen members. Each group was in limited contact with the others: at the time, only thirteen per cent of East Germans even had a phone. All they knew was that on Monday nights, outside St. Nicholas Church in downtown Leipzig, people gathered to voice their anger at the state. And the primary determinant of who showed up was "critical friends"—the more friends you had who were critical of the regime the more likely you were to join the protest.

So one crucial fact about the four freshmen at the Greensboro lunch counter—David Richmond, Franklin McCain, Ezell Blair, and Joseph McNeil—was their relationship with one another. McNeil was a roommate of Blair's in A. & T.'s Scott Hall dormitory. Richmond roomed with McCain one floor up, and Blair, Richmond, and McCain had all gone to Dudley High School. The four would smuggle beer into the dorm and talk late into the night in Blair and McNeil's room. They would all have remembered the murder of Emmett Till in 1955, the Montgomery bus boycott that same year, and the showdown in Little Rock in 1957. It was McNeil who brought up the idea of a sit-in at Woolworth's. They'd discussed it for nearly a month. Then McNeil came into the dorm room and asked the others if they were ready. There was a pause, and McCain said, in a way that works only with people who talk late into the night with one another, "Are you guys chicken or not?" Ezell Blair worked up the courage the next day to ask for a cup of coffee because he was flanked by his roommate and two good friends from high school.

The kind of activism associated with social media isn't like this at all. The platforms of social media are built around weak ties. Twitter is a way of following (or being followed by) people you may never have met. Facebook is a tool for efficiently managing your acquaintances, for keeping up with the people you would not otherwise be able to stay in touch with. That's why you can have a thousand "friends" on Facebook, as you never could in real life.

This is in many ways a wonderful thing. There is strength in weak ties, as the sociologist Mark Granovetter has observed. Our acquaintances—not our friends—are our greatest source of new ideas and information. The Internet lets us exploit the power of these kinds of distant connections with marvellous efficiency. It's terrific at the diffusion of innovation, interdisciplinary collaboration, seamlessly matching up buyers and sellers, and the logistical functions of the dating world. But weak ties seldom lead to high-risk activism.

In a new book called "The Dragonfly Effect: Quick, Effective, and Powerful Ways to Use Social Media to Drive Social Change," the business consultant Andy Smith and the Stanford Business School professor Jennifer Aaker tell the story of Sameer Bhatia, a young Silicon Valley entrepreneur who came down with acute myelogenous leukemia. It's a perfect illustration of social media's strengths. Bhatia needed a bone-marrow transplant, but he could not find a match among his relatives and friends. The odds were best with a donor of his ethnicity, and there were few South Asians in the national bone-marrow database. So Bhatia's business partner sent out an e-mail explaining Bhatia's plight to more than four hundred of their acquaintances, who forwarded the e-mail to their personal contacts; Facebook pages and YouTube videos were devoted to the Help Sameer campaign. Eventually, nearly twenty-five thousand new people were registered in the bone-marrow database, and Bhatia found a match.

But how did the campaign get so many people to sign up? By not asking too much of them. That's the only way you can get someone you don't really know to do something on your behalf. You can get thousands of people to sign up for a donor registry, because doing so is pretty easy. You have to send in a cheek swab and—in the highly unlikely event that your bone marrow is a good match for someone in need—spend a few hours at the hospital. Donating bone marrow isn't a trivial matter. But it doesn't involve financial or personal risk; it doesn't mean spending a summer being chased by armed men in pickup trucks. It doesn't require that you confront socially entrenched norms and practices. In fact, it's the kind of commitment that will bring only social acknowledgment and praise.

The evangelists of social media don't understand this distinction; they seem to believe that a Facebook friend is the same as a real friend and that signing up for a donor registry in Silicon Valley today is activism in the same sense as sitting at a segregated lunch counter in Greensboro in 1960. "Social networks are particularly effective at increasing motivation," Aaker and Smith write. But that's not true. Social networks are effective at increasing *participation*—by lessening the level of motivation that participation requires. The Facebook page of the Save Darfur Coalition has 1,282,339 members, who have donated an average of nine cents apiece. The next biggest Darfur charity on Facebook has 22,073 members, who have donated an average of thirty-five cents. Help Save Darfur has 2,797 members, who have given, on average, fifteen cents. A spokesperson for the Save Darfur Coalition told *Newsweek*, "We wouldn't necessarily gauge someone's value to the advocacy movement based on what they've given. This is a powerful mechanism to engage this critical population. They inform their community, attend events, volunteer. It's not something you can measure by looking at a ledger." In other words, Facebook activism succeeds not by motivating people to make a real sacrifice but by motivating them to do the things that people do when they are not motivated enough to make a real sacrifice. We are a long way from the lunch counters of Greensboro.

The students who joined the sit-ins across the South during the winter of 1960 described the movement as a "fever." But the civil-rights movement was more like a military campaign than like a contagion. In the late nineteen-fifties, there had been sixteen sit-ins in various cities throughout the South, fifteen of which were formally organized by civil-rights organizations like the N.A.A.C.P. and CORE. Possible locations for activism were scouted. Plans were drawn up. Movement activists held training sessions and retreats for would-be protesters. The Greensboro Four were a product of this groundwork: all were members of the N.A.A.C.P. Youth Council. They had close ties with the head of the local N.A.A.C.P. chapter. They had been briefed on the earlier wave of sit-ins in Durham, and had been part of a series of movement meetings in activist churches. When the sit-in movement spread from Greensboro throughout the South, it did not spread indiscriminately. It spread to those cities which had preëxisting "movement centers"—a core of dedicated and trained activists ready to turn the "fever" into action.

The civil-rights movement was high-risk activism. It was also, crucially, strategic activism: a challenge to the establishment mounted with precision and discipline. The N.A.A.C.P. was a centralized organization, run from New York according to highly formalized operating procedures. At the Southern Christian Leadership Conference, Martin Luther King, Jr., was the unquestioned authority. At the center of the movement was the black church, which had, as Aldon D. Morris points out in his superb 1984 study, "The Origins of the Civil Rights Movement," a carefully demarcated division of labor, with various standing committees and disciplined groups. "Each group was task-oriented and coordinated its activities through authority structures," Morris writes. "Individuals were held accountable for their assigned duties, and important conflicts were resolved by the minister, who usually exercised ultimate authority over the congregation."

This is the second crucial distinction between traditional activism and its online variant: social media are not about this kind of hierarchical organization. Facebook and the like are tools for building *networks*, which are the opposite, in structure and character, of hierarchies. Unlike hierarchies, with their rules and procedures, networks aren't controlled by a single central authority. Decisions are made through consensus, and the ties that bind people to the group are loose.

This structure makes networks enormously resilient and adaptable in low-risk situations. Wikipedia is a perfect example. It doesn't have an editor, sitting in New York, who directs and corrects each entry. The effort of putting together each entry is self-organized. If every entry in Wikipedia were to be erased tomorrow, the content would swiftly be restored, because that's what happens when a network of thousands spontaneously devote their time to a task.

There are many things, though, that networks don't do well. Car companies sensibly use a network to organize their hundreds of suppliers, but not to design their cars. No one believes that the articulation of a coherent design philosophy is best handled by a sprawling, leaderless organizational system. Because networks don't have a centralized leadership structure and clear lines of authority, they have real difficulty reaching consensus and setting goals. They can't think strategically; they are chronically prone to conflict and error. How do you make difficult choices about tactics or strategy or philosophical direction when everyone has an equal say?

The Palestine Liberation Organization originated as a network, and the international-relations scholars Mette Eilstrup-Sangiovanni and Calvert Jones argue in a recent essay in *International Security* that this is why it ran into such trouble as it grew: "Structural features typical of networks—the absence of central authority, the unchecked autonomy of rival groups, and the inability to arbitrate quarrels through formal mechanisms—made the P.L.O. excessively vulnerable to outside manipulation and internal strife."

In Germany in the nineteen-seventies, they go on, "the far more unified and successful left-wing terrorists tended to organize hierarchically, with professional management and clear divisions of labor. They were concentrated geographically in universities, where they could establish central leadership, trust, and camaraderie through regular, face-to-face meetings." They seldom betrayed their comrades in arms during police interrogations. Their counterparts on the right were organized as decentralized networks, and had no such discipline. These groups were regularly infiltrated, and members, once arrested, easily gave up their comrades. Similarly, Al Qaeda was most dangerous when it was a unified hierarchy. Now that it has dissipated into a network, it has proved far less effective.

The drawbacks of networks scarcely matter if the network isn't interested in systemic change—if it just wants to frighten or humiliate or make a splash—or if it doesn't need to think strategically. But if you're taking on a powerful and organized establishment you have to be a hierarchy. The Montgomery bus boycott required the participation of tens of thousands of people who depended on public transit to get to and from work each day. It lasted a *year*. In order to persuade those people to stay true to the cause, the boycott's organizers tasked each local black church with maintaining morale, and put together a free alternative private carpool service, with forty-eight dispatchers and forty-two pickup stations. Even the White Citizens Council, King later said, conceded that the carpool system moved with "military precision." By the time King came to Birmingham, for the climactic showdown with Police Commissioner Eugene (Bull) Connor, he had a budget of a million dollars, and a hundred full-time staff members on the ground, divided into operational units. The operation itself was divided into steadily escalating phases, mapped out in advance. Support was maintained through consecutive mass meetings rotating from church to church around the city.

Boycotts and sit-ins and nonviolent confrontations—which were the weapons of choice for the civil-rights movement—are high-risk strategies. They leave little room for conflict and error. The moment even one protester deviates from the script and responds to provocation, the moral legitimacy of the entire protest is compromised. Enthusiasts for social media would no doubt have us believe that King's task in Birmingham would have been made infinitely easier had he been able to communicate with his followers through Facebook, and contented himself with tweets from a Birmingham jail. But networks are messy: think of the ceaseless pattern of correction and revision, amendment and debate, that characterizes Wikipedia. If Martin Luther King, Jr., had tried to do a wiki-boycott in Montgomery, he would have been steamrollered by the white power structure. And of what use would a digital communication tool be in a town where ninety-eight per cent of the black community could be reached every Sunday morning at church? The things that King needed in Birmingham—discipline and strategy—were things that online social media cannot provide.

The bible of the social-media movement is Clay Shirky's "Here Comes Everybody." Shirky, who teaches at New York University, sets out to demonstrate the organizing power of the Internet, and he begins with the story of Evan, who worked on Wall Street, and his friend Ivanna, after she left her smart phone, an expensive Sidekick, on the back seat of a New York City taxicab. The telephone company transferred the data on Ivanna's lost phone to a new phone, whereupon she and Evan discovered that the Sidekick was now in the hands of a teenager from Queens, who was using it to take photographs of herself and her friends.

When Evan e-mailed the teen-ager, Sasha, asking for the phone back, she replied that his "white ass" didn't deserve to have it back. Miffed, he set up a Web page with her picture and a description of what had happened. He forwarded the link to his friends, and they forwarded it to their friends. Someone found the MySpace page of Sasha's boyfriend, and a link to it found its way onto the site. Someone found her address online and took a video of her home while driving by; Evan posted the video on the site. The story was picked up by the news filter Digg. Evan was now up to ten e-mails a minute. He created a bulletin board for his readers to share their stories, but it crashed under the weight of responses. Evan and Ivanna went to the police, but the police filed the report under "lost," rather than "stolen," which essentially closed the case. "By this point millions of readers were watching," Shirky writes, "and dozens of mainstream news outlets had covered the story." Bowing to the pressure, the N.Y.P.D. reclassified the item as "stolen." Sasha was arrested, and Evan got his friend's Sidekick back.

Shirky's argument is that this is the kind of thing that could never have happened in the pre-Internet age—and he's right. Evan could never have tracked down Sasha. The story of the Sidekick would never have been publicized. An army of people could never have been assembled to wage this fight. The police wouldn't have bowed to the pressure of a lone person who had misplaced something as trivial as a cell phone. The story, to Shirky, illustrates "the ease and speed with which a group can be mobilized for the right kind of cause" in the Internet age.

Shirky considers this model of activism an upgrade. But it is simply a form of organizing which favors the weak-tie connections that give us access to information over the strong-tie connections that help us persevere in the face of danger. It shifts our energies from organizations that promote strategic and disciplined activity and toward those which promote resilience and adaptability. It makes it easier for activists to express themselves, and harder for that expression to have any impact. The instruments of social media are well suited to making the existing social order more efficient. They are not a natural enemy of the status quo. If you are of the opinion that all the world needs is a little buffing around the edges, this should not trouble you. But if you think that there are still lunch counters out there that need integrating it ought to give you pause.

Shirky ends the story of the lost Sidekick by asking, portentously, "What happens next?"—no doubt imagining future waves of digital protesters. But he has already answered the question. What happens next is more of the same. A networked, weak-tie world is good at things like helping Wall Streeters get phones back from teen-age girls. *Viva la revolución.*

Critical Thinking

1. This article was quite controversial when it appeared in October 2010. Use the Internet to research the responses. Are you convinced by Gladwell? By his critics?

2. Gladwell says that genuine activism is a strong-tie phenomenon. What does he mean by that?

3. Gladwell makes much of the fact that the "Facebook page of the Save Darfur Coalition has 1,282,339 members, who have donated an average of nine cents apiece." The amount of the donation appears to be, in Gladwell's eyes, a proxy for the strength of the tie. Does this persuade you?

4. Gladwell says that "the instruments of social media are well suited to making the existing social order more efficient." What story did he tell to illustrate this tendency? Are you persuaded?

From *The New Yorker*, October 4, 2010. Copyright © 2010 by Malcolm Gladwell. All rights reserved. Reprinted by permission.

Relationships, Community, and Identity in the New Virtual Society

As we spend more of our social lives online, the definitions of relationships and families are shifting. A business futurist offers an overview of these trends and what they imply for organizations in the coming years.

ARNOLD BROWN

In India, where for centuries marriages have been arranged by families, online dating services such as BharatMatrimony .com are profoundly changing embedded traditions.

MyGamma, a Singapore-based mobile phone social networking site, has millions of users throughout Asia and Africa, giving social networking capability to people across continents—no personal computer necessary.

In China, individuals have been participating in *wang hun* (online role-play marriages). These gaming sites are causing actual married couples to get divorced on the grounds that this constitutes adultery—even though no face-to-face meetings ever took place.

And Web sites such as GeneTree.com and Ancestry.com, which offer inexpensive cheek-swab DNA tests, link up people throughout the world who have similar DNA, thus combining genealogy, medical technology, and social networking.

Clearly the Internet has radically reshaped our social lives over the span of just a couple of decades, luring us into a virtual metaworld where traditional interactions—living, loving, belonging, and separating, as well as finding customers and keeping them—require new protocols.

Relationships Take on a Digital Dimension

The future of falling in love may be online. Dating sites, once considered a gimmicky way to meet and connect with new people, have grown immensely in popularity, thanks in part to the convergence of information technologies and digital entertainment. Facilitating and managing relationships online is projected to become close to a billion-dollar industry in the United States in 2011.

In the new Virtual Society, we will see an increasing transition from basic matchmaking sites to sites that enable people to actually go out on online "dates" without ever leaving their desks. While face-to-face dating will never entirely disappear, the process—and even relationships themselves—will happen more and more in virtual space.

Especially for young people, relationships made in virtual space can be just as powerful and meaningful as those formed in the real world. Additionally, as more people gain access to broadband technologies, an increasing number are seeking social connectivity this way. There are already at least 500 million mobile broadband users globally. The speed and flexibility with which people communicate and socialize online will likely only continue to increase.

Technology doesn't just bring people together, though. As Douglas Rushkoff points out in *Program or Be Programmed* (OR Books, 2010), cyberspace creates a temporal and spatial separation from which it becomes seemingly easier to accomplish unpleasant interpersonal tasks. Hence, the *techno brush-off*: breaking up with a significant other via e-mail or text message.

This will increasingly be a dominant fixture of the global youth culture. Young people everywhere link up through IM, Twitter, blogs, smart-phones, and social networking sites that are proliferating at an accelerating rate. This is a critical point for businesses to understand. The emerging generation is part of what is, in essence, a vast new cross-border empire. It is marked by an instant awareness of what's new, what's hot, what's desirable—and what's not. This is the group that pollster John Zogby, in his book *The Way We'll Be* (Random House, 2008), calls the First Globals. His research shows that their expectations of products and services will be vastly different and that they will force businesses to redefine their offerings.

Young people will not, as their elders did, simply adapt to the technology. The new youth cyberculture will continue to find ways to adapt the technology to their needs and desires. For example, Ning, created in 2005 by Netscape co-founder Marc Andreessen, enables people to create their own individual social network—not join a preexisting world but actually build their own. A Web site called paper.li creates a personalized newspaper for you everyday based on whom you follow on Twitter and whether or not they said anything particularly important in the last 24 hours (as measured by retweets). Your friend's brilliant blog post about last night's St. Patrick's Day party could appear directly next to Tim O'Reilly or Bruce Sterling's most recent missive on China's Internet policy. It's hard to imagine a local newspaper providing that sort of personalized content.

But online relationships are not exclusively reserved for young people. As the elderly become more comfortable with the Internet, they will increasingly turn to alternative spaces, such as virtual worlds, to find company or meet people with similar interests. By 2008, more than 20 million social networkers in the United States were over the age of 50, according to a study by Deloitte. There have been a slew of media reports playing up the fact that many seniors are joining Facebook and Twitter, as well as becoming an increasingly significant part of the growing commercial activity in virtual worlds.

Commercializing Communities

More and more people regard the virtual world as a place where they can establish and maintain safer, less demanding relationships on their own time. Ease, flexibility, and relative anonymity will continue to be three key components of dating online. Monetization will happen quickly, as virtual restaurants, movie theaters, concerts, and even wedding chapels are established.

In addition to using virtual worlds as test markets for real-life products and services, as is done now, businesses will offer a much wider variety of virtual products and services. Having these options would give a substantive feel to online relationships. The more real and satisfying these relationships can be made to seem, the more they will attract and hold people, and the more money they will generate.

Commercialized virtual venues such as upscale bars and coffeehouses could even be looked to as testing grounds to develop the social skills necessary to form meaningful human relationships. Businesses could use game applications like Mall World or Café World on Facebook as platforms to advertise various specials that occur in virtual space, ranging from coupons for those aforementioned simulations of bars and coffeehouses to discounts for two to "live" streaming concert events. Advertising boards could promote online activities and events such as speed dating in a virtual nightclub setting. All this will dramatically change the nature of relationships.

As social researchers have pointed out, the Internet is programming us as well, starting at an early age. For example, there are combination social networking and gaming sites for children such as Disney's Club Penguin. Children are developing social skills within these virtual worlds. What this will mean in terms of how they will start, maintain, and end "real" friendships and relationships in the future is anyone's guess.

But the Internet can also strengthen family ties because it provides a continuously connected presence. In Norway, for example, one study showed that college students were in touch with their parents on average 10 times a week. Young people use mobile devices to Skype, text, upload photos and videos to Facebook, and more, with increasing frequency. Cyberspace enables families and friends to converse, in effect, as if they were in the same room. This is part of the reason that the Millennial generation reported feeling closer to their parents than did their older siblings during adolescence, according to the Pew Internet and American Life Survey.

So what does all this tell us? For one thing, the temporal and spatial "here-and-now" limitations that formerly characterized social interactions such as dating and family get-togethers have broken down. The composition of, and behavior in, relationships and households in the future will therefore change seriously. These trends are powerfully affecting how companies and organizations will design, sell, and market a wide range of products and services to consumers, with a growing emphasis on individualization and personalization. For instance, if relationships and families are more virtual, we should see an increase in the construction of new kinds of single-person housing units or dual sleeping quarters.

Family formation will need to be flexible and adaptive. The nuclear family was a response to the Industrial Age, in large measure replacing the extended family that characterized the Agricultural Era. It spurred vast economic shifts and led to new multibillion-dollar industries, from autos to washing machines to personal telephones. We are already seeing indications that the family is morphing into other forms as the Virtual Age approaches. Employers and governments will see their social, human resources, financial services, and benefits programs challenged, as the new economy takes great advantage of these multiple, newly unfolding personal relationships. For instance, should a "virtual spouse" be able to claim the Social Security benefits of a partner? The easy answer is, of course not. But what if it's the virtual spouse who is charged with monitoring the health of an aged parent remotely? What if he or she does the household bill-paying, or even contributes half of the household income? In other words, what if the virtual spouse performs many if not all of the tasks associated with a traditional spouse? And should the same polygamy laws applied to regular marriages also apply to virtual marriages? Should such marriages be subject to the same taxation laws?

With the advent of an electronic era, many social scientists and other "experts" decried what they saw as a loss of social capital—the so-called "Bowling Alone" theory—because people were supposedly decreasing their participation in such things as bowling leagues. The big mistake that the fearful always make is to equate change with destruction. The social turmoil of the 1970s was heralded by such observers as "the destruction of the family." But the family did not die; it just changed—and it is still changing.

Similarly, social capital is not going away; it is too intrinsic to human nature, although aspects of it may well be changing, and it is important that you view these changes objectively if you want to understand what they are and what they mean to you.

Social ties are being created, strengthened, and—yes—weakened in an almost unbelievable variety of ways. This has to entail, as well, the remaking and establishing of both a deeper and a shallower social capital. Someone with more than

The Reality of Virtual Feelings

Advances in brain research and multisensory perception could play an important role in the development of virtual relationships. Neural devices already allow people to control electronic equipment such as wheelchairs, televisions, and video games via brain–computer interfaces.

One day soon, avatars may also be controllable this way. Virtual reality may become so advanced that it could trick the brain into thinking the invented images it is responding to are real—and human emotions would follow accordingly. Avatars will cause people to feel love, hate, jealousy, etc. And as haptic technologies improve, our abilities to respond physically to our virtual partners will also improve.

Sexual pleasure may be routinely available without any inter-human stimulation at all.

If it becomes possible to connect virtual reality programs directly to the brain, thoughts and emotions may also be digitized, rendered binary and reduced to 0s and 1s. Feelings of satisfaction and pleasure (two key components in any relationship) could be created between avatars without any "real" stimulus at all. But would they be real or mimetic?

Once humans begin to perceive virtual social interactions as actually having occurred, it will greatly impact individuals, relationships, communities, and society as a whole.

—Arnold Brown

3,000 Facebook friends probably has more than 2,000 shallow friendships, but there's a tremendous amount of variety in that number; some of these friendships are viable clients, others may be service providers, others may be long-term friend prospects, or secret crushes, or members of a social circle to which the person with 3,000 friendships wants access; some of them will be annoying people encountered only once at a party, be grudgingly given the status of "friend" to avoid seeming rude. All of these friendships have their own unique value. But Facebook sees little difference among them outside of how they are designated in privacy settings (some people can see more private posts than others). Outside institutions don't recognize any distinction among these virtual friendships, if they recognize such friendships at all.

Sociologist Richard Ling has labeled the new communication phenomenon *micro-coordination*—as people are constantly planning, coordinating, and changing plans because their cyberconnections are always on. University of Southern California sociologist Manuel Castells says that adolescents today build and rebuild social networks via constant messaging. This is helped by the fact that they have what he calls "a safe autonomous pattern," in that their parents are only a speed dial away.

Sociologists describe two kinds of social ties: strong ties of family members and those with shared values, beliefs, and identities; and weak ties to acquaintances and other people with shallower connections. According to some researchers, the Internet and, in particular, mobile devices are enabling the strong community ties to be reinforced, often at the expense of the weak ties. At a time when technology is being lauded for encouraging diversity and facilitating cross-cultural communication, there is, consequently, a strong and growing counter-trend: digital tribalism. Aside from strengthening ties to family and close friends, people are using the technology to find others with whom they share important affinities, ranging from genomes to beliefs to lifestyle choices. This digital form of tribalism is an unexpectedly strong trend, as observed by social critics such as Christine Rosen.

Information—including product and service information—spreads electronically with speed and power. Effectively getting a positive message on a tribal network could well be tomorrow's best marketing strategy. Although the tribal identity can be deep and solid, brand connections may not necessarily be so. Maintaining the connection will require constant monitoring of the electronic tribal village and quickness to reposition or reinforce when required.

Bridal showers, for instance, can be attended by distant guests through Skype, and e-registries allow gift givers to view what others have bought. There is much room for innovation here, in terms of bringing people together who would not otherwise be in the same place for business meetings, financial planning, meal sharing, celebrations, and more. Associations might capitalize on online events for far-flung and numerous businesses, professionals, and friends and families of members. Employers might do the same for their employees' personal networks, perhaps offering discounts, education, job postings, and new products to all "friends of friends."

Expat workers and members of the armed forces might be more easily enabled to stay in touch with their families if their employers organized better around online communications and communities. This would ease the burden on relocated personnel, improve morale, attract more people, increase productivity, and spin the sale of products and service to these populations. This could also be true for alumni networks and other diaspora groups.

The Identity Industry

Social scientists make the distinction between a found identity and a made identity. The found identity is one created by your circumstances—who your parents were, your ethnic background, your religion, your sex, where you went to school, your profession, and all the other external factors that people use to categorize and describe you. The made identity, on the other hand, is the one you create for yourself. It is how you wish to see yourself and how you want others to see you.

In the past, people who wanted to escape what they saw as the trap of their found identity did such things as change their name or appearance. They moved somewhere else. Now, and increasingly in the future, technology will let you make and remake your identity at will—virtually. This extraordinary, even revolutionary, development will profoundly affect fundamental societal values such as trust and reliability.

In addition to engaging directly online with other individuals, you can also interact with them through avatars, the images that represent you (or an idealized version of yourself) in virtual worlds. Each virtual world requires a separate avatar, so in effect you can be as many different people as there are virtual worlds. In the future, you will be able to create avatars that will literally take on lives of their own. They will, once created, be able to "think" on their own, without further input from you. They may be able to perform intensive research tasks for you, start and even manage online companies, maintain your social relationships by reading your Facebook updates and blog posts and analyzing them for significant news so you don't have to.

Increasingly, over time, distinctions between real and virtual identity will become less sharply defined, particularly for people who spend substantial amounts of time in the virtual world—or some enhanced combination of the real and the virtual. A company called Total Immersion combines 3-D and augmented reality technology on the Internet, inserting people and physical objects into live video feeds. According to the company's Web site, "this digital processing mixes real and virtual worlds together, in real time."

All this could lead to growing confusion about identity. We will go from "Who am I?" to "Who, when, and where am I?" What in the twentieth century was seen as a problem that needed treatment—multiple personalities—will increasingly be seen in the twenty-first century as a coping mechanism, greatly affecting the evolving economy, as multiple personas split their expenditures in multiple ways. Companies that provide such services will be a great growth industry as we move further into the "Who are you, really?" era.

Critical Thinking

1. Count the number of times the future tense is used in this article. Now use the Internet to listen to: http://freakonomicsradio.com/hour-lonq-special-the-folly-of-prediction.html. What is Freakonomics?

2. Brown says that "Clearly the Internet has radically reshaped our social lives over the span of just a couple of decades. . . ." Who is "our"? Ask your parents if their social lives are different now than they were two decades ago.

3. Brown says "face-to-face dating will never entirely disappear." This suggests that it has been around for millennia. Do some research to find out when face-to-face dating, as you understand it, first appeared in the United States and Europe.

4. Arnold distinguishes between *found* and *made* identities. What are they?

5. Do you distinguish between your real and virtual identity? How is your online presentation different from your "real" identity? Why do you suppose *real* is enclosed within quotes?

ARNOLD BROWN is the chairman of Weiner, Edrich, Brown, Inc., and the coauthor (with Edie Weiner) of *FutureThink: How to Think Clearly in a Time of Change* (Pearson Prentice Hall, 2006). E-mail arnold@weineredrichbrown.com. Web site www.weineredrichbrown.com.

Originally published in the March/April 2011 issue of *The Futurist*. Copyright © 2011 by World Future Society, Bethesda, MD. Used with permission. www.wfs.org

R U Friends 4 Real?

Psychologists are learning more about how teen friendships are changed by social networking and text messaging.

AMY NOVOTNEY

As the parents of most teenagers know, today's two-hour telephone calls with friends are often now conducted via marathon text messaging or Facebook sessions. And that cultural shift has psychologists asking lots of questions: What happens to adolescent friendships when so much interpersonal communication is via text? Or when fights between best friends explode via Facebook for all to see? And can "OMG—ROTFL" ("Oh my God! I'm rolling on the floor laughing!") via text really convey the same amusement as hearing the giggles of a best friend?

So far, the answers to those questions are mixed. Margarita Azmitia, PhD, a psychology professor at the University of California, Santa Cruz, who studies adolescent friendships, is among those who contend that these technologies have only changed some of the ways teens interact. Today's youth still count the friends they see and talk to every day among their closest, she says.

"The [qualities] teens value in friendships, like loyalty and trust, remain the same," Azmitia says. "Technology has just changed some of the ways kids can be friends with each other."

Other psychologists, however, say today's ways of communicating can change the message, and wonder what effect that has on adolescent friendships, and even teens' social development. For example, instead of learning how to handle the give and take of conversation—one of our most basic human attributes and a connection we all crave—teens instead are crafting and often constantly editing witty text responses, says Massachusetts Institute of Technology social psychologist Sherry Turkle, PhD.

"We're losing our sense of the human voice and what it means—the inflections, hesitations and the proof that someone isn't just giving you stock answers," says Turkle, whose book "Alone Together" (2011) is based on 15 years of research and observation of children and adult interactions with technology. "That's a radical thing to do to our relationships."

Outcasts Reaching Out

One of social networking's greatest benefits is its ability to bring meaningful friendships to people who might otherwise be shunned as outcasts. As research has shown, being friendless in high school can have lifelong consequences on a person's cognitive, social and moral development. In one study, published in *School Psychology Review*, educational psychologist Beth Doll, PhD, of the University of Nebraska–Lincoln, found that friendless adolescents are more likely to be unemployed, aggressive or have poor mental health as adults.

But thanks to text messaging and the Internet, socially anxious teens who might have been left out now have a voice. In a 2010 study with 626 children and teens, researchers at the Queensland University of Technology in Australia found that lonely adolescents reported using the Internet to make new friends, and that they communicated online significantly more frequently about personal and intimate topics than those who did not report loneliness. These teens also indicated that they communicated online more frequently because they did not feel as shy, were able to talk more comfortably and dared to say more (*Cyberpsychology, Behavior, and Social Networking,* 2010).

Further, in a 2010 study in *Computers in Human Behavior,* Malinda Desjarlais, PhD, a psychology professor at the University of Northern British Columbia, found that socially anxious teen boys who played computer games with friends reported better friendships than their socially anxious peers who used the computer by themselves. Online games, Desjarlais says, typically allow players to speak to each other via the computer—and the opportunity to communicate without making eye contact may put socially anxious boys at ease.

The Internet's capacity for social connection doesn't only benefit shy and lonely teens. In a study of 63 Cornell University undergraduates, researchers found that people reported higher self-esteem after spending time on their Facebook profile than after time spent looking into a mirror (*Cyberpsychology, Behavior and Social Networking*, 2011).

"Unlike a mirror, which reminds us of who we really are and may have a negative effect on self-esteem if that image does not match with our ideal, Facebook can show a positive version of ourselves," says Cornell communications professor Jeffrey Hancock, PhD, one of the study's co-authors. "We're not saying that it's a deceptive version of self, but it's a positive one."

New research also suggests that youth who use blogs, websites and email to discuss politics and current events become more socially engaged over time. Students who spent more time seeking out information and participating in political and civic discussions in online communities, for example, reported higher levels of volunteerism, including raising money for charity, working on a local political campaign and increased voting participation, even after controlling for their level of political interest and involvement. The three-year as-yet-unpublished study of 2,500 teens was led by Joseph Kahne, PhD, an education professor at Mills College.

Lyn Mikel Brown, EdD, has seen first-hand the positive effects of the Internet on teen relationships and civic engagement in her job as director of Hardy Girls Healthy Women, a nonprofit girls' advocacy organization based in Waterville, Maine. In one national media literacy program titled Powered by Girls and sponsored by Hardy Girls, teenage girls throughout the United States connect online via the social networking site Ning to discuss pop culture's positive and negative media representations of girls and women and create their own e-zine to raise awareness of these issues.

"It's easy to say that the Internet is bad and filled with porn, and that's the stuff that makes the news," says Brown, professor of education at Colby College. "What doesn't make the news is the degree to which girls are blogging and building coalitions around social and political projects. No, they may not be intimate, long-term relationships, but they impact girls' sense of self in really positive ways because they connect with people who really get them."

A Crisis of Connection?

But while the Internet may give teens a forum, it may also rob them of the richness of real-life friendships. Time spent online, after all, is time not spent *with* friends and could lessen the social support teens feel.

For example, a 2010 study with 99 undergraduates led by Holly Schiffrin, PhD, a psychology professor at the University of Mary Washington, found that those who spent more time on the Internet reported decreased well-being. Most of

the students also reported that the Internet was less useful than face-to-face communication for building relationships and increasing emotional closeness with others (*Cyberpsychology, Behavior, and Social Networking*, 2010).

"I definitely think that technology can be used to build and maintain in-person relations, but it's not a satisfactory substitute for in-person relationships," Schiffrin says.

The Internet—and particularly online social networking websites—may also exacerbate the problems identified in a 2011 study in *Personality and Psychology Bulletin*. It found that people think their peers are happier than they really are, and this distortion of reality makes people lonely and dissatisfied with life. In the study, Dartmouth College business professor Alexander Jordan, PhD (a student in Stanford's graduate psychology department at the time) asked 80 college freshmen about how often they thought other students had negative experiences, such as getting dumped, receiving a bad grade or feeling overloaded with work.

Students were also asked to estimate how often their peers had positive experiences, such as going out with friends or acing tests.

Overall, the researchers found that students underestimated their peers' negative feelings (by 17 percent) and overestimated their positive emotions (by 6 percent).

"Online social networks are a great example of the type of public venue where people play up the positive and hide the negative, which can lead to the sense that one is alone in one's own struggles," Jordan says.

These findings also suggest that even though we all know we hide our own sad or lonely feelings from others, we don't realize how often others are doing the same.

"This anxiety around always 'performing' for others via social networking sites may lead to teenagers whose identities are shaped not by self-exploration and time alone to process their thoughts, but by how they are perceived by the online collective," Turkle says.

What remains to be seen is how well adolescent friendships managed via Facebook and text message affect teen development, and ultimately, how today's teens will develop relationships in adulthood, says New York University developmental psychologist Niobe Way, PhD, who has been studying friendships among teenagers for more than two decades. In a 2009 study in *Child Development*, Way and colleagues found that, among both American and Chinese middle-school students, the emotional support they got from close friends boosted their self-esteem and grade point averages more than support from their parents. Way, author of "Deep Secrets: Boys' Friendships and the Crisis of Connection" (2011), has also found that teenage boys who feel supported by and intimate with their friends are more likely to be academically engaged and do their homework than teens who report low support. Yet as social networking drives teens to decrease their face-to-face time with friends, how much intimacy do they really share?

"We know from the developmental literature that empathy and intimacy are fostered by looking at people's faces and reading people's emotions and spending time together physically," Way says, but it remains to be seen whether that can really be accomplished online. "We also know from the sociological literature that Americans are becoming less empathic and more emotionally disconnected from each other. We are facing a crisis of connection that most assuredly is not effectively addressed by less face-to-face contact."

Online friends can also make it less likely for young adults to create new adult friendships—a move that Way says may even put psychological and physical health in jeopardy.

"It's evident in the research that building real connections can help us thrive in life," Way says. "Friendships are a core part of that, and we just don't take them seriously enough."

Critical Thinking

1. How might the quality of conversation differ between phone, text, and social networking channels? In what ways is phone better? In what ways is texting better? Are concepts such as loyalty and trust valued differently by teen that choose one channel of interaction over another?
2. Are Facebook friendships meaningful friendships? Why do you answer the way you do?
3. Do teens who use texting fail to learn the give and take of social communication, as Sherry Turkle suggests?

AMY NOVOTNEY is a writer in Chicago.

From *Monitor on Psychology*, February 2012, pp. 62–65. Copyright © 2012 by American Psychological Association. Reproduced with permission. No further reproduction or distribution without written permission from the American Psychological Association.

The YouTube Cure

Popular demand for an unproved surgical treatment for multiple sclerosis shows the growing power of social media to shape medical practice—for good and ill.

KATIE MOISSE

When vascular surgeon Paolo Zamboni reported in December 2009 that inflating a tiny balloon inside twisted veins in the neck provided relief from multiple sclerosis, he created quite a stir. The idea that surgically straightening crooked veins could somehow benefit a degenerative nerve problem was astounding. Physicians were skeptical. Zamboni himself concluded that his findings should be subjected to more rigorous testing. Regardless, many people with MS, which affects at least 250,000 people in the United States, immediately began clamoring for the unproved treatment. Their demands, amplified through a wide range of social-networking platforms, soon proved impossible to resist. In the past year, for instance, hospitals in California, New York, Italy and Poland have offered the Zamboni treatment—at a cost of $10,000 or more because it is not covered by insurance.

Doctors found themselves playing catch-up every step of the way. Even before Zamboni published his results in the *Journal of Vascular Surgery,* a post on PatientsLikeMe.com (an online patient community) boasted news of his research, useful links and a dedicated Facebook URL. Community networks traded contact information detailing who would offer the procedure and where. Before-and-after videos were posted on YouTube. Like AIDS activists of 30 years ago but armed with much more powerful communications tools, patients challenged researchers and medical centers to explain why it was taking so long to offer Zamboni's approach. Yet most MS experts believe that undergoing the procedure at the moment is a very risky proposition.

This episode highlights a growing challenge for patients: how to temper enthusiasm for experimental therapies, now widely and effectively marketed through personal testimonials posted online, until evidence shows that the treatments are likely to do more good than harm. "You can never blame people for being excited about something that sounds like good news, especially when they have a serious disease," says Aaron Miller, a professor of neurology at Mount Sinai School of Medicine and chief medical officer for the National MS Society. "I think these social-media sites can have a positive function in that they allow patients to discuss research and share their experiences." But, he adds, "they have a very major risk in leading patients to embark on therapeutic courses that are not necessarily appropriate for them or haven't been established as being scientifically valid."

A Dangerous Game

In the case of Zamboni's work, it is easy to see how patients might be tempted to jump the gun and seek a treatment that initially sounds exciting. After all, the study findings came from a reputable surgeon (though not an MS researcher) publishing in a respected journal. As Daniel Simon, an interventional radiologist in Edison, N.J., says of the work: "It wasn't *Bob's Journal of MS and Autobody Repair;* it was the premier journal of vascular surgery."

It is also easy to see why racing to get treatment can be a dangerous game to play. In the first place, one study, even a well-done one, does not show that a therapy is ready for prime time. Often in medicine, early positive findings wash away later. And Zamboni himself pointed out that the study had limitations. The small trial was not randomized, double-blinded or placebo-controlled—the combination of which is considered the gold standard in clinical research. Participants also continued to take immune system-modulating therapies known to reduce symptoms.

In the case of MS, as with some other disorders, the difficulty of knowing whether a treatment that seemed to work really did have an effect in a study is compounded by the erratic nature of the disease. The most common form—relapse-remitting MS—has a variable course marked by flare-ups amid symptom-free periods. So it is difficult to know if a certain treatment actually works or was simply taken during a naturally occurring remission. Patients taking placebo have often reported substantial improvements, according to Mount Sinai's Miller.

Furthermore, the ultimate cause of the disease remains obscure, which makes it hard to gauge the appropriateness of an intervention. Everyone agrees that MS destroys the fatty myelin sheath that enwraps many nerve fibers. Stripped of their insulation, the wires of the nervous system lose their ability to transmit the electrical signals needed for movement, sensation and vision. Most researchers assume some kind of autoimmune response, in which a person's own defense system attacks rather than ignores the body's own tissues, is at work.

Given that current MS treatments are a far cry from a cure and do not work for everyone, some people with MS feel there is no harm in trying something that might improve their quality of life. The answer, of course, is that it could also make their quality of life much, much worse. Any surgery carries the risk of infection, and the procedure itself can actually damage the blood vessels, making them more vulnerable to clots and aneurysms.

Without more rigorous clinical trials, it is almost impossible to weigh accurately the potential costs and benefits. The operation to straighten out and puff up crooked and collapsed veins, called venoplasty, is almost identical to cardiac angioplasty—a common treatment for diseased coronary arteries. (Side effects for both include blood clots, infections and severe internal bleeding.) After piercing through a vein in the pelvis, a spaghetti-size catheter is threaded up through a vein near the spine and into the neck, where a balloon on the catheter's tip is inflated to pop the neck vein back to its normal shape—just like squatting in jeans that have shrunk in the wash stretches them, Simon explains.

But veins, which are more pliable than arteries, often regain their tortuous shape within months after venoplasty, requiring multiple procedures. One MS patient in the United States reportedly died from a brain hemorrhage while recovering, and another needed emergency surgery after a stent implanted to permanently straighten a vein dislodged and migrated to the heart.

Ready for Testing

One thing in favor of Zamboni's approach is it has a reasonable scientific rationale, which not all potential therapies touted on the Internet have. A close look at the characteristic plaques of scar tissue that lend the disease its name shows that they typically cluster around blood vessels. And that, Zamboni says, is key. Veins are flexible and can get twisted, slowing the rate of blood flow and potentially leaving waste and compounds such as iron to accumulate in the brain. Isn't it possible, he wonders, the buildup triggers an inflammatory response? And if the inflammation lasted long enough, it could eventually end up targeting the myelin wrapping of the nerves. A similar mechanism had been linked to myelopathies, degenerative conditions of the spinal cord, which bear a pathological semblance to MS.

That is a lot of "if's." But some physicians consider Zamboni's hypothesis and treatment plausible enough to test. And the National MS Society and the Multiple Sclerosis Society of Canada have pledged $2.4 million over the next two years to examine the role that problems with venous circulation might play in multiple sclerosis. "There is little doubt that the intense interest in [venoplasty for MS] played a role in the decisions by the National MS Society and the Canadian MS Society to fund further research," Miller says. Still, it is just too soon, he believes, to offer the procedure unless it is a part of a clinical trial.

A lesson from this episode, Miller says, is that it is important for neurologists and other physicians to be aware of what patients are seeing and reading online. "We can't bury ourselves in an ivory tower and function as though [social-media sites] don't exist," he notes. "What our patients are thinking, we need to address. We have to be aware of it and be prepared to discuss it with them logically." Miller says his patients almost invariably have been able to engage with him. After he explains the lack of certainty about venoplasty for MS, he observes, they usually agree with his advice to wait. Just how long they will continue to do so, however, may depend a lot on what social media push next.

Critical Thinking

1. Should new medical treatments be developed in secret, or should the public know about treatment experiments before final results are determined?

2. It is illegal to practice medicine in the United States without a license. Should there be restrictions about who can post medical information into social media?

3. Should some editing authority exist to control or limit what medical information can be posted to the Web?

If so, who should that authority be and what decision rules should they apply to determine whether medical information is publishable?

4. How should we, in the United States, deal with incorrect or misleading medical information posted on foreign-based websites?

5. When you see incorrect medical information posted to a social networking site, what do you consider your responsibility to be for correcting that information?

From *Scientific American*, February 2011, pp. 34, 37. Copyright © 2011 by Scientific American, a division of Nature America, Inc. All rights reserved. Reprinted by permission.

Everyone's a Player

Games are sneaking into every part of our lives—at home, school, and work. Cisco, Ibm, Microsoft, and even the Army depend on games. And pretty soon, you'll be a part of one. We guarantee it.

ADAM L. PENENBERG

Jesse Schell peered out at the 400 or so attendees of last February's DICE (design, innovate, communicate, entertain) Summit, the video-game industry's answer to TED. Dressed in a crinkly button-down shirt and chinos, the 40-year-old game designer and Carnegie Mellon professor had no idea how his speech would be received. Organizers had invited him to share insights about his work at Disney Imagineering, where he had helped design large-scale theme-park rides such as Pirates of the Caribbean, but he knew the Mouse would have his head if he violated any nondisclosure agreements. So the day before, on the flight from Pittsburgh to Las Vegas, he'd sketched out something radically different, something he titled "Beyond Facebook."

He began his speech with the premise that a real-life game could be stacked on top of reality. You'd get points for, well, just about everything you normally do in the course of 24 hours. This was already happening, he explained, and the games were altering human behavior. What were American Express points and frequent-flier miles but games that reward loyalty? Weight Watchers? A game. Fantasy football? A game stacked on top of a game that influences the way you watch a game. In the Ford Fusion, a virtual tree is embedded in the dash. The more gas you save, the more the tree grows. They put a virtual pet in your car, he marveled, and it actually changes the way people drive!

Sensors, he said, have gotten so cheap that they are being embedded in all sorts of products. Pretty soon, every soda can and cereal box could have a built-in CPU, screen, and camera, along with Wi-Fi connectivity. And at that point, the gaming of life takes off. "You'll get up in the morning to brush your teeth and the toothbrush can sense that you're brushing," Schell said. "So, 'Hey, good job for you! Ten points'" from the toothpaste maker. You sit down to breakfast and get 10 points from Kellogg's for eating your Corn Flakes, then grab the bus because you get enviro-points from the government, which can be used as a tax deduction. Get to work on time, your employer gives you points. Drink Dr

Pepper at lunch, points from the soda maker. Walk to a meeting instead of grabbing the shuttle, points from your health-insurance provider. Who knows how far this might run? Schell said. He offered psychedelic scenarios, like the one in which you recall a dream from the previous night where your mother was dancing with a giant Pepsi can: "You remember the REM-tertainment system, which is this thing you put in your ear that can sense when you enter REM sleep, and then [it] starts putting little advertisements out there to try and influence your dreams." If the ads take hold, you win big points for discounts at your local grocery store. "Then there's your office mate," Schell continued, "and he's like, 'Check out this new digital tattoo'" that he got from Tatoogle AdSense, and when you show him yours, you realize you're both wearing Pop-Tart ads. You get paid for the ads, plus 30 additional points just for noticing.

After work, you go shopping. Points. Your daughter gets good grades in school and practices the piano? More points. You plop down on your sofa for some television, and "it's just points, points, points, points," because eye sensors ensure that you actually watch the ads. In the meantime, you chat with other viewers, play games designed around the ads, and tally more points. Sure, it's crass commercialization run amok, Schell conceded, but "this stuff is coming. Man, it's gotta come. What's going to stop it?"

The applause was nothing compared to the reception his speech got online. The video went viral and was downloaded millions of times. Om Malik, founder of the blog GigaOM and an astute observer of all things tech, called it "the most mind-blowing thing I've seen in a long, long time." Others found it sinister: "the most disturbing presentation of the year," a "tech nightmare," a "Skinner Box" dooming us to live our lives inside a game.

Dystopian? Not to many game designers. Schell believes that embedding games in our lives has the potential to make us better people. Seth Priebatsch, the 22-year-old founder of Scvngr, a social location-based gaming platform for mobile devices (Google is an investor), has said that he dropped out of Princeton "to build a game layer over the world." Jane McGonigal, director of games research and development at the Institute for the Future, in Palo Alto, believes collaborative gaming can help solve the most vexing challenges of our times—global warming, war, poverty, disease. Yes, she really does.

The players have taken their places, the pieces are set, the cards dealt, the dice tossed. It's time to see who will win, and lose, in this version of the game of life.

Simulated Living

If Schell's vision seems a little, well, out there, consider this: Much of what he discusses already exists, having infiltrated our culture and our business landscape in ways that are barely recognized. Sure, 97 percent of 12- to 17-year-olds play computer games, but so do almost 70 percent of the heads of American households, according to the Entertainment Software Association. The average gamer is 34 and has been at it a dozen years; 40 percent are women. One survey found that 35 percent of C-suite executives play video games.

> **"Advances in technology will soon make all of life a game. Or has it happened already?"**
>
> —Jesse Schell

As McGonigal points out in her new book, *Reality Is Broken: Why Games Make Us Better and How They Can Change the World,* whether we intended to or not, we have raised a nation of gaming experts. Before turning 21, the average American has spent 2,000 to 3,000 hours reading books—and more than three times as much playing computer and video games. Ten thousand hours of practice, according to *Outliers* author Malcolm Gladwell, is a defining trait of virtuosos. Globally, 350 million people spend a combined 3 *billion* hours per week playing these games. Pricewaterhouse-Coopers estimates that global sales of video games will grow from 2007's $41.9 billion to $68.4 billion in 2012, at which point they would exceed the combined global revenues of film box office and DVDs.

The massive multiplayer online game *World of Warcraft* boasts 12 million registered users paying $15 a month to spend an average of 80 hours a month inside the game. Since the game's release in 2004, users have racked up some 50 billion hours of playing time—the equivalent of 5.93 million years. McGonigal points out that 5.93 million years ago is when early primates began to walk upright. "We've spent as much time playing *World of Warcraft*," she notes, "as we've spent evolving as a species." The social games FarmVille and Mafia Wars have together amassed almost 80 million active players, while media darling Foursquare has made a game

out of recording the inane aspects of our lives, like dropping into a Rite-Aid to fill prescriptions or buying Big Macs.

There is reliable evidence, which may horrify some, that playing video games can be beneficial. Studies indicate that video games improve decision making, vision, and hand-eye coordination. One study funded by New York's Beth Israel Medical Center and the National Institute on Media and the Family at Iowa State University found that surgeons who play such games three hours a week commit 37 percent fewer errors and work 27 percent faster in laparoscopic surgery—which requires deft use of a joystick, instruments, and a tiny camera—than doctors who don't.

Surgeons are players in an emerging niche of the industry called "serious games." The Entertainment Software Association claims that 70 percent of major employers use interactive software and games for training. Many are simulations that enable users to perfect skills in 2-D before taking on the 3-D challenges of real life—doctors, for example, may practice cutting open avatars instead of cadavers before turning to living, breathing humans. Such simulations make up a billion-dollar-plus business that is growing fast.

Japanese automaker Lexus performs safety tests on its vehicles in what it brags is the worlds most advanced driving simulator at the Toyota research campus in Japan. Canon's repair techies learn by dragging and dropping parts into place on a virtual copier. FedEx and airlines have simulators to train pilots, and UPS deploys its own version for new drivers—one even mimics the experience of walking on ice. Cisco developed a "sim" called *myPlanNet,* in which players become CEOs of service providers. Schell, who has a real role as chief of his 60-employee videogame-development firm, created *Hazmat: Hotzone,* an antiterror team-training game for firefighters.

> **"Games have all these amazing superpowers, blissful productivity, the ability to weave a tight social fabric, this feeling of urgent optimism, and the desire for epic meaning."**
>
> —Jane McGonigal

No company has embraced simulations more than IBM. The company recently released *CityOne,* a free interactive game targeting business leaders, city planners, and government agencies, with more than a hundred crisis scenarios that require the application of new technologies to create more efficient water use, lessen traffic congestion, and develop alternative-energy sources. Players review various "smart city" technologies such as cloud computing and supply-chain-management software. These are, of course, products and services sold by IBM.

Serious games have also become a staple in education: To practice running virtual businesses, students at more than 1,000 colleges and universities around the world play another IBM sim called *Innov8*. Even America's three-letter agencies are gaga over gaming. The Defense Intelligence Agency trains spies with PC-based games such as *Sudden Thrust,* written by David Freed, a B-list television writer. *Thrust* users play a DIA analyst confronting terrorists who hijack a tanker brimming with natural gas and steer it into New York Harbor. The CIA and FBI have also commissioned video games to help train agents in counterterror techniques.

The military has led this charge. "Militainment" is a key recruitment and training tool—perfect for young men and women who have already mastered the art of simulated war. Today, Army life can imitate art. Operating the gunnery on a tank or firing missiles from a naval destroyer resembles a first-person-shooter game, while piloting a predator drone over Pakistan from the comfort of a computer 9,000 miles away is a skill that brings to mind *Missile Command,* a staple of arcades in the 1980s.

The Army has gone so far as to budget $50 million for a video-game unit that will develop games. Lockheed Martin manufactures *Virtual Combat Convoy Trainer,* a system in which soldiers who may soon ship out to Afghanistan simulate battles over the same terrain—even the same streets—as the ones they will patrol, grappling with everything from improvised explosive devices to snipers to suicide bombers.

It's telling that the Army's most successful recruitment tool is a first-person-shooter game where players get points for blowing up enemy combatants. One study concluded that the game, called *America's Army,* has done more to influence recruits "than all other forms of Army advertising combined," with "30 percent of all Americans aged 16 to 24 having a more positive impression of the Army because of the game." Extremely popular—more than 7 million people, including 40 percent of new enlistees, have played the game since its 2002 release—it's also cost effective: *America's Army* cost $6 million to create, and the website is a mere $4,000 a year to maintain.

But all this—from *World of Warcraft* to IBM and UPS—is only the beginning. Games are on the verge of transforming our concepts of work, education, and commerce. To understand how, you have to know a little bit about what makes a great game and what happens to your brain when you're playing one.

This Is Your Brain on Games

Schell greets me outside his office at the Entertainment Technology Center (ETC) at Carnegie Mellon University. It's late August, yet Schell's skin has a Casper the Friendly Ghost pallor. He guides me through the ETC geekorama,

talking with the speed of an auctioneer as we walk past full-size R2-D2 and C-3PO *Star Wars* robots, a Commodore 64 console, walls covered with photos of movie stars and video-game characters, and a student lounge that seems to have been designed by Gene Roddenberry, *Star Trek*'s creator.

ETC is a feeder farm for Disney, Electronic Arts, and other top gaming outfits. One alum was a lead designer on Zynga's Mafia Wars; Schell calls another "the Alan Greenspan of FarmVille," because she sets prices for everything from the seeds to tractors and land.

Schell, whose official title is assistant professor of the practice of entertainment technology ("My business card is 6 inches long," he says), is a juggler and a magician who has been designing games all his life. As a kid in New Jersey, Schell and his younger brother would play Monopoly with two boards or three dice. He would change the rules of anything so that neighborhood kids, for instance, would have to hide *and* seek simultaneously. When his parents' marriage hit a rough patch, the two boys would wander a local mall unsupervised, gravitating to the Atari 400s and Commodore 64s on display at JCPenney, dedicating hours to testing programs he cut out of computer magazines. "That was where I learned to type," he says.

At 13, Schell designed his first computer game, a rudimentary fishing competition. After the divorce, his mother whisked the boys to Springfield, Massachusetts, where Schell fell into hacking. He also continued to create more games: one helped his brother with his math homework, while another was based on *Dr. Who*. "A good game," Schell says, "gives us meaningful accomplishment, clear achievement that we don't necessarily get from real life. In a game, you've beaten level four, the boss monster is dead, you have a badge, and now you have a super laser sword. Real life isn't like that, right?"

He was learning that a game is, at its root, a structured experience with clear goals, rules that force a player to overcome challenges, and instant feedback. What he couldn't have known then is that because they offer those clearly articulated rewards for each point players score and new level they achieve, games trigger the release of dopamine, a hormone in the brain that encourages us to explore and try new things. Since we like the feeling we get when our brains are awash in dopamine, we'll do whatever it takes to get it, over and over again. Video and computer games, as well as slot machines, are particularly good at this. They offer "threshold effects," where prizes or level changes are dribbled out to keep us hooked. It's the same system that drives compulsive gamblers and cocaine addicts.

It's also what makes it possible for gamers to enter a mental state called "flow," in which they're completely immersed in what they are doing and lose track of time. (In sports, it's called the "zone," when a basketball player, for example, feels as if he can't miss a shot.) In 2003, two researchers at the University of Southern California studied the impact of

71

violent video games on brain activity. Test subjects climbed into an MRI machine and played a popular shoot-'em-up. These machines tend to be cramped and noisy; people usually want a break after 20 minutes. But the test subjects were happy to remain crammed inside one for an hour or more.

Such is the power of games to influence behavior. Games, says Schell, "are a powerful psychological magnet that can connect into anything that we do." And now the game designers are tapping into just that—from the workplace to the doctor's office even to the classroom.

The Video-Game Workplace

At IBM, Chuck Hamilton has the curious title of v-learning strategy leader. (The *v* stands for virtual.) One of the stranger parts of his gig is to manage 16,000 avatars that IBMers have created for themselves. Like Cisco Systems and many other companies, IBM saves on travel and hotel expenses by holding the occasional convention or meeting in a virtual space; a couple hundred employees, each represented by an avatar, can attend. "In the early days," Hamilton says, "people showed up as whatever they chose—dogs, cats, penguins. It was a playful, exploratory time." But now that these virtual conventions are common fare, IBMers' avatars are getting, well, more traditionally IBMish. "They modify their avatars to get as close as they can get to the way they really look," he says. "I do get email from people in Japan and China asking where they can get a particular eye shape or skin color."

> **"If you follow human desire and trigger dopamine response, everyone eats Twinkies all day."**
>
> —NYU Professor Alexander Galloway

Some companies invent their own games to train employees. Sun Microsystems has conjured up two, *Dawn of the Shadow Specters* and *Rise of the Shadow Specters,* which take place in an alternate universe called Solaris, colonized by a race of people who happen to reflect the company's values. At McKinsey & Co., potential recruits play *Team Leader,* in which they manage a team whose fictitious client, Wang Fo, faces serious challenges. The players must answer 10 questions, each of which involves a set of decisions. At the end, players see (anonymously) how their scores stack up.

Archrivals Google and Microsoft use game design to tangibly improve company processes. In 2006, Google created a game to help it tag pictures and photos on the web. Search engines have a difficult time with image searches, and while facial-recognition software has made strides over the past decade, a new computer can't scan a photo of, say, Robert Pattinson and tell you who it is. It can't tell you what car he's

driving, if he's a celebrity, or what kind—athlete, chef, actor, singer. (If you don't know, of course, you may be beyond the help of computers.) Google's solution: Tap the manpower of the web by making image-tagging a game. The Google Image Labeler, which it licensed from MacArthur fellow and Carnegie Mellon professor Luis von Ahn, randomly pairs anonymous volunteers, both of whom are shown an identical set of images. They have two minutes to label each shot. Players receive points when their labels match— validation that a tag makes sense. The more descriptive a tag, the more points the team earns. A leaderboard keeps track of the best scores.

Microsoft's *Code Review Game* tackles a very different problem. In 2007, Ross Smith was appointed a team leader in Microsoft's Vista group, overseeing a group of 85 highly educated programmers who handled mind-numbing work, intensely scrutinizing thousands of lines of code for security glitches. It was as if Harvard Law grads were working traffic court. Smith wanted to see if game design could improve the quality, productivity, and job satisfaction of his crew.

In the *Code Review Game,* four teams choose a section of code to attack. They receive points based on the type of bugs they discover. Different groups can come up with different strategies: One focused on code produced by error-prone developers, while another team waited until a flaw was identified and then hunted similar bugs, since the coder who contributed to the section would likely repeat the same mistake. The project went so well that the company has used such teams to vet at least six other major releases.

"Work can be tough. It can be boring, repetitive, complex; you have to collaborate," says Stanford professor Byron Reeves, coauthor of *Total Engagement: Using Games and Virtual Worlds to Change the Way People Work and Businesses Compete.* "If you are not engaged, it doesn't go well."

Reeves and his coauthor, J. Leighton Read, believe game design will eventually put employees *inside* video games. In their book, they create two scenarios for a mythical call-center employee named Jennifer.

In the first scenario, Jennifer spends eight regimented hours a day at a typical corporate cubicle farm. She fields 75 calls a day. Her performance is tracked on a gargantuan, lighted board that lists data like handling time, number of calls on hold, projected-versus-actual call volume. She must log out for lunch, so the exact start of her break can be recorded. If she's late, she can be suspended. Turnover at this office is high, and there's no opportunity to get to know coworkers. For the three months she is working there, she is talking constantly, surrounded by a sea of other people. Yet she's lonely and bored.

In the second scenario, Jennifer works from home. When she logs in, she is greeted by her personalized avatar and joins her 20-person team. While they congregate on a pirate ship (this week's theme), they are in reality spread across three different time zones. But they can chat with one another, so Jennifer forges friendships. As with the

Microsoft bug testers, her team competes with others and her success depends on the success of her teammates. As calls are routed to her screen, she accumulates points for inputting data accurately and following company protocols. There's even voice-stress-analysis software, so that if Jennifer handles a caller deftly, she scores more. The more points she scores, the more she helps her team, whose progress is expressed by how quickly its ship sails to an island, where they are rewarded with a real-world perk: free holiday airline travel.

In both scenarios, Jennifer performs the same job. The only difference is that in the second, she's engaged by her work. Her mundane task seems like fun, and the constant feedback she receives in the form of points can give her a growing sense of accomplishment. She's a motivated, loyal, productive team member. Better for her, better for the company.

Playing around with Your Health

As any dieter knows, the problem with staying healthy is motivation. From iPhone apps to sophisticated simulations, games are increasingly being deployed to motivate patients and even doctors.

HealthSeeker is a Facebook game developed for the Diabetes Hands Foundation by Vancouver-based Ayogo in conjunction with the Joslin Diabetes Center (affiliated with Harvard Medical School). Players receive rewards for healthy activity and can reward the healthy behavior of others. The aim isn't to cure drug abuse or persuade smokers to quit. "We're trying to leverage what we understand about how our brains work and motivate very small actions by giving very small rewards," says company founder Michael Fergusson.

Lea Bakalyar, a 36-year-old stay-at-home mom from Atkinson, New Hampshire, claims the game has helped her make small changes that have a big impact, like modifying how she serves food to her family. Instead of putting the whole meal on the table, she now offers portioned plates from the stove. "It has helped take away the feeling of 'If it's in front of me, I'll eat it,'" she says. Tanya Ortiz, 24, a housewife from Queens, New York, with type 2 diabetes and high blood pressure, likes the social-networking component, which creates "a comforting atmosphere with people who share similar dilemmas," she says.

The world is full of games like Weight Watchers that encourage healthy lifestyles, of course. A game called *ZamZee* broadens the Weight Watchers model with middle-school students, pushing them to be more physically active by having them wear an activity monitor that is connected to a website where they can redeem points for rewards. HopeLab, the not-for-profit that created the game, claims a 30 percent increase in players' physical activity. Then there's *Pick Chow,* which lets kids drag-and-drop virtual food onto a plate and learn the nutritional value of each item; the *Snack Neutralizer,* a classroom aid to teach

Play the Games They Play at Cisco, IBM, and the U.S Army

Want to get ready for the game-ization of life? You can play most of the games cited in this article—for free! Go to fastcompany.com/workgames for links to some very interesting sims, apps, and shooters.

children the consequences of eating poorly; and *Trainer,* in which players are responsible for the dietary and fitness needs of a creature—when the creature exercises, so does the player. There are even iPhone apps that drive you to do more pushups (*Hundred PushUps*) or your child to brush her teeth (*Motivetrix,* designed by a German psychiatrist).

Finally, Nintendo's Wii is so widely used in rehabilitation that some have dubbed it "Wii-hab." Patients who have suffered strokes, paralysis, torn rotator cuffs, broken bones, and combat injuries play Wii baseball, boxing, bowling, and tennis. Since they earn points, they can easily chart their progress in managing the motion of the game controller. Grueling rehabilitative exercise becomes a game—a competition so engrossing patients can forget they are engaged in occupational therapy.

Teaching by Playing

Quest to Learn, a noncharter public school for grades 6–12 in Manhattan, bases its entire pedagogy on game design. Its students assume the roles of truth seekers—explorers, evolutionary biologists, historians, writers, and mathematicians—and engage in problem solving. There are no grades. Instead, students are rated at levels from novice to master. A typical class may be devoted to a multiplayer game where the students work in teams to defeat hostile aliens, or to a simulation in which the kids run an entire city. The kids even code their own games, which involve math, English, computer science, and art.

Even parents who routinely play video and computer games may have trouble grokking that. But a growing number of academics, led by James Paul Gee at Arizona State University, believe that gaming can drive problem-based learning, in which students develop skills as they work collaboratively to confront challenges. (Gee is quick to point out that he is not advocating for the likes of *Halo 3* in the classroom.)

"The problem is that our schools are focused on relating facts and how well students retain this info," says Gee. "Teachers are teaching to the test." When Gee started playing video games seven years ago, he was struck by the fact that games are often long and demanding—not nearly as dumb as stereotyped—yet designed to be so intuitive that no manual is ever needed. You learn by playing.

In countries such as Singapore, China, and Finland—all of whose children do better in math and science than American kids—problem solving is the key to learning. In America, we take the opposite approach. We teach math as a theory, then throw in problem sets as homework to reinforce what students have learned. The schools are, in essence, teaching the manual without exposing children to the game. Gee reasons that kids would learn more if they had to solve challenges that required them to use hard skills.

There's growing evidence to support this approach. According to a 2006 report by the Federation of American Scientists, students recall just 10 percent of what they read and 20 percent of what they hear. If visuals accompany an oral presentation, retention rises to 30 percent. But "if they do the job themselves, even if only as a simulation," students can remember 90 percent. While reliable numbers are hard to come by, several games claim improvements over traditional classroom learning. *Supercharged,* a game designed to teach physics, claims to be 28 percent more effective than lectures; *Virtual Cell* (biology) boasts a 30 percent to 63 percent improvement; and *Geography Explorer,* a 15 percent to 40 percent gain. Game-based methods may benefit the poorest-performing students most. *River City,* a game that exposes students to ecology and scientific inquiry, cites a 370 percent boost for D-students' test scores, while B-students' scores rose just 14 percent versus lectures.

Of course, not everyone is convinced. "Who said education is supposed to be fun and not hard work?" says Alexander Galloway, a professor at New York University. "At some point, you have to buckle down and memorize facts." Not to mention that video games unleash almost double the levels of dopamine experienced by humans at rest. Yes, this can increase performance in meaningful ways. But what would happen if nefarious companies and marketers realized the potential of hooking us through dopamine release? Therein lies the danger.

Game Over

We humans are pretty susceptible to addictive tricks, so surely people trying to make money will exploit that to the fullest. In fact, they already do," says David Sirlin, an independent game designer. "The best defense is to raise awareness about the dangers of being manipulated by external reward systems." But he isn't hopeful. There's too much money to be made.

What worries Sirlin excites Priebatsch, Scvngr's self-appointed "chief ninja." The next 10 years, he argues, will usher in the era of game design, and result in a pervasive net of behavior-altering mechanisms. As he points out, the game-ization of commerce is under way. Credit-card schemes, airline mile programs, and coupon cards—they all touch upon game dynamics, but "they just suck," he said in a July TED speech. (Priebatsch did not respond to numerous requests for an interview.)

Scvngr is, essentially, a mobile-commerce system fueled by real-world challenges. As its press page urges: "Go places. Do challenges. Earn points! You'll unlock badges and rewards and share where you are and what you're up to with friends." Get a point for checking into a 7-Eleven. Earn two for snapping a photo of a Coca-Cola can. Bump phones with a friend—two points for each of you. The points can be redeemed for real goods at selected merchants. Scvngr has signed up 1,000 corporate customers, and more than 500,000 users have downloaded the company's iPhone and Android apps. (Imagine pairing Scvngr with the payment card Citibank began testing in November: The standard-size card is a game itself, with two buttons and tiny lights that allow users to choose at checkout whether to pay with credit or rewards points.)

"Six hours a week should be spent playing games we love, and one hour should be spent playing serious, world-changing, life-changing games."

—Jane McGonigal

Growing rapidly, Scvngr seems cool. But it verges on a marketing ploy, obviously trying to alter its users' behavior to benefit corporate sponsors. Will the public grow wise to this and walk away? As NYU's Galloway says, "If you follow human desire and trigger dopamine response, everyone eats Twinkies all day." Or will Scvngr pull off a neat trick and be viewed not as a game manipulating its users but as one that engages them while also sharing its bounty?

Where Priebatsch sees economic opportunity, McGonigal of the Institute for the Future sees nothing less than a way to save the human race. She believes that if we want to conquer problems such as climate change, hunger, obesity, poverty, and war, we need to play at least 21 billion hours of video games a week.

Say what? McGonigal would like to see roughly half the planet play an hour a day, which is a low-end estimate of the time spent by gamers now—that's how she gets to 21 billion hours a week. "I reckon that roughly six hours a week should be spent playing games we love, to develop our gamer skills," McGonigal says, "and one hour a week should be spent playing serious, world-changing, life-changing, or reality-changing games." For example, she prescribes Evoke, a game she designed with the World Bank Institute that takes place in Africa and has users undertake 10 missions in 10 weeks involving water sustainability, disaster relief, and human rights. A game called *World Without Oil* simulates how we could survive without nonrenewable resources, while *Lost Joules* encourages players to save energy by awarding points for turning down thermostats, or for using appliances like washers and dryers during off-peak hours.

McGonigal argues that games like *World of Warcraft,* which are designed to give us the constant rush of being on the edge of an epic win, can be better than reality. With so many of us dedicating so much time to these virtual realms, all this collaborative play is causing us to evolve as a species. Playing games with others fosters trust and cooperation, and builds stronger social relationships. If designers set the problems within the fabric of a game, she believes our combined efforts could lead to solutions.

The night before his speech at DICE, Schell stayed up until 2 a.m. He couldn't think of an ending, a kicker that would put his many examples of the gaming of life in the right context. He felt certain that he was right, that this was the next big trend after the social connectivity unleashed by Facebook. He knew that some people would view a world of ubiquitous gaming with fear, and he knew that this unique gathering of the world's best game designers would have a say in whether the pessimists' fears would be realized, to tragic effect—or whether the outcome would be far better. And he knew something else: With sensors and tracking technology, our grandkids could discover where we had gone, what we had bought, how—and how well—we had spent our time. Perhaps the knowledge that we could be remembered so specifically would shame us into leading better lives.

"And so," Schell concluded the next day, "it could be that these systems are all crass commercialization and terrible, but it's possible that they'll inspire us to be better people if the game systems are designed right." He looked out at the crowd again. "The only question I care about right now is, Who in this room is going to lead us to get there?"

Critical Thinking

1. Should game-based methods be used more in school? Which of your courses do you think is most applicable to be taught with a well-conceived computer game? Have you taken any courses for which you think learning by computer game would be completely inappropriate?

2. At what age or grade level do you think educational computer games should be introduced? Why?

From *Fast Company*, December 2010/January 2011, pp. 135–141. Copyright © 2011 by Mansueto Ventures LLC. Reprinted by permission via Copyright Clearance Center.

UNIT 5
Privacy and Security

Unit Selections

Learning Outcomes

After reading this Unit, you will be able to:

- Know the risks of maintaining an online presence.

- Understand of the historical and legal issues surrounding privacy in the digital age.

- Understand that offshore oil extraction depends upon highly complex, sometimes inadequately tested software.

- Understand the contours of cyber warfare and cyber espionage.

- Be able to articulate the moral dilemmas invoked by governmental use of computer viruses for military advantage.

- Understand the depth of personal information stored by governments and businesses on the Internet.

- Understand the tradeoffs between advantages and risks of sharing information on social networks. Understand how you pay to visit the most popular websites through the sale of your preferences to advertisers.

- Be able to articulate the issues surrounding the Internet and risk youthful behavior.

Student Website
www.mhhe.com/cls

Internet References

Center for Democracy and Technology
www.cdt.org

Cyber Warfare
http://en.wikipedia.org/wiki/Cyberwarfare

A Declaration of Cyber-War
www.vanityfair.com/culture/features/2011/04/stuxnet-201104

Electronic Frontier Foundation
www.eff.org

Electronic Privacy Information Center (EPIC)
http://epic.org

Survive Spyware
http://reviews.cnet.com/4520-3688_7-6456087-1.html

In a recent New Yorker article, Nicholas Thompson noted that "privacy snafus are to social networks as violence is to football. The whole point of social networks is to share stuff about people that's interesting, just as the whole point of football is to upend the guy with the ball. Every so often, someone gets paralyzed, which prompts us to add padding to the helmets or set new rules about tackling. Then we move on."[1] But we change the rules and add more security—both in football and in our computer networks and the injuries not only keep occurring, but they become larger and more dangerous than before.

Edward Tenner published a book chronicling what he calls "revenge effects" 17 years ago. Revenge effects occur, he writes, "because new structures, devices, and organisms react with real people in real situations in ways we could not foresee."[2] Thus when stronger football helmets were developed in the 1960s and 1970s, players began charging with their heads forward and spines straight, resulting in more broken necks and damaged spinal columns. Similarly soldiers in Iraq have suffered more frequent brain injuries than those who served in Vietnam, largely the result of body armor and rapid evacuation of the wounded. We equip our soldiers with body armor to withstand small weapons fire and insurgents respond with head-trauma inducing rocket-propelled grenades and IEDs.[3] The moral of Tenner's story is to look beyond technological fixes for our predicaments to the social and economic systems in which they are embedded. "Technology giveth and technology taketh away."

Our networks and data repositories have become larger and more tightly coupled with the economic, social, and civic fabric of our lives. Our modern Internet-based society is dominated by several types of complementary networks and data repositories, many of them coexisting in the shared public space we call the Internet. Among those data repositories are the vast collections of information held by Google, Apple, Facebook, LinkedIn, Amazon, eBay, and others about our personal surfing, posting, and shopping habits. Also potentially accessible out there in more secured spaces are our credit card and banking information, our credit histories, our medical histories, and government data such as property holdings, license and registration data, criminal and traffic history, and voter registration records. Thompson's analogy to football might seem a bit abstract at first, but all of us our players in this privacy and security game—and all of us run the risk of getting hurt.

Beyond our personal data that is stored out there at many places in the Internet cloud are institutional and public data. The aforementioned medical, insurance, and credit information is held for the most part by private companies doing the best job they can (we hope) to successfully steward our data. Further many banks, retail stores, and other institutions network security cameras tracking the comings and goings of their patrons. Beyond that are the police and criminal databases often referred to during cop shows on TV. And there exist databases and active networks used to manage civic security cameras, and public works such as water and power distribution. And our national security infrastructure makes use of networks (sometimes, but not always, separate and more secure than the Internet) to undertake their mission. This includes, but is not limited to, work

© Yvan Dube/Getty Images

by Homeland Security departments, the Military, and the various government spy agencies.

None of these networks is 100 percent secure. Many, perhaps most, of these networks are under regular attack—though security protocols automatically block the common and more amateur attacks. There have been multiple reports of late, however, of more skilled and determined attacks on our public networks from groups within China and, perhaps, Iran.[4,5,6] The U.S. security forces as well, apparently, have been engaged in cyberattacks of their own. Many will remember the Stuxnet virus, thought to target Iran's nuclear weapons program. One report notes that Iran replaced about 1,000 centrifuges in late 2009 or early 2010, perhaps as a result of the attack. As it happens, our "electrical power grid is easier to break into than any nuclear enrichment facility." Read "Hacking the Lights Out" for a disturbing story of just how vulnerable power networks might be.

Stuxnet made the news in 2010 as a mysterious very focused attack upon the Iranian nuclear program that must have come from the Americans or Israelis, though neither government owned up to sponsoring it. Both of our first two articles reference the attack, but by now it is old news. Much more interesting is an even more follow up attack upon the Iranian nuclear program called Flame by the Russian computer security firm that uncovered and publicized its existence. Jonathan Last calls it "Bride of Stuxnet", which might be a more apt title given its monstrous abilities. As you read Last's article consider: is this what the future of warfare is going to be like? How will we feel when such an attack is launched upon us, if one has not already been launched?

Privacy and security concerns exist not just in the realm of our collective relationships with government. Large corporations have as much—perhaps more—information about us. Google's vast database of our Web browsing and related history, as Gleick discussed in Unit 2, contains far more detailed personal interests and behaviors than any government could know. And Facebook, as Simonite summarized as well, is aiming to capture every one of everyone's relationships with objects, organizations, and each other. What are the implications of having such personal and complete information about most all of us sitting in corporate databases? Read "Me and My Data" to see what James Ball found out when he petitioned Google and Facebook to see all of the data they've acquired about him over the years.

As the Patriot Act enacted during the Bush years has shown, a normal response of government during times of threatened public safety is to threaten civil liberties. In theory, a free press, a concerned citizenry, and the normal checks and balances built into our system should prevent the worst abuses. If only the federal government were all we had to worry about. In a world of networked computers, e-commerce, and social networking, we blithely hand over valuable data to providers of services we usually think of as free. To take a simple example, imagine that you're a Gmail subscriber. You may well think you have deleted private messages. But they are stored on a server, who knows where for who knows how long, with access by who knows whom. We Americans (but not Europeans and Canadians whose governments were farsighted enough to pass privacy legislation in the 1980s and 1990s) are in a privacy fix. Read "The Web's New Gold Mine" to learn how all that free stuff on the Internet got to be free. Turns out that the 50 most visited websites install on average 64 "pieces of tracking technology" onto our computers. Who is the worst offender? Dictionary.com installs 234 files. The best-behaved is Wikipedia, which installs no tracking technology at all.

We end this unit with a piece on a subject that has been part of the national conversation about the Internet since the beginning, sexual predation, harassment, and youth exposure to adult content: "The Conundrum of Visibility". The authors contend that despite real dangers associated with unrestricted access to the Internet, technology has made an old problem more visible.

What is a reasonable person to make of all of this? We can communicate with almost anyone almost anywhere on the planet at almost no cost. The wealth of the world is available on Amazon or eBay for those with credit cards. Google, Wikipedia, and an ocean of other sites provide information in abundance and at a speed that would have seemed like science fiction a generation ago. Yet thieves get hold of digitally-stored personal information. Our digital records are disintegrating even as we digitize more and more of them. The government compiles massive databases about terrorism and catches the innocent in its nets. Disruption of the global communications network could be catastrophic, as financial markets and global supply chains collapse. And one, if not several, governments are sabotaging nuclear centrifuges of their enemies. One strives for the equanimity of Neil Postman: "Technology giveth and technology taketh away."

Notes

1. Nicholas Thompson, How to get Privacy Right, *New Yorker Magazine*, March 5, 2012.

2. Edward Tenner, *Why Things Bite Back,* Vintage, 1996, p. 4.

3. Emily Singer, *Technology Review,* Brain Trauma in Iraq, 2008.

4. S. Gorman, J. Barnes, Iran Blamed for Cyberattacks, *Wall Street Journal*, October 13, 2012.

5. E. Nakashima, China testing cyber-attack capabilities, report says, *Washington Post*, March 7, 2012.

6. J. Winter, J. Kaplan, Washington confirms Chinese hack attack on White House computer, FoxNews .com (accessed 10/13/12 at http://www.foxnews.com/ tech/2012/10/01/washington-confirms-chinese-hack-attack-on-white-house-computer/#ixzz29D5gQjKp).

Hacking the Lights Out

Computer viruses have taken out hardened industrial control systems. The electrical power grid may be next.

Every facet of the modern electrical grid is controlled by computers. It is our greatest example of physical infrastructure interlinked with electronics.

The Stuxnet virus that infected Iran's nuclear program showed just how vulnerable machines could be to a well-crafted electronic virus. The grid shares many of the vulnerabilities that Stuxnet exposed; being larger, its vulnerabilities are, if anything, more numerous. Although a sophisticated attack could bring down a large chunk of the U.S. electrical grid, security is being ramped up.

DAVID M. NICOL

Last year word broke of a computer virus that had managed to slip into Iran's highly secure nuclear enrichment facilities. Most viruses multiply without prejudice, but the Stuxnet virus had a specific target in its sights—one that is not connected to the Internet. Stuxnet was planted on a USB stick that was handed to an unsuspecting technician, who plugged it into a computer at a secure facility. Once inside, the virus spread silently for months, searching for a computer that was connected to a prosaic piece of machinery: a programmable logic controller, a special-purpose collection of microelectronics that commonly controls the cogs of industry—valves, gears, motors and switches. When Stuxnet identified its prey, it slipped in, unnoticed, and seized control.

The targeted controllers were attached to the centrifuges at the heart of Iran's nuclear ambitions. Thousands of these centrifuges are needed to process uranium ore into the highly enriched uranium needed to create a nuclear weapon. Under normal operating conditions, the centrifuges spin so fast that their outer edges travel just below the speed of sound. Stuxnet bumped this speed up to nearly 1,000 miles per hour, past the point where the rotor would likely fly apart, according to a December report by the Institute for Science and International Security. At the same time, Stuxnet sent false signals to control systems indicating that everything was normal. Although the total extent of the damage to Iran's nuclear program remains unclear, the report notes that Iran had to replace about 1,000 centrifuges at its Natanz enrichment facility in late 2009 or early 2010.

Stuxnet demonstrates the extent to which common industrial machines are vulnerable to the threat of electronic attack.

The virus targeted and destroyed supposedly secure equipment while evading detection for months. It provides a dispiriting blueprint for how a rogue state or terrorist group might use similar technology against critical civilian infrastructure anywhere in the world.

Unfortunately, the electrical power grid is easier to break into than any nuclear enrichment facility. We may think of the grid as one gigantic circuit, but in truth the grid is made from thousands of components hundreds of miles apart acting in unerring coordination. The supply of power flowing into the grid must rise and fall in lockstep with demand. Generators must dole their energy out in precise coordination with the 60-cycle-per-second beat that the rest of the grid dances to. And while the failure of any single component will have limited repercussions to this vast circuit, a coordinated cyberattack on multiple points in the grid could damage equipment so extensively that our nation's ability to generate and deliver power would be severely compromised for weeks—perhaps even months.

Considering the size and complexity of the grid, a coordinated attack would probably require significant time and effort to mount. Stuxnet was perhaps the most advanced computer virus ever seen, leading to speculation that it was the work of either the Israeli or U.S. intelligence agencies—or both. But Stuxnet's code is now available on the Internet, raising the chance that a rogue group could customize it for an attack on a new target. A less technologically sophisticated group such as al Qaeda probably does not have the expertise to inflict significant damage to the grid at the moment, but black hat hackers for hire in China or the former Soviet Union might. It is beyond time we secured the country's power supply.

The Break-In

A year ago I took part in a test exercise that centered on a fictitious cyberattack on the grid. Participants included representatives from utility companies, U.S. government agencies and the military. (Military bases rely on power from the commercial grid, a fact that has not escaped the Pentagon's notice.) In the test scenario, malicious agents hacked into a number of transmission substations, knocking out the specialized and expensive devices that ensure voltage stays constant as electricity flows across long high-power transmission lines. By the end of the exercise half a dozen devices had been destroyed, depriving power to an entire Western state for several weeks.

Computers control the grid's mechanical devices at every level, from massive generators fed by fossil fuels or uranium all the way down to the transmission lines on your street. Most of these computers use common operating systems such as Windows and Linux, which makes them as vulnerable to malware as your desktop PC is. Attack code such as Stuxnet is successful for three main reasons: these operating systems implicitly trust running software to be legitimate; they often have flaws that admit penetration by a rogue program; and industrial settings often do not allow for the use of readily available defenses.

Even knowing all this, the average control system engineer would have once dismissed out of hand the possibility of remotely launched malware getting close to critical controllers, arguing that the system is not directly connected to the Internet. Then Stuxnet showed that control networks with no permanent connection to anything else are still vulnerable. Malware can piggyback on a USB stick that technicians plug into the control system, for example. When it comes to critical electronic circuits, even the smallest back door can let an enterprising burglar in.

Consider the case of a transmission substation, a waypoint on electricity's journey from power plant to your home. Substations take in high-voltage electricity coming from one or more power plants, reduce the voltage and split the power into multiple output lines for local distribution. A circuit breaker guards each of these lines, standing ready to cut power in case of a fault. When one output line's breaker trips, all of the power it would have carried flows to the remaining lines. It is not hard to see that if all the lines are carrying power close to their capacity, then a cyberattack that trips out half of the output lines and keeps the remaining ones in the circuit may overload them.

These circuit breakers have historically been controlled by devices connected to telephone modems so that technicians can dial in. It is not difficult to find those numbers; hackers invented programs 30 years ago to dial up all phone numbers within an exchange and make note of the ones to which modems respond. Modems in substations often have a unique message in their dial-up response that reveals their function. Coupled with weak means of authentication (such as well-known passwords or no passwords at all), an attacker can use these modems to break into a substation's network. From there it may be possible to change device configurations so that a danger condition that would otherwise open a circuit breaker to protect equipment gets ignored.

New systems are not necessarily more secure than modems. Increasingly, new devices deployed in substations may communicate with one another via low-powered radio, which does not stop at the boundaries of the substation. An attacker can reach the network simply by hiding in nearby bushes with his computer. Encrypted Wi-Fi networks are more secure, but a sophisticated attacker can still crack their encryption using readily available software tools. From here he can execute a man-in-the-middle attack that causes all communication between two legitimate devices to pass through his computer or fool other devices into accepting his computer as legitimate. He can craft malicious control messages that hijack the circuit breakers—tripping a carefully chosen few to overload the other lines perhaps or making sure they do not trip in an emergency.

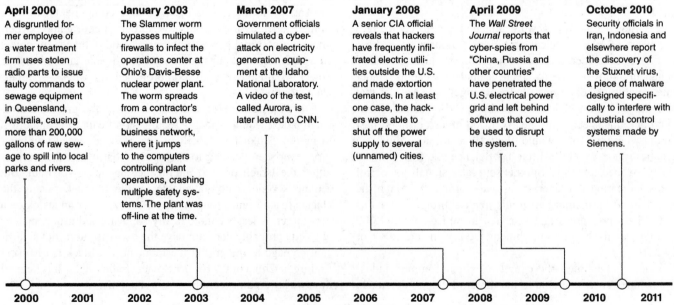

Digital Attacks, Physical Harm   As industrial machinery goes online, the potential for wreaking havoc grows. Intrusions over the past decade show that the grid is not the only vulnerability—anything with a microchip can be a target.

April 2000
A disgruntled former employee of a water treatment firm uses stolen radio parts to issue faulty commands to sewage equipment in Queensland, Australia, causing more than 200,000 gallons of raw sewage to spill into local parks and rivers.

January 2003
The Slammer worm bypasses multiple firewalls to infect the operations center at Ohio's Davis-Besse nuclear power plant. The worm spreads from a contractor's computer into the business network, where it jumps to the computers controlling plant operations, crashing multiple safety systems. The plant was off-line at the time.

March 2007
Government officials simulated a cyberattack on electricity generation equipment at the Idaho National Laboratory. A video of the test, called Aurora, is later leaked to CNN.

January 2008
A senior CIA official reveals that hackers have frequently infiltrated electric utilities outside the U.S. and made extortion demands. In at least one case, the hackers were able to shut off the power supply to several (unnamed) cities.

April 2009
The *Wall Street Journal* reports that cyber-spies from "China, Russia and other countries" have penetrated the U.S. electrical power grid and left behind software that could be used to disrupt the system.

October 2010
Security officials in Iran, Indonesia and elsewhere report the discovery of the Stuxnet virus, a piece of malware designed specifically to interfere with industrial control systems made by Siemens.

2000 2001 2002 2003 2004 2005 2006 2007 2008 2009 2010 2011

Once an intruder or malware sneaks in through the back door, its first step is usually to spread as widely as possible. Stuxnet again illustrates some of the well-known strategies. It proliferated by using an operating system mechanism called autoexec. Windows computers read and execute the file named AUTOEXEC.BAT every time a new user logs in. Typically the program locates printer drivers, runs a virus scan or performs other basic functions. Yet Windows assumes that any program with the right name is trusted code. Hackers thus find ways to alter the AUTOEXEC.BAT file so that it runs the attackers' code.

Attackers can also use clever methods that exploit the economics of the power industry. Because of deregulation, competing utilities share responsibility for grid operation. Power is generated, transmitted and distributed under contracts obtained in online auctions. These markets operate at multiple timescales—one market might trade energy for immediate delivery and another for tomorrow's needs. A utility's business unit must have a constant flow of real-time information from its operations unit to make smart trades. (And vice versa: operations need to know how much power they need to produce to fulfill the business unit's orders.) Here the vulnerability lies. An enterprising hacker might break into the business network, ferret out user names and passwords, and use these stolen identities to access the operations network.

Other attacks might spread by exploiting the small programs called scripts that come embedded in files. These scripts are ubiquitous—PDF files routinely contain scripts that aid in file display, for example—but they are also a potential danger. One computer security company recently estimated that more than 60 percent of all targeted attacks use scripts buried in PDF files. Simply reading a corrupted file may admit an attacker onto your computer.

Consider the hypothetical case where a would-be grid attacker first penetrates the Website of a software vendor and replaces an online manual with a malicious one that appears exactly like the first. The cyberattacker then sends an engineer at the power plant a forged e-mail that tricks the engineer into fetching and opening the booby-trapped manual. Just by going online to download an updated software manual, the unwitting engineer opens his power plant's gates to the Trojan horse. Once inside, the attack begins.

Search and Destroy

An intruder on a control network can issue commands with potentially devastating results. In 2007 the Department of Homeland Security staged a cyberattack code-named Aurora at the Idaho National laboratory. During the exercise, a researcher posing as a malicious hacker burrowed his way into a network connected to a medium-size power generator. Like all generators, it creates alternating current operating at almost exactly 60 cycles per second. In every cycle, the flow of electrons starts out moving in one direction, reverses course, and then returns to its original state. The generator has to be moving electrons in exactly the same direction at exactly the same time as the rest of the grid.

During the Aurora attack, our hacker issued a rapid succession of on/off commands to the circuit breakers of a test generator at the laboratory. This pushed it out of sync with the power grid's own oscillations. The grid pulled one way, the generator another. In effect, the generator's mechanical inertia fought the grid's electrical inertia. The generator lost. Declassified video shows the hulking steel machine shuddering as though a train hit the building. Seconds later steam and smoke fill the room.

Industrial systems can also fail when they are pushed beyond their limits—when centrifuges spin too fast, they disintegrate. Similarly, an attacker could make an electric generator produce a surge of power that exceeds the limit of what the transmission lines can carry. Excess power would then have to escape as heat. Enough excess over a long enough period causes the line to sag and eventually to melt. If the sagging line comes into contact with anything— a tree, a billboard, a house—it could create a massive short circuit.

Protection relays typically prevent these shorts, but a cyberattack could interfere with the working of the relays, which means damage would be done. Furthermore, a cyberattack could also alter the information going to the control station, keeping operators from knowing that anything is amiss. We have all seen the movies where crooks send a false video feed to a guard.

Control stations are also vulnerable to attack. These are command and control rooms with huge displays, like the war room in *Dr. Strangelove*. Control station operators use the displays to monitor data gathered from the substations, then issue commands to change substation control settings. Often these stations are responsible for monitoring hundreds of substations spread over a good part of a state.

Data communications between the control station and substations use specialized protocols that themselves may have vulnerabilities. If an intruder succeeds in launching a man-in-the-middle attack, that individual can insert a message into an exchange (or corrupt an existing message) that causes one or both of the computers at either end to fail. An attacker can also try just injecting a properly formatted message that is out of context— a digital non sequitur that crashes the machine.

Attackers could also simply attempt to delay messages traveling between control stations and the substations. Ordinarily the lag time between a substation's measurement of electricity flow and the control station's use of the data to adjust flows is small—otherwise it would be like driving a car and seeing only where you were 10 seconds ago. (This kind of lack of situational awareness was a contributor to the Northeast Blackout of 2003.)

Many of these attacks do not require fancy software such as Stuxnet but merely the standard hacker's tool kit. For instance, hackers frequently take command over networks of thousands or even millions of ordinary PCs (a botnet), which they then instruct to do their bidding. The simplest type of botnet attack is to flood an ordinary Website with bogus messages, blocking or slowing the ordinary flow of information. These "denial of service" attacks could also be used to slow traffic moving between the control station and substations.

Botnets could also take root in the substation computers themselves. At one point in 2009 the Conficker botnet had

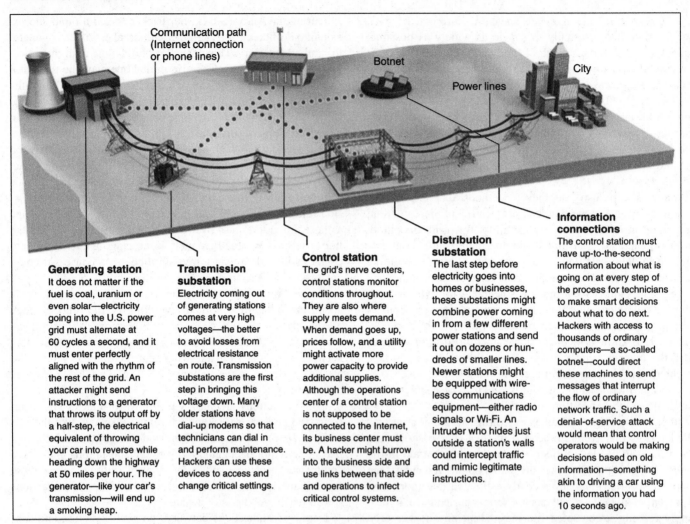

Generating station
It does not matter if the fuel is coal, uranium or even solar—electricity going into the U.S. power grid must alternate at 60 cycles a second, and it must enter perfectly aligned with the rhythm of the rest of the grid. An attacker might send instructions to a generator that throws its output off by a half-step, the electrical equivalent of throwing your car into reverse while heading down the highway at 50 miles per hour. The generator—like your car's transmission—will end up a smoking heap.

Transmission substation
Electricity coming out of generating stations comes at very high voltages—the better to avoid losses from electrical resistance en route. Transmission substations are the first step in bringing this voltage down. Many older stations have dial-up modems so that technicians can dial in and perform maintenance. Hackers can use these devices to access and change critical settings.

Control station
The grid's nerve centers, control stations monitor conditions throughout. They are also where supply meets demand. When demand goes up, prices follow, and a utility might activate more power capacity to provide additional supplies. Although the operations center of a control station is not supposed to be connected to the Internet, its business center must be. A hacker might burrow into the business side and use links between that side and operations to infect critical control systems.

Distribution substation
The last step before electricity goes into homes or businesses, these substations might combine power coming in from a few different power stations and send it out on dozens or hundreds of smaller lines. Newer stations might be equipped with wireless communications equipment—either radio signals or Wi-Fi. An intruder who hides just outside a station's walls could intercept traffic and mimic legitimate instructions.

Information connections
The control station must have up-to-the-second information about what is going on at every step of the process for technicians to make smart decisions about what to do next. Hackers with access to thousands of ordinary computers—a so-called botnet—could direct these machines to send messages that interrupt the flow of ordinary network traffic. Such a denial-of-service attack would mean that control operators would be making decisions based on old information—something akin to driving a car using the information you had 10 seconds ago.

Holes in the Grid. The modern electrical grid involves an intricate balance between the amount of energy needed by society and the amount generated at power plants. Dozens of components orchestrate the flow of electrons over distances of hundreds of miles, aligning the alternating currents and making sure no single component gets stretched beyond its limits. Any one of these parts might suffer from the attention of malicious actors. Here are some of the most troublesome choke points and the ways they might be compromised.

insinuated itself into 10 million computers; the individuals, as yet unknown, who control it could have ordered it to erase the hard drives of every computer in the network, on command. A botnet such as Conficker could establish itself within substations and then have its controller direct them simultaneously to do anything at any time. According to a 2004 study by researchers at Pennsylvania State University and the National Renewable Energy Laboratory in Golden, Colo., an attack that incapacitated a carefully chosen minority of all transmission substations—about 2 percent, or 200 in total—would bring down 60 percent of the grid. Losing 8 percent would trigger a nationwide blackout.

What to Do

When microsoft learns of a potential security liability in its Windows software, it typically releases a software patch. Individual users and IT departments the world over download the patch, update their software and protect themselves from the threat. Unfortunately, things are not that simple on the grid.

Whereas the power grid uses the same type of off-the-shelf hardware and software as the rest of the world, IT managers at power stations cannot simply patch the faulty software when bugs crop up. Grid control systems cannot come down for three hours every week for maintenance; they have to run continuously. Grid operators also have a deep-rooted institutional conservatism. Control networks have been in place for a long time, and operators are familiar and comfortable with how they work. They tend to avoid anything that threatens availability or might interfere with ordinary operations.

In the face of a clear and present danger, the North American Electric Reliability Corporation (NERC), an umbrella body of grid operators, has devised a set of standards designed to protect critical infrastructure. Utilities are now required to identify their critical assets and demonstrate to NERC-appointed auditors that they can protect them from unauthorized access.

Yet security audits, like financial audits, cannot possibly be exhaustive. When an audit does go into technical details, it does so only selectively. Compliance is in the eye of the auditor.

The most common protection strategy is to employ an electronic security perimeter, a kind of cybersecurity Maginot line. The first line of defense is a firewall, a device through which all electronic messages pass. Each message has a header indicating where it came from, where it is going, and what protocol is used to interpret the message. Based on this information, the firewall allows some messages through and stops others. An auditor's job is partly to make sure the firewalls in a utility are configured properly so that they do not let any unwanted traffic in or out. Typically the auditors would identify a few critical assets, get a hold of the firewall configuration files, and attempt to sort through by hand the ways in which a hacker might be able to break through the firewall.

Firewalls, though, are so complex that it is difficult for an auditor to parse all the myriad possibilities. Automated software tools might help. Our team at the University of Illinois at Urbana-Champaign has developed the Network Access Policy Tool, which is just now being used by utilities and assessment teams. The software needs only a utility's firewall configuration files—it does not even have to connect to the network. Already it has found a number of unknown or long-forgotten pathways that attackers might have exploited.

The DOE has come out with a roadmap that lays out a strategy for enhancing grid security by 2015. (A revision due this year extends this deadline to 2020.) One focus: creating a system that recognizes an intrusion attempt and reacts to it automatically. That would block a Stuxnet-like virus as soon as it jumped from the USB stick. But how can an operating system know which programs are to be trusted?

One solution is to use a one-way hash function, a cryptographic technique. A hash function takes a fantastically huge number—for example, all the millions of 1s and 0s of a computer program, expressed as a number—and converts it to a much smaller number, which acts as a signature. Because programs are so large, it is highly unlikely that two different ones would result in the same signature value. Imagine that every program that wants to run on a system must first go through the hash function. Its signature then gets checked against a master list; if it does not check out, the attack stops there.

The DOE also recommends other security measures, such as physical security checks at operator workstations (think radio chips in identification badges). It also highlights the need to exert tighter control over communication between devices inside the network. The 2007 Aurora demonstration involved a rogue device tricking a generator's network into believing it was sending authoritative commands. These commands eventually led to the destruction of the generator.

These worthwhile steps will require time and money and effort. If we are going to achieve the DOE roadmap to a more secure grid in the next decade, we are going to have to pick up the pace. Let us hope we have even that much time.

References

Roadmap to Secure Control Systems in the Energy Sector. Jack Eisenhauer et al. Energetics Incorporated, January 2006. www.oe.energy.gov/csroadmap.htm

Security of Critical Control Systems Sparks Concern. David Geer in *IEEE Computer,* Vol. 39, No. 1, pages 20–23; January 2006.

Trustworthy Cyber Infrastructure for the Power Grid. Multiuniversity research project funded by the U.S. Department of Energy. www.tcipg.org

What Is the Electric Grid, and What Are Some Challenges It Faces? U.S. Department of Energy. www.eia.doe.gov/energy_in_brief/power_grid.cfm

Scientific American Online

For an extended look at the history of electronic attacks on physical structures, visit ScientificAmerican.com/jul2011/lights-out

Critical Thinking

1. Use the Internet to research the Stuxnet virus. Who is thought to have been responsible for it?

2. The author mentions a type of cyber-attack known as at Trojan horse. Use the Internet to read about the Trojan horse attack. While you're at it, where was the first Trojan horse described?

3. The author uses the phrase "clear and present danger." Use the Internet to learn who first used it and in what context. Is the phrase being misused in the article?

4. Think about technology biting back. Is there a simpler solution to protecting the grid than those proposed? Again, use the Internet to do some research.

DAVID M. NICOL is director of the Information Trust Institute and a professor in the department of electrical and computer engineering at the University of Illinois at Urbana-Champaign. He has worked as a consultant for the U.S. Department of Homeland Security and Department of Energy.

From *Scientific American*, July 2011, pp. 70–75. Copyright © 2011 by Scientific American, a division of Nature America, Inc. All rights reserved. Reprinted by permission.

Bride of Stuxnet

Webcraft as spycraft.

JONATHAN V. LAST

Last April, the Iranian Oil Ministry and the National Iranian Oil Company noticed a problem with some of their computers: A small number of machines were spontaneously erasing themselves. Spooked by the recent Stuxnet attack, which had wrecked centrifuges in their nuclear labs, the Iranians suspected a piece of computer malware was to blame. They went to the United Nations' International Telecommunications Union and asked for help. After an initial investigation, it was determined that the Iranians had been hit with a new piece of malicious software; it was temporarily labeled Wiper. Or Viper. After translating the moniker into different languages, no one is quite sure what the original nickname was.

The experts from Turtle Bay quickly realized they were out of their depth with Wiper/Viper and contracted a Russian computer security firm, Kaspersky Lab, to help. As the techs at Kaspersky investigated, they began to find bits and pieces of a much bigger program. What they eventually uncovered forced them to put aside Wiper/Viper and send out an all-hands call to the tech community: a cyber-weapon that made Stuxnet look primitive. They called it Flame.

Stuxnet was like a guided missile with a targeted payload. It was created to spread rapidly, but always to be seeking a particular set of computers—machines made by Siemens and used to control centrifuge operations at a uranium enrichment plant. Once Stuxnet reached its destination, it had very precise instructions: It altered the speed of the centrifuges in such a manner as to slowly degrade the equipment and destroy the uranium they contained—all while sending false readings back to the operating console so that neither the computer nor the human supervisors would notice the damage being done.

If Stuxnet was like a missile, then Flame is more like a surveillance satellite.

Once a computer is infected by Flame, the program begins a process of taking over the entire machine. Flame records every keystroke by the user, creating a perfect log of all activity. It takes pictures of the screen every 60 seconds—and every 15 seconds when instant message or email programs are in use. It records all administrative action on the computer—taking note of network passwords, for instance. And it rummages through the computer's hard drive copying documents and files.

But that's not all. Flame also takes control of the machine's Bluetooth capability and turns it into a hub for a small wireless network, bonding with other Bluetooth-enabled devices in the vicinity, such as cell phones. It then uses the Bluetooth connection to case whatever information is on the remote device—say, an address book, calendar, or email list. Most spectacularly, Flame is able to turn on the computer's built-in microphone and record the user, or anyone else who happens to be chatting in the vicinity.

Flame then compiles all of this information—the passwords, the documents, the keystroke logs, the screenshots, and the audio recordings—encrypts it, and secretly uploads it to a command-and-control server (C&C), where someone is waiting to analyze it.

The first thing the white hats noticed about Flame was its size. Most malware is designed to be tiny—the smaller the package of code, the harder it is for your computer's constantly updating security protocols to intercept it. It took half a megabyte of code to build Stuxnet, which was a remarkably large footprint by the standards of malware. When completely deployed, Flame takes up 20 megabytes. Which is positively gargantuan.

But Flame is deployed in stages. When it works its way onto a new machine, Flame comes in an initial package of six megabytes. After the worm takes control of the box, it inventories the machine and the surrounding networks, and then begins communicating with a remote C&C server. On the other end of the line, a team takes in the data being sent by Flame, makes a determination of the new host's value, and then returns instructions to the waiting worm. Depending on what the C&C team see, they might instruct Flame to install any of 14 additional modules—mini add-on programs which, for instance, would give Flame the ability to take over the computer's microphone, or Bluetooth functionality. One module, named "browse32," is a kill module. When activated by the C&C, browse32 systematically moves through the computer, deleting every trace of Flame's existence. Its wipe is so thorough that once it's been triggered, no one—not even computer security techs—can tell if Flame was ever there in the first place.

No one is sure how long Flame has been operational. There is evidence of its existence in the wild dating to March 2010, but Flame may be older than that. (Stuxnet was discovered in June 2010 and is believed to have been released 12 months before then.) It's difficult to date Flame because its makers went to some trouble to disguise its age. Computer code typically has meta-data describing its "compilation date"—that is, the time and date it was assembled in final form. Flame's 20 modules all have compilation dates set in 1994 and 1995. Which is impossible, because they're written in a language that was released just a few years ago.

Neither are analysts certain exactly how Flame spreads. It has the ability to move from one computer to another by piggybacking onto a USB flash drive (just like Stuxnet). Alternately, it can migrate across a local network by exploiting a shared printer (again, like Stuxnet). But Flame is also able to spread across a network without a printer if it finds itself on a computer that has administrative privileges. When that happens, the worm is smart enough to create backdoor accounts for all the other computers on the network and copy itself into those machines.

As for the question of security—how does Flame talk its way past the computer's antivirus protections? No one knows. The techs at Kaspersky Lab watched Flame attack a PC running the fully updated Windows 7 security suite. The worm took over the computer effortlessly. This suggests that the worm's designers have access to one or more vulnerabilities in the operating system that even the people who designed the OS don't know about. (Stuxnet utilized four of these so-called zero-day exploits.)

Engineers are only two weeks into the teardown, but they already believe that Flame and Stuxnet were created by different development teams. The code and workings are dissimilar. And besides, the timelines on the two projects are too close. It is estimated that coding Stuxnet required 10,000 man-hours. For a team of 30 to 50 programmers, that's a year or two of work. The same squad simply would not have had the time to build both Stuxnet and the much larger Flame.

That said, Kaspersky Lab notes that the worms do share two interesting similarities: They use the same rootkit-based exploit to hijack USB drives and the same print-spooler vulnerability to spread over a network's shared printer. There are three possible explanations for this: (1) The teams that developed Flame and Stuxnet discovered these identical mechanisms independently; (2) the team which developed Flame learned about them from analyzing an early version of Stuxnet; (3) the teams that developed the two worms were working in parallel, for the same organization(s), and thus were able to share information about these mechanisms.

Yet the most interesting aspect of Flame is the strategic ways it differs from Stuxnet. As a weapon, Stuxnet was a tool conceived in urgency. Every piece of malware has to balance virulence with stealth. The more aggressively a worm propagates, the more likely it is to be caught. Stuxnet was designed to spread at a fairly robust rate. Its creators wanted it to get on lots of different computers and they were willing to risk quicker discovery on the chance that the worm would find its way to the very specific system it was meant for and deliver its payload. In the end, Stuxnet's engineers made a good trade. Because it eventually spread to 100,000 computers, Stuxnet was caught reasonably quickly. Yet this aggressive approach got it to its target—Iran's Natanz refinery—where it wrecked at least a year's worth of work.

Flame, on the other hand, is a study in stealth and patience. Unlike Stuxnet, with its single-minded search for a specific computer system, Flame seems to have wandered in many directions: onto computers used by governments, universities, and private companies. It moved slowly, and the overall number of infected systems seems to be quite low. Current estimates put it at 1,000 computers, nearly all of them located in Iran, the Palestinian territories, Sudan, Syria, and Lebanon. Flame kept the number of infections low because it never moved from one computer to another without explicit instructions from its C&C. According to Kaspersky Lab, the method went something like this:

> [T]hey infect several dozen [machines], then conduct analysis of the data of the victim, [and] uninstall Flame from the systems that aren't interesting, leaving the most important ones in place. After which they start a new series of infections.

It was a detailed, deliberate process of identifying and exploiting targets that must have required significant manpower and intelligence capability on the C&C side. In other words, the design and deployment of Flame was only half of the job. Another team, with a different skill set, was needed to run the operation once it was in the field.

But once Flame was running, it was like something out of science fiction. Flame could watch a target even when he was completely alone. It could listen to every word he said on the telephone, or through Skype, or to a colleague walking past his desk. It could rifle through his computer files and find any document. Or peek into a cell phone sitting in someone's pocket in the next room. It never had to worry about getting caught in the act. And on a moment's notice, it could erase any sign that it was ever there. It kept up constant communication with its handlers, even when they were thousands of miles away, and it always followed orders.

Whoever engineered Flame didn't just build the most spectacular computer worm ever made. They created the perfect spy.

Critical Thinking

1. Build an ethical argument for infiltrating the computer networks of an enemy we are not at war with? Build an ethical argument against such an infiltration.

2. What are the risks back to us when we inject software code into computer networks of another country? Are these risks worthwhile?

3. How would the American public react if we found out spies from another country infiltrated the networks used by our military or nuclear scientists? Beyond the initial reaction, what would an appropriate governmental response be to such an infiltration?

4. As these software techniques become better known among hackers, inevitably a commercial system will be infiltrated in a similar manner either by outside thieves looking to profit, or by a competitor looking for intelligence. How does such a commercial attack compare to military-style attacks of this sort by government?

JONATHAN V. LAST is a senior writer at *The Weekly Standard.*

From *The Weekly Standard*, June 11, 2012, pp. 18–19. Copyright © 2012 by Weekly Standard. Reprinted by permission.

Me and My Data: How Much Do the Internet Giants Really Know?

James Ball discovered that the information Google and Facebook hold on him is disturbing but also comforting.

JAMES BALL

To briefly state the obvious, the internet giants are seriously big: Google is not only the world's largest search engine, it's one of the top three email providers, a social network, and owner of the Blogger platform and the world's largest video site, YouTube. Facebook has the social contacts, messages, wallposts and photos of more than 750 million people.

Given that such information could be used to sell us stuff, accessed by government or law enforcement bodies (perhaps without warrants, under legal changes), or—theoretically, at least—picked up by hackers or others, it's not unreasonable to wonder exactly how much the internet giants know about us.

US users of the sites are out of luck: there's no legal right under US law to ask a company to hand over all the information it holds on you. Users do have some say in how much companies are allowed to take, usually contained in the terms of service. But EU citizens are in a better position—under Europe-wide data protection rules, anyone can send a written request for their full data and, for a small fee, the company has to ship it out, usually within 40 days.

It's a great chance to see exactly how much Google and Facebook really know about us, and all we need is a test subject. Perhaps an EU citizen who's been on Facebook since it came to the UK in 2005; who's had a YouTube account almost as long; and was on Gmail back when invitations to the service were something to beg, borrow and steal, rather than a nuisance. They'd also have to be enough of an idiot to write about what they dig up in public. This left one obvious, unlucky test case in the Guardian offices: me.

Things didn't get off to a great start with Google. The company has a main US branch, Google Inc, and subsidiaries within other countries. In the UK, that's Google UK Ltd. Here's the catch: Google UK Ltd, which is subject to the EU rules that let you access your data, doesn't hold it. As Google says in a statement: "Please note that Google UK Ltd does not process any personal data in relation to Google services, which are provided by Google Inc, a US-incorporated company whose address you can find in the Google privacy policy."

While we can find Google Inc's address, that doesn't necessarily help: a spokeswoman for the UK regulator, the ICO, confirmed that EU laws on subject access requests do not extend to the US parent company. This means there's no real chance of getting hold of user data from Google through this route.

Thankfully, Google isn't totally unhelpful. It has two tools that help show the information it holds on you, which a helpful staffer walked me through. The first, Google Dashboard, has run for about three years and gathers information from almost all of Google's services in one place. Another feature, the "account activity report", has launched recently, and shows Google's information on my logins in the past month, including countries, browsers, platforms and how much I've used the services.

Running these tools on my work email account (the Guardian's emails are managed by Google) is disconcerting, but not too much so. The dashboard can see I'm a member of a few internal Google groups, and have a blogger account used to collaborate with some researchers on Twitter riot data.

Data showing my work gmail account has 877 contacts—and listing them—gives me some pause for thought, as does a list of the 398 Google docs I've opened. The site also lists my most recent sent and received emails (in both cases a "no subject" conversation thread with a colleague).

A little more disconcerting is a chat history logging 500 conversations with 177 colleagues. Google chat is a handy way to collaborate in a large building, especially one full of journalists who seem to prefer to talk online (as Twitter activity testifies) rather than in the flesh. But there's more than a little gossip going on too. I make a mental note to check how to delete those logs.

The big relief comes when I note Google isn't tracking the internet searches I've made on my work account, which for journalists the world over tends towards the incredibly odd.

Repeating this exercise for my personal Google account is less relaxing. There are several bits of extra info here. The most innocuous is a heavily neglected Google+ profile with a few hundred connections but almost no posts.

Slightly more embarrassing is a seemingly connected You-Tube account, apparently set up at a time when I thought using character names from role-playing games was a good account-naming policy. It has only one surviving video—a student interview with Heather Brooke—but does link to my viewing history, which includes the Tottenham riots, Dire Straits, Pomplamoose and, bafflingly, a Q&A from the Ryan commission into child abuse in Ireland.

Worst of all is a lengthy list of my search results. Looking through anyone's list of searches gives a distressing degree of insight into odder parts of their personality. Google helpfully lists my most recent searches across its different services on one page. For web search: "paul daniels wiki". For images: "harry styles" (explainer: I was trying to see who he was, after my 15-year-old niece mentioned him).

News was "youtube user figures", showing I am meticulous in my research, while even my maps search history is present—last result "Portland House, SW1". Mortifyingly, my last blogs search was a vanity one: "james ball". Google also holds information on my login IPs, and other anonymised non-logged-in data, but doesn't (yet) make this available.

There was some relief from the gloom though. Google insists the tracking for its display adverts—it is the market leader in online advertising—doesn't draw from user data, but comes instead from cookies, files that anonymously monitor the sites you visit. Google's ad preference page believes I am interested in online video, TV reality shows, printers, Egypt, politics and England. From this, it has concluded I am likely to be over 65 and male. I find myself more reassured than offended that Google has got this more or less wrong.

Facebook is a much trickier prospect. Unlike Google, Facebook actually processes some data in the EU, through its Irish branch, making it subject to access laws. These are currently taking a long time—apparently up to three months—due to a large volume of requests from campaigners, so I once again resorted to the site's own tools.

Facebook's main download tool was familiar, if slightly embarrassing. A downloaded archive that opens into something looking oddly like a stripped-down, uncluttered Facebook, this lists all my friends, every post ever made on my wall, by myself or others (some dating back almost seven years are not comfortable viewing), my private messages and the small number (fewer than 10) of photos I've uploaded to the site myself.

The Facebook extended archive is a little creepier, including "poke info", each instance of tracking cookies they possess, previous names, and full login and logout info. Every event to which I've ever been invited is neatly listed, alongside its location, time, and whether I said I would attend .

One piece of information—a supposed engagement to a schoolfriend, Amy Holmes—stands out. A Facebook "joke" that seemed faintly funny for about a week several years ago was undone by hiding it from any and all Facebook users, friends or otherwise (to avoid an ". . . is now single!" status update). The forgotten relationship helpfully explains why Facebook has served me up with badly targeted bridalwear adverts for several years, and reassures me that Facebook doesn't know quite everything.

Or does it? There are gaping holes in what Facebook has made available to me. No posts from other users in which I'm mentioned are included, not even from my friends. None of the 300+ photographs in which I feature, uploaded by friends and family, are there. On the upside, this means I escape yet another viewing of the naked baby photos my ruthless older sister decided to share with the world. On the downside, it reminds me that huge swaths of my information on these networks are outside my control.

Campaigners estimate that only around 29% of the information Facebook possesses on any given user is accessible through the site's tools.

The tour through a decent swath of my personal data is at once disturbing and comforting. Disturbing because it reminds me mine is a life lived online. Among the huge tranche of information available to Google and Facebook alone is virtually everyone I know, a huge amount of what I've said to (and about) them, and a vast amount of data on where I've been. Such detailed tracking would have been an impossibility even 10 years ago, and we're largely clueless as to its effects.

This is the core of the main comfort: despite their mountain of data, Google and Facebook seem largely clueless, too—they've had no more luck making any sense out of it than I have. And that, for now, is a relief.

Critical Thinking

1. The subhead of this article is "James Ball discovered that the information Google and Facebook hold on him is disturbing but also comforting." If you were to petition Google or Facebook to provide you with all of the data they know about you, do you think you would find the result more disturbing or more comforting?

2. What do you see as the biggest upsides to having large amounts of your information stored online by commercial organizations? What do you see as the biggest downsides?

3. When you delete information from your online accounts, for example when you delete an email message or Google doc or Facebook post, copies of that information persist on archived versions of the large corporate databases. While such archived data is not at all easy to access, it is still out there. Is this a good or a bad thing?

4. After reading this article are you more likely to add more information to your Google and Facebook accounts, or work to remove information?

From *The Guardian*, April 22, 2012. Copyright © 2012 by Guardian News & Media Ltd. Reprinted by permission.

The Web's New Gold Mine: Your Secrets

A Journal investigation finds that one of the fastest-growing businesses on the Internet is the business of spying on consumers. First in a series.

JULIA ANGWIN

Hidden inside Ashley Hayes-Beaty's computer, a tiny file helps gather personal details about her, all to be put up for sale for a tenth of a penny.

The file consists of a single code—4c812db292272995e-5416a323e79bd37—that secretly identifies her as a 26-year-old female in Nashville, Tenn.

The code knows that her favorite movies include "The Princess Bride," "50 First Dates" and "10 Things I Hate About You." It knows she enjoys the "Sex and the City" series. It knows she browses entertainment news and likes to take quizzes.

"Well, I like to think I have some mystery left to me, but apparently not!" Ms. Hayes-Beaty said when told what that snippet of code reveals about her. "The profile is eerily correct."

Ms. Hayes-Beaty is being monitored by Lotame Solutions Inc., a New York company that uses sophisticated software called a "beacon" to capture what people are typing on a website—their comments on movies, say, or their interest in parenting and pregnancy. Lotame packages that data into profiles about individuals, without determining a person's name, and sells the profiles to companies seeking customers. Ms. Hayes-Beaty's tastes can be sold wholesale (a batch of movie lovers is $1 per thousand) or customized (26-year-old Southern fans of "50 First Dates").

"We can segment it all the way down to one person," says Eric Porres, Lotame's chief marketing officer.

One of the fastest-growing businesses on the Internet, a Wall Street Journal investigation has found, is the business of spying on Internet users.

The Journal conducted a comprehensive study that assesses and analyzes the broad array of cookies and other surveillance technology that companies are deploying on Internet users. It reveals that the tracking of consumers has grown both far more pervasive and far more intrusive than is realized by all but a handful of people in the vanguard of the industry.

- The study found that the nation's 50 top websites on average installed 64 pieces of tracking technology onto the computers of visitors, usually with no warning. A dozen sites each installed more than a hundred. The nonprofit Wikipedia installed none.

- Tracking technology is getting smarter and more intrusive. Monitoring used to be limited mainly to "cookie" files that record websites people visit. But the Journal found new tools that scan in real time what people are doing on a Web page, then instantly assess location, income, shopping interests and even medical conditions. Some tools surreptitiously re-spawn themselves even after users try to delete them.

- These profiles of individuals, constantly refreshed, are bought and sold on stock-market-like exchanges that have sprung up in the past 18 months.

The new technologies are transforming the Internet economy. Advertisers once primarily bought ads on specific Web pages—a car ad on a car site. Now, advertisers are paying a premium to follow people around the Internet, wherever they go, with highly specific marketing messages.

In between the Internet user and the advertiser, the Journal identified more than 100 middlemen—tracking companies, data brokers and advertising networks—competing to meet the growing demand for data on individual behavior and interests.

The data on Ms. Hayes-Beaty's film-watching habits, for instance, is being offered to advertisers on BlueKai Inc., one of the new data exchanges.

"It is a sea change in the way the industry works," says Omar Tawakol, CEO of BlueKai. "Advertisers want to buy access to people, not Web pages."

The Journal examined the 50 most popular U.S. websites, which account for about 40% of the Web pages viewed by Americans. (The Journal also tested its own site, WSJ.com.) It then analyzed the tracking files and programs these sites downloaded onto a test computer.

As a group, the top 50 sites placed 3,180 tracking files in total on the Journal's test computer. Nearly a third of these were innocuous, deployed to remember the password to a favorite site or tally most-popular articles.

But over two-thirds—2,224—were installed by 131 companies, many of which are in the business of tracking Web users to create rich databases of consumer profiles that can be sold.

The top venue for such technology, the Journal found, was IAC/InterActive Corp.'s Dictionary.com. A visit to the online dictionary site resulted in 234 files or programs being downloaded onto the Journal's test computer, 223 of which were from companies that track Web users.

The information that companies gather is anonymous, in the sense that Internet users are identified by a number assigned to their computer, not by a specific person's name. Lotame, for instance, says it doesn't know the name of users such as Ms. Hayes-Beaty—only their behavior and attributes, identified by code number. People who don't want to be tracked can remove themselves from Lotame's system.

And the industry says the data are used harmlessly. David Moore, chairman of 24/7 RealMedia Inc., an ad network owned by WPP PLC, says tracking gives Internet users better advertising.

"When an ad is targeted properly, it ceases to be an ad, it becomes important information," he says.

Tracking isn't new. But the technology is growing so powerful and ubiquitous that even some of America's biggest sites say they were unaware, until informed by the Journal, that they were installing intrusive files on visitors' computers.

The Journal found that Microsoft Corp.'s popular Web portal, MSN.com, planted a tracking file packed with data: It had a prediction of a surfer's age, ZIP Code and gender, plus a code containing estimates of income, marital status, presence of children and home ownership, according to the tracking company that created the file, Targus Information Corp.

Both Targus and Microsoft said they didn't know how the file got onto MSN.com, and added that the tool didn't contain "personally identifiable" information.

Tracking is done by tiny files and programs known as "cookies," "Flash cookies" and "beacons." They are placed on a computer when a user visits a website. U.S. courts have ruled that it is legal to deploy the simplest type, cookies, just as someone using a telephone might allow a friend to listen in on a conversation. Courts haven't ruled on the more complex trackers.

The most intrusive monitoring comes from what are known in the business as "third party" tracking files. They work like this: The first time a site is visited, it installs a tracking file, which assigns the computer a unique ID number. Later, when the user visits another site affiliated with the same tracking company, it can take note of where that user was before, and where he is now. This way, over time the company can build a robust profile.

One such ecosystem is Yahoo Inc.'s ad network, which collects fees by placing targeted advertisements on websites. Yahoo's network knows many things about recent high-school graduate Cate Reid. One is that she is a 13- to 18-year-old female interested in weight loss. Ms. Reid was able to determine this when a reporter showed her a little-known feature on Yahoo's website, the Ad Interest Manager, that displays some of the information Yahoo had collected about her.

Yahoo's take on Ms. Reid, who was 17 years old at the time, hit the mark: She was, in fact, worried that she may be 15 pounds too heavy for her 5-foot, 6-inch frame. She says she often does online research about weight loss.

"Every time I go on the Internet," she says, she sees weight-loss ads. "I'm self-conscious about my weight," says Ms. Reid, whose father asked that her hometown not be given. "I try not to think about it. . . . Then [the ads] make me start thinking about it."

Yahoo spokeswoman Amber Allman says Yahoo doesn't knowingly target weight-loss ads at people under 18, though it does target adults.

"It's likely this user received an untargeted ad," Ms. Allman says. It's also possible Ms. Reid saw ads targeted at her by other tracking companies.

Information about people's moment-to-moment thoughts and actions, as revealed by their online activity, can change hands quickly. Within seconds of visiting eBay.com or Expedia.com, information detailing a Web surfer's activity there is likely to be auctioned on the data exchange run by BlueKai, the Seattle startup.

Each day, BlueKai sells 50 million pieces of information like this about specific individuals' browsing habits, for as little as a tenth of a cent apiece. The auctions can happen instantly, as a website is visited.

Spokespeople for eBay Inc. and Expedia Inc. both say the profiles BlueKai sells are anonymous and the people aren't identified as visitors of their sites. BlueKai says its own website gives consumers an easy way to see what it monitors about them.

Tracking files get onto websites, and downloaded to a computer, in several ways. Often, companies simply pay sites to distribute their tracking files.

But tracking companies sometimes hide their files within free software offered to websites, or hide them within other tracking files or ads. When this happens, websites aren't always aware that they're installing the files on visitors' computers.

Often staffed by "quants," or math gurus with expertise in quantitative analysis, some tracking companies use probability algorithms to try to pair what they know about a person's online behavior with data from offline sources about household income, geography and education, among other things.

The goal is to make sophisticated assumptions in real time—plans for a summer vacation, the likelihood of repaying a loan—and sell those conclusions.

Some financial companies are starting to use this formula to show entirely different pages to visitors, based on assumptions about their income and education levels.

Life-insurance site AccuquoteLife.com, a unit of Byron Udell & Associates Inc., last month tested a system showing visitors it determined to be suburban, college-educated baby-boomers a default policy of $2 million to $3 million, says Accuquote executive Sean Cheyney. A rural, working-class senior citizen might see a default policy for $250,000, he says.

"We're driving people down different lanes of the highway," Mr. Cheyney says.

Consumer tracking is the foundation of an online advertising economy that racked up $23 billion in ad spending last year. Tracking activity is exploding. Researchers at AT&T Labs and Worcester Polytechnic Institute last fall found tracking technology on 80% of 1,000 popular sites, up from 40% of those sites in 2005.

The Journal found tracking files that collect sensitive health and financial data. On Encyclopaedia Britannica Inc.'s dictionary website Merriam-Webster.com, one tracking file from Healthline Networks Inc., an ad network, scans the page a user is viewing and targets ads related to what it sees there. So, for example, a person looking up depression-related words could see Healthline ads for depression treatments on that page—and on subsequent pages viewed on other sites.

Healthline says it doesn't let advertisers track users around the Internet who have viewed sensitive topics such as HIV/AIDS, sexually transmitted diseases, eating disorders and impotence. The company does let advertisers track people with bipolar disorder, overactive bladder and anxiety, according to its marketing materials.

Targeted ads can get personal. Last year, Julia Preston, a 32-year-old education-software designer in Austin, Texas, researched uterine disorders online. Soon after, she started noticing fertility ads on sites she visited. She now knows she doesn't have a disorder, but still gets the ads.

It's "unnerving," she says.

Tracking became possible in 1994 when the tiny text files called cookies were introduced in an early browser, Netscape Navigator. Their purpose was user convenience: remembering contents of Web shopping carts.

Back then, online advertising barely existed. The first banner ad appeared the same year. When online ads got rolling during the dot-com boom of the late 1990s, advertisers were buying ads based on proximity to content—shoe ads on fashion sites.

The dot-com bust triggered a power shift in online advertising, away from websites and toward advertisers. Advertisers began paying for ads only if someone clicked on them. Sites and ad networks began using cookies aggressively in hopes of showing ads to people most likely to click on them, thus getting paid.

Targeted ads command a premium. Last year, the average cost of a targeted ad was $4.12 per thousand viewers, compared with $1.98 per thousand viewers for an untargeted ad, according to an ad-industry-sponsored study in March.

The Journal examined three kinds of tracking technology— basic cookies as well as more powerful "Flash cookies" and bits of software code called "beacons."

More than half of the sites examined by the Journal installed 23 or more "third party" cookies. Dictionary.com installed the most, placing 159 third-party cookies.

Cookies are typically used by tracking companies to build lists of pages visited from a specific computer. A newer type of technology, beacons, can watch even more activity.

Beacons, also known as "Web bugs" and "pixels," are small pieces of software that run on a Web page. They can track what a user is doing on the page, including what is being typed or where the mouse is moving.

The majority of sites examined by the Journal placed at least seven beacons from outside companies. Dictionary.com had the most, 41, including several from companies that track health conditions and one that says it can target consumers by dozens of factors, including zip code and race.

Dictionary.com President Shravan Goli attributed the presence of so many tracking tools to the fact that the site was working with a large number of ad networks, each of which places its own cookies and beacons. After the Journal contacted the company, it cut the number of networks it uses and beefed up its privacy policy to more fully disclose its practices.

The widespread use of Adobe Systems Inc.'s Flash software to play videos online offers another opportunity to track people. Flash cookies originally were meant to remember users' preferences, such as volume settings for online videos.

But Flash cookies can also be used by data collectors to re-install regular cookies that a user has deleted. This can circumvent a user's attempt to avoid being tracked online. Adobe condemns the practice.

Most sites examined by the Journal installed no Flash cookies. Comcast.net installed 55.

That finding surprised the company, which said it was unaware of them. Comcast Corp. subsequently determined that it had used a piece of free software from a company called Clearspring Technologies Inc. to display a slideshow of celebrity photos on Comcast.net. The Flash cookies were installed on Comcast's site by that slideshow, according to Comcast.

Clearspring, based in McLean, Va., says the 55 Flash cookies were a mistake. The company says it no longer uses Flash cookies for tracking.

CEO Hooman Radfar says Clearspring provides software and services to websites at no charge. In exchange, Clearspring collects data on consumers. It plans eventually to sell the data it collects to advertisers, he says, so that site users can be shown "ads that don't suck." Comcast's data won't be used, Clearspring says.

Wittingly or not, people pay a price in reduced privacy for the information and services they receive online. Dictionary.com, the site with the most tracking files, is a case study.

The site's annual revenue, about $9 million in 2009 according to an SEC filing, means the site is too small to support an extensive ad-sales team. So it needs to rely on the national ad-placing networks, whose business model is built on tracking.

"Think about how these technologies and the associated analytics can be used in other industries and social settings (e.g. education) for real beneficial impacts. This is nothing new for the web, now that it has matured, it can be a positive game-changer."

—Mitchell Weisberg

Dictionary.com executives say the trade-off is fair for their users, who get free access to its dictionary and thesaurus service.

"Whether it's one or 10 cookies, it doesn't have any impact on the customer experience, and we disclose we do it," says Dictionary.com spokesman Nicholas Graham. "So what's the beef?"

The problem, say some industry veterans, is that so much consumer data is now up for sale, and there are no legal limits on how that data can be used.

Until recently, targeting consumers by health or financial status was considered off-limits by many large Internet ad companies. Now, some aim to take targeting to a new level by tapping online social networks.

Media6Degrees Inc., whose technology was found on three sites by the Journal, is pitching banks to use its data to size up consumers based on their social connections. The idea is that the creditworthy tend to hang out with the creditworthy, and deadbeats with deadbeats.

"There are applications of this technology that can be very powerful," says Tom Phillips, CEO of Media6Degrees. "Who knows how far we'd take it?"

Critical Thinking

1. What is a cookie (in the context of a web browser)?

2. What is a beacon?

3. Many websites, like broadcast TV, appear to be free. The bills are paid through advertising. Would you prefer to pay directly to use websites or to continue to allow their owners to collect and sell information about you?

Acknowledgements—*Emily Steel, Jennifer Valentino-DeVries* and *Tom McGinty* contributed to this report.

From *The Wall Street Journal*, August 1, 2010. Copyright © 2010 by Dow Jones & Company, Inc. Reprinted by permission via Rightslink.

The Conundrum of Visibility: Youth Safety and the Internet

Danah Boyd and Alice Marwick

The complexities of the Internet continue to be a source of consternation for parents, educators, and policy makers. Some embrace the Internet, evangelizing about its tremendous potential. Others fear it, preaching en masse about its dangers. These cycles of polarizing doctrine make it difficult to understand that the Internet is quickly becoming just another aspect of everyday life, mirroring dynamics that shape every environment that people inhabit. Are there risks and dangers online? Certainly—just as there are offline. There is little doubt that technology inflects age-old issues in new ways, and these shifts must be understood. But when we focus exclusively on technology, we lose track of the bigger picture. For many youth, technology is part of their everyday lives, and must be examined in that context. The key to addressing online safety is to take a few steps back and make sense of the lives of youth, the risks and dangers they face, and the personal, social, and cultural logic behind their practices.

Four issues dominate contemporary conversations about online safety: 1) sexual solicitation; 2) harassment; 3) exposure to inappropriate content; and 4) youth-generated problematic content. Data on these issues have been well-documented, especially in the U.S. (Shrock and Boyd 2008), but let's look briefly at each of these concerns before turning to think about the most significant opportunity provided by the Internet: visibility.

Sexual Solicitation

The image of the online predator is pervasive. He is portrayed as an older, unattractive man who falsifies his identity to deceive, groom, kidnap, and rape children. A handful of devastating but rare cases that fit this stereotype are put forward as proof that the Internet is dangerous. Statistics about sexual solicitation are misinterpreted to convey the idea that these men are lurking everywhere online. The image is perpetrated by TV shows where fake profiles of children are used to "catch a predator." The danger of this manufactured image is that it is misleading and obscures the very real risks youth face with regard to sexual solicitation.

Consider the findings of the Crimes Against Children Research Center, who found that one in seven minors in a national U.S. sample are sexually solicited online (Wolak et al. 2006). Peers and young adults—not older adults—account for 90% of solicitations in which approximate age is known (Wolak et al. 2006). Many acts of online solicitation are harassing or teasing communications that are not designed to seduce youth into offline sexual encounters; 69% of solicitations involve no attempt at offline contact and youth typically ignore or deflect the experience without distress (Wolak et al. 2006). A study of U.S. criminal cases in which adult sex offenders were arrested after meeting young victims online found that victims were adolescents—not children; few (5%) were deceived by offenders claiming to be teens or lying about their sexual intentions; and 73% of youth who met an offender in person did so more than once (Wolak et al. 2008b). Interviews with police indicate that most victims are underage adolescents who knowingly meet adults for sexual encounters. These offenses tended to fit a model of statutory rape involving a post-pubescent minor having nonforcible sexual relations with an adult, most frequently adults in their twenties (Wolak et al. 2008a).

Let us not dismiss these crimes, for they are crimes. Statutory rape is illegal in many countries because our society believes that minors cannot truly consent to sexual relations with adults. But this problem is not unique to the Internet. Most youth are not at-risk online, and those who are tend to also have problems offline (Mitchell et al. 2007). In other words, the Internet provides a new forum for a type of problematic interaction that predates the technology. But the Internet is also a tremendous tool to see at-risk youth engaging in risky behaviors. Instead of deploring the Internet as the cause of age-old problems, we should use it to understand why youth do these things, and how we can reach out to prevent them from happening.

Harassment

Bullying, gossip-mongering, and harassment have been a cruel presence in the lives of children for a very long time. While the numbers vary wildly, as do the definitions for bullying or harassment, there is little doubt that the Internet has provided new ways for youths to torment each other. Ignoring highly celebrated and exceptional examples, the vast majority of online harassment targeted at children and teens stems from other youth.

While the Internet is certainly used for harassment, the term "cyberbullying" implies that what takes place online radically departs from offline behavior. Anonymity is often cited as a core difference. Yet, while online perpetrators may appear to be anonymous, this does not mean that victims do not know the perpetrators or cannot figure out who is harassing them. Hinduja and Patchin (2009) found that 82% of victims in their U.S. sample knew their perpetrator (and that 41% of all perpetrators were friends or former friends). Others claim that online harassment is more harmful. There is little doubt that online harassment can be more persistent and is thus visible to more people, including peers and adults. One could reasonably argue that the potential reputational damage of visible harassment is greater than physical and emotional blows shelled out in the locker room. But visibility is a double-edged sword. Increasing the transparency of harassment means that more people can observe the harm and intervene. More importantly, it is easier for adults—parents, teachers, counselors—to see what takes place online than what goes on in private. This is an amazing opportunity to address a long-standing problem, but adults must stop blaming the technology and focus on the youth hurting and being hurt.

Exposure to Inappropriate Content

As a society, we believe that some content that is acceptable for adults is inappropriate for minors. The increased flow of information facilitated by the Internet means that content of all types is easier to access now than ever, including inappropriate content. We worry that youth might gain access to forbidden content or be inadvertently exposed to it during otherwise innocuous activities.

Pornographic content is usually front and center in this discussion. Encounters with pornography are not universal and rates of exposure are heavily debated. Wolak et al. (2006) found that 42% of youth in a U.S. sample reported unwanted or wanted exposure or both; of these, 66% reported only unwanted exposure, and only 9% of those indicated being "very or extremely upset." Furthermore, rates of unwanted exposure were higher among youth who were older, suffered from depression, and reported being harassed or solicited online or victimized offline (Wolak et al. 2007). This suggests that unwanted exposure might be linked to specific activities, particularly at-risk online behavior.

While use of the Internet is assumed to increase the likelihood of unwanted exposure to pornography, this may not be true among all demographics. Younger children report encountering pornographic content offline more frequently than online (Ybarra and Mitchell 2005) and a study of seventh and eighth graders in the U.S. found that of those who are exposed to nudity (intentionally or not), more are exposed through TV (63%) and movies (46%) than on the Internet (35%) (Pardun et al. 2005). This raises questions about whether the boundaries that we assume offline actually exist.

Youth-Generated Problematic Content

One of the Internet's core benefits it is that it enables consumers of culture to become producers and distributors. But not all user-generated content is considered healthy, particularly when youth produce content that society deems immoral, illegal, or detrimental. Eating disorders and self-harm have a long history, but the Internet provides a way for youth to document their "lifestyles" and find like-minded others. Teens once used Polaroids to capture their burgeoning sexuality; today, youth leverage mobile phones to capture and disseminate naked photographs, both for fun and harm. Gangs, violence, and hate are not new, but they are now documented and disseminated through fight videos and shock content. The content that results from these activities is undoubtedly disturbing, as is the ease with which it can be disseminated but shouldn't we be more concerned with the underlying issues than the content itself?

Most troubling is the determination by some lawyers to prosecute minors who produce and disseminate naked photos of themselves and their peers as child pornographers. The legal apparatus around child pornography is meant to uncover, prosecute, and severely punish those who produce and consume content that records—or appears to record—the sexual assault of a child by an adult. When minors are prosecuted, child pornography laws are devalued and minors are victimized in entirely new ways.

Youth-generated problematic content is indeed disturbing. And technology does make it easier to distribute. But the underlying problems are the same. Once again, just because technology makes an issue more noticeable does not mean that we should focus on eliminating its visibility. Instead, we should use visibility to get to the root of the problem.

The Conundrum of Visibility

Many of our fears and concerns regarding online safety stem from the ways in which the Internet uncovers many things that were previously hidden. Simply put, we see more risky behaviors not because risky acts have increased, but because the technology makes them more conspicuous. Most of the risks youth take and face online parallel those they take and face offline. But many of us do not see at-risk youth seeking the attention of older men offline. Many of us are unaware of all of the hateful gossip and bullying that takes place in our schools. Many of us are oblivious to the availability of inappropriate content to those seeking it. And, finally, many of us do not realize how many youth are struggling with mental health issues, making risky decisions, or living in worlds of hate and violence. It's easier not to notice.

The Internet demands that we notice. It illuminates that which we least want to see. It shows many of our youth struggling and hurting and crying out for help. Of course, the Internet does not do this by itself. It does it because we're looking. But we're not seeing. We're giving agency to the Internet so that we can blame it for what it reveals, rather than forcing ourselves to contend with what we see. At the end of the day, the Internet is not the issue. The issue is us. We cannot provide perfect protection for our children. We don't have the social or organizational infrastructure to help all youth who are in need. We don't know how to stop bullying. We don't have a magic bullet to end mental illness or insecurity or anger. And we, the adults of the world, are scared. We want something to blame. So we blame what we don't understand, that which is forcing us to see. We blame the Internet because we are unwilling to blame ourselves for not knowing how to solve the problems of this world.

Perhaps it's time that we look beyond the Internet and begin addressing the fundamental problems of our society. Thanks to the Internet, they are staring us right in the face. It's high time we do something about it.

Bibliography

Hinduja, Sameer and Justin Patchin. 2009. *Bullying Beyond the Schoolyard: Preventing and Responding to Cyberbullying.* Thousand Oaks, CA: Sage.

Mitchell, Kimberly J., Janis Wolak, and David Finkelhor. 2007. "Trends in Youth Reports of Sexual Solicitations, Harassment, and Unwanted Exposure to Pornography on the Internet." *Journal of Adolescent Health* 40(2): 116–126.

Pardun, Carol J., Kelly Ladin L'Engle, and Jane D. Brown. 2005. "Linking Exposure to Outcomes: Early Adolescents' Consumption of Sexual Content in Six Media." *Mass Communication & Society* 8(2): 75–91.

Schrock, Andrew and Danah Boyd. 2008. "Online Threats to Youth: Solicitation, Harassment, and Problematic Content." Report of the Internet Safety Technical Task Force, 62–142. (http://cyber.law.harvard.edu/pubrelease/isttf/).

Wolak, Janis, David Finkelhor, and Kimberly Mitchell. 2008a. "Is Talking Online to Unknown People Always Risky? Distinguishing Online Interaction Styles in a National Sample of Youth Internet Users." *CyberPsychology & Behavior* 11(3): 340–343.

Wolak, Janis, David Finkelhor, Kimberly Mitchell, and Michele Ybarra. 2008b. "Online 'Predators' and Their Victims: Myths, Realities, and Implications for Prevention and Treatment." *American Psychologist* 63(2): 111–128.

Wolak, Janis, Kimberly J. Mitchell, and David Finkelhor. 2007. "Unwanted and Wanted Exposure to Online Pornography in a National Sample of Youth Internet Users." *Pediatrics* 119(2): 247–257.

Wolak, Janis, Kimberly Mitchell, and David Finkelhor. 2006. "Online Victimization of Youth: Five Years Later." National Center for Missing and Exploited Children, #07-06-025. (www.unh.edu/ccrc/pdf/CV138.pdf).

Ybarra, Michele and Kimberly J. Mitchell. 2005. "Exposure to Internet Pornography among Children and Adolescents: A National Survey." *CyberPsychology & Behavior* 8(5): 473–486.

Critical Thinking

1. The authors argue that the image of the adult predator is greatly overstated and, that, in fact, most of the solicitation of minors online is done by other minors and young adults. Further, most victims seem to be adolescents, not young children. Are you comforted?

2. Do you think minors should be prosecuted as child pornographers for disseminating "naked photos of themselves and their peers"? Use the Internet to see if you can find out how common such prosecutions are.

3. The authors argue, toward the end of the article, "the Internet is not the issue. The issue is us." Have you been persuaded?

4. Are the authors arguing that the Internet is only a tool and it is how we use it that counts?

5. Continuing the previous questions, are the authors arguing that the Internet is transformative in that it brings to light the more problematic side of our culture that reproduces itself online?

DANAH BOYD and **ALICE MARWICK** (2009). "The Conundrum of Visibility." *Journal of Children & Media, 3*(4): 410–414.

From *Journal of Children and Media*, 2009, pp. 410–414. Copyright © 2009 by Taylor & Francis Group. Reprinted by permission via Rightslink.

UNIT 6

Public Policy and Law

Unit Selections

Learning Outcomes

After reading this Unit, you will be able to:

- Know the rights of an individual with digital media when being searched by police.

- Know the risks of maintaining an online presence.

- Understand the objectives driving IP legislation such as SOPA and PIPA and understand the objections raised against that legislation.

- Understand the complexities of protecting IP of digital media across international boundaries.

- Understand how the IT industry is being impacted by the current status of patent law, and how that impact might change under the America Invents Act going into effect in 2013.

Student Website

www.mhhe.com/cls

Internet References

Berkman Center for Internet and Society at Harvard University World Intellectual Property Organization
www.wipo.org

BitLaw
www.bitlaw.com

Did You Say "Intellectual Property"? It's a Seductive Mirage
www.gnu.org/philosophy/not-ipr.html

Trans-Pacific Partnership (Pro and Con Sites)
Office of the United States Trade Representative (pro)
www.ustr.gov/tpp

EFF: Trans Pacific Partnership Agreement (con)
www.eff.org/issues/tpp

United States Copyright Office: Resources
www.copyright.gov/resces.html

United States Patent and Trademark Office
www.uspto.gov

We begin this unit be reviewing how the Fourth Amendment to the U.S. Constitution prohibiting unreasonable search and seizure might impact you—or someone like you—who maintains information on a digital device (a computer, tablet, or telephone). While the American courts have continuously reinterpreted the provisions of the Fourth Amendment over the past 230 years, shifts in our society over the past 30 years toward storing personal and commercial information in digital form, and largely over the past five years in storing information in mobile devices has required considerable rethinking of the law. The courts, which are naturally rather conservative institutions in that they are very slow to shift from the status quo, have been unable to keep up with the fast pace of technological change.

The Electronic Frontier Foundation is a rights organization at the forefront of fighting for individual civil and consumer rights in the digital world. As you review their "Know Your Rights!" webpage, consider which of the issues they discuss are most impacted by technological change outstepping the law's ability to keep pace.

Much of this Unit focuses on the dynamic between unsteady pace of technological change and the law within the realm of intellectual property. In the area of copyright several technological governors, such as digital rights management (DRM), have been attempted with mixed results—every technical improvement in DRM protection over the past 20 years has been met with similar gains in the ability to defeat that protection. And several legislative fixes have been proposed, with some of them such as the Digital Millennium Copyright Act of 1998 (DMCA) and the PRO IP Act of 2008 becoming law. In 2011, two companion pieces of legislation, the Stop Online Piracy Act (SOPA) and the Protect IP Act (PIPA) we proposed. In "The Yin and Yang of Copyright and Technology", Randal Picker describes the landscape that led to these proposals. This legislation set the digital content industries, led by the Motion Picture Association of America (MPAA) and the Recording Industry Association of America (RIAA), against the hardware and Internet service industries. The software companies found they had feet in both camps.

The content producers argued that their content was being stolen en masse by Internet users who share music and videos without regard for (or payment to) the holders of the copyright on that material. They lobbied for—and got in SOPA and PIPA—strong new protections for their intellectual property by empowering the government to more effectively police copyright violations on the Internet. The Internet service industry argued the content lobbyists were overstating their financial losses and, more importantly, that the Internet presages a new technological era that requires new business models—the old models the content industries are using just don't work anymore. The impending votes on SOPA and PIPA set the stage for a concerted effort on the part of Internet users, in January 2012, to lobby Congress against the legislation. In "The Online Copyright War: The Day the Internet Hit Back at Big Media", Dominic Rushe describes the protests that emerged. (And you have already read about aspects of this in Unit 5).

© Stockbyte/Getty Images

While many arguments were made by the protesters, one interesting argument made was along the lines of:

> Sure, content sharing is violation as the rules are currently written, but it is impossible to stop people from making perfect copies of digital media. So it is foolish to try to apply the rules of the last epoch to the realities of today. People are going to copy media. Therefore, what makes more sense is for the rules to change, and for business models to change in reaction to this new reality.

This argument is addressed, in part, in "Can Online Piracy Be Stopped by Laws?" Samuelson provides yet another take on SOPA and PIPA, but she also explores the question of whether there is a third route to a solution.

While Samuelson wrote an article to describe the dilemmas of Internet piracy, Aaron Swartz became a pirate himself. Swartz, an accomplished Internet programmer engaged in the civil disobedient act of downloading 4.8 million journal articles and making them freely available on the Internet. While the article "Aaron Swartz Hacks the Attention Economy" is, on the surface, another SOPA/PIPA read, it is actually much more than that. Consider the title *Technology Review* decided to apply to this interview. As you read the article, notice that Swartz sees himself as the leader of a movement and consider what that movement might be. The key questions, perhaps, are who controls the Internet? And who ought to control the Internet?

We finish this Unit moving from the quagmire of copyright in the digital age to the separate, but similar quagmire of patent law in the digital age. Patents are intended to encourage innovation by protecting the inventor and giving her an ample head start to earn back development costs, while at the same time promoting more innovation by requiring the details of each invention be revealed and limiting the amount of time monopoly right can be maintained.

Over the past 230 years inventors have found all sorts of games to play to hoard their inventions for maximum benefit possible. But the system more or less worked, and in some industries—bio-tech, for example—it still more or less works. In the computer hardware and software industries existing patent law has been problematic. A typical new computing device (such as a tablet or cell phone) may contain hundreds of patents, and a networking technology could contain many more. As of 2008, a 4G wireless network utilized over 18,000 patents on top of the 80,000 patents used in its underlying backbone.[1] How can a new network vendor innovate in this environment without violating a patent (or worse, having a threatened competitor perceive their patent was violated)?

Patent lawsuits have become the norm for most all large scale IT development efforts. Many large firms, Google, Apple, and Microsoft among them, have purchased companies simply to acquire their patent holdings and protect their own development efforts. Further exacerbating the situation are the presence of patent trolls: small companies who have acquired patents from others and exist solely to sue others for violation of their patent. Often the validity of these suits is questionable, but just as often it is perceived by the defendant to be cheaper to settle and pay a few thousand dollars for a patent license than to fight back in court.

Notes

1. L. Gilroy, T. D'Amato, How many patents does it take to build an iPhone?, *Intellectual Property Today*, November 2009 (accessed on October 13, 2012 at http://www.iptoday.com/issues/2009/11/articles/how-many-patents-take-build-iPhone.asp)

Know Your Rights!

Your computer, your phone, and your other digital devices hold vast amounts of personal information about you and your family. This is sensitive data that's worth protecting from prying eyes—including those of the government.

Hanni Fakhoury

The Fourth Amendment to the Constitution protects you from unreasonable government searches and seizures, and this protection extends to your computer and portable devices. But how does this work in the real world? What should you do if the police or other law enforcement officers show up at your door and want to search your computer?

EFF has designed this guide to help you understand your rights if officers try to search the data stored on your computer or portable electronic device, or seize it for further examination somewhere else.

Because anything you say can be used against you in a criminal or civil case, before speaking to any law enforcement official, you should consult with an attorney.

Q: Can the police enter my home to search my computer or portable device, like a laptop or cell phone?

A: No, in most instances, unless they have a warrant. But there are two major exceptions: (1) you consent to the search;[1] or (2) the police have probable cause to believe there is incriminating evidence on the computer that is under immediate threat of destruction.[2]

Q: What if the police have a search warrant to enter my home, but not to search my computer? Can they search it then?

A: No, typically, because a search warrant only allows the police to search the area or items described in the warrant.[3] But if the warrant authorizes the police to search for evidence of a particular crime, and such evidence is likely to be found on your computer, some courts have allowed the police to search the computer without a warrant.[4] Additionally, while the police are searching your home, if they observe something in plain view on the computer that is suspicious or incriminating, they may take it for further examination and can rely on their observations to later get a search warrant.[5] And of course, if you consent, any search of your computer is permissible.

Q: Can my roommate/guest/spouse/partner allow the police access to my computer?

A: Maybe. A third party can consent to a search as long as the officers reasonably believe the third person has control over the thing to be searched.[6] However, the police cannot search if one person with control (for example a spouse) consents, but another individual (the other spouse) with control does not.[7] One court, however, has said that this rule applies only to a residence, and not personal property, such as a hard drive placed into someone else's computer.[8]

Q: What if the police want to search my computer, but I'm not the subject of their investigation?

A: It typically does not matter whether the police are investigating you, or think there is evidence they want to use against someone else located on your computer. If they have a warrant, you consent to the search, or they think there is something incriminating on your computer that may be immediately destroyed, the police can search it. Regardless of whether you're the subject of an investigation, you can always seek the assistance of a lawyer.

Q: Can I see the warrant?

A: Yes. The police must take the warrant with them when executing it and give you a copy of it.[9] They must also knock and announce their entry before entering your home[10] and must serve the warrant during the day in most circumstances.[11]

Q: Can the police take my computer with them and search it somewhere else?

A: Yes. As long as the police have a warrant, they can seize the computer and take it somewhere else to search it more thoroughly. As part of that inspection, the police may make a copy of media or other files stored on your computer.[12]

Q: Do I have to cooperate with them when they are searching?

A: No, you do not have to help the police conduct the search. But you should not physically interfere with them, obstruct the search, or try to destroy evidence, since that can lead to your arrest. This is true even if the police don't have a warrant and you do not consent to the search, but the police insist on searching anyway. In that instance, do not interfere but write down the names and badge numbers of the officers and immediately call a lawyer.

PROPERTY OF ... COMMUNITY COLLEGE

PROPERTY OF
CENTRAL COMMUNITY COLLEGE

Q: Do I have to answer their questions while they are searching my home without a warrant?

A: No, you do not have to answer any questions. In fact, because anything you say can be used against you and other individuals, it is best to say nothing at all until you have a chance to talk to a lawyer. However, if you do decide to answer questions, be sure to tell the truth. It is a crime to lie to a police officer and you may find yourself in more trouble for lying to law enforcement than for whatever it was they wanted on your computer.[13]

Q: If the police ask for my encryption keys or passwords, do I have to turn them over?

A: No. The police can't force you to divulge anything. However, a judge or a grand jury may be able to. The Fifth Amendment protects you from being forced to give the government self-incriminating testimony. If turning over an encryption key or password triggers this right, not even a court can force you to divulge the information. But whether that right is triggered is a difficult question to answer. If turning over an encryption key or password will reveal to the government information it does not have (such as demonstrating that you have control over files on a computer), there is a strong argument that the Fifth Amendment protects you.[14] If, however, turning over passwords and encryption keys will not incriminate you, then the Fifth Amendment does not protect you. Moreover, even if you have a Fifth Amendment right that protects your encryption keys or passwords, a grand jury or judge may still order you to disclose your data in an unencrypted format under certain circumstances.[15] If you find yourself in a situation where the police are demanding that you turn over encryption keys or passwords, let EFF know.

Q: If my computer is taken and searched, can I get it back?

A: Perhaps. If your computer was illegally seized, then you can file a motion with the court to have the property returned.[16] If the police believe that evidence of a crime has been found on your computer (such as "digital contraband" like pirated music and movies, or digital images of child pornography), the police can keep the computer as evidence. They may also attempt to make you forfeit the computer, but you can challenge that in court.[17]

Q: What about my work computer?

A: It depends. Generally, you have some Fourth Amendment protection in your office or workspace.[18] This means the police need a warrant to search your office and work computer unless one of the exceptions described above applies. But the extent of Fourth Amendment protection depends on the physical details of your work environment, as well as any employer policies. For example, the police will have difficulty justifying a warrant-less search of a private office with doors and a lock and a private computer that you have exclusive access to. On the other hand, if you share a computer with other co-workers, you will have a weaker expectation of privacy in that computer, and thus less Fourth Amendment protection.[19] However, be aware that your employer can consent to a police request to search an office or workspace.[20] Moreover, if you work for a public entity or government agency, no warrant is required to search your computer or office as long as the search is for a non-investigative, work-related matter.[21]

Q: I've been arrested. Can the police search my cell phone without a warrant?

A: Maybe. After a person has been arrested, the police generally may search the items on her person and in her pockets, as well as anything within her immediate control.[22] This means that the police can physically take your cell phone and anything else in your pockets. Some courts go one step further and allow the police to search the contents of your cell phone, like text messages, call logs, emails, and other data stored on your phone, without a warrant.[23] Other courts disagree, and require the police to seek a warrant.[24] It depends on the circumstances and where you live.

Q: The police pulled me over while I was driving. Can they search my cell phone?

A: Maybe. If the police believe there is probably evidence of a crime in your car, they may search areas within a driver or passenger's reach where they believe they might find it—like the glove box, center console, and other "containers."[25] Some courts have found cell phones to be "containers" that police may search without a warrant.[26]

Q: Can the police search my computer or portable devices at the border without a warrant?

A: Yes. So far, courts have ruled that almost any search at the border is "reasonable"—so government agents don't need to get a warrant. This means that officials can inspect your computer or electronic equipment, even if they have no reason to suspect there is anything illegal on it.[27] An international airport may be considered the functional equivalent of a border, even if it is many miles from the actual border.[28]

Q: Can the police take my electronic device away from the border or airport for further examination without a warrant?

A: At least one federal court has said yes, they can send it elsewhere for further inspection if necessary.[29] Even though you may be permitted to enter the country, your computer or portable device may not be.

References

1. Schneckloth v. Bustamonte, 412 United States 218, 219 (1973); United States v. Vanvilet, 542 F.3d 259 (1st Cir. 2008).
2. Ker v. California, 374 United States 23 (1963); see also United States v. Vallimont, 378 Fed.Appx. 972 (11th Cir. 2010) (unpublished); United States v. Smith, 2010 WL 1949364 (9th Cir. 2010) (unpublished).
3. See Maryland v. Garrison, 480 United States 79, 84–85 (1987) (citing cases).
4. See e.g., United States v. Mann, 592 F.3d 779 (7th Cir. 2010); see also Brown v. City of Fort Wayne, 752 F.Supp.2d 925 (N.D. Ind. 2010).

5. Horton v. California, 496 United States 128 (1990); see also United States v. Walser, 275 F.3d 981 (10th Cir. 2001); United States v. Carey, 172 F.3d 1268 (10th Cir. 1999).

6. Illinois v. Rodriguez, 497 United States 177 (1990); United States v. Stabile, 633 F.3d 219 (3d Cir. 2011); United States v. Andrus, 483 F.3d 711 (10th Cir. 2007).

7. Georgia v. Randolph, 547 United States 103 (2006).

8. United States v. King, 604 F.3d 125 (3d Cir. 2010) (court approved search and seizure where two housemates shared a desktop computer, and one housemate granted the police access to the entire computer over the other housemate's objections, even though the objecting housemate was the sole owner of a hard drive in the computer).

9. Federal Rule of Criminal Procedure 41(f)(1)(C).

10. Wilson v. Arkansas, 514 United States 927 (1995).

11. Federal Rule of Criminal Procedure 41(e)(2)(A)(ii).

12. See e.g., United States v. Hill, 459 F.3d 966 (9th Cir. 2006); In re Search of 3817 W. West End, First Floor Chicago, Illinois 60621, 321 F.Supp.2d 953 (N.D. Ill. 2004); see also Federal Rule of Criminal Procedure 41(e)(2)(B).

13. Compare 18 United StatesC. § 1001(a) (maximum punishment for first offense of lying to federal officer is 5 or 8 years) with 18 United StatesC. §§ 1030(a)(2) and (c)(2)(A) (maximum punishment for first offense of simply exceeding authorized computer access is generally 1 year).

14. See United States v. Kirschner, 2010 WL 1257355 (E.D. Mich. Mar. 30, 2010) (unpublished) (relying on United States v. Hubbell, 530 United States 27 (2000)).

15. See e.g., United States v. Hatfield, 2010 WL 1423103 (E.D.N.Y. April 7, 2010) (unpublished); In re Boucher, 2009 WL 424718 (D. Vt. Feb. 19, 2009) (unpublished).

16. Federal Rule of Criminal Procedure 41(g).

17. See 18 United StatesC. § 983, Federal Rule of Criminal Procedure 32.2.

18. Mancusi v. DeForte, 392 United States 364 (1968); United States v. Ziegler, 474 F.3d 1184 (9th Cir. 2007).

19. See e.g., Schowengerdt v. United States, 944 F.2d 483 (9th Cir. 1991).

20. See Ziegler, 474 F.3d at 1191 (citing Mancusi).

21. City of Ontario v. Quon, 130 S.Ct. 2619 (2010); O'Connor v. Ortega, 480 United States 709 (1987).

22. Chimel v. California, 395 United States 752 (1969).

23. See e.g., United States v. Murphy, 552 F.3d 405 (4th Cir. 2009); United States v. Wurie, 612 F.Supp.2d 104 (D. Mass. 2009); People v. Diaz, 51 Cal.4th 84, 244 P.3d 501 (2011).

24. See e.g., United States v. Wall, 2008 WL 5381412 (S.D.Fla. Dec. 22, 2008) (unpublished); United States v. Park, 2007 WL 1521573 (N.D. Cal. May 23, 2007) (unpublished); State v. Smith, 124 Ohio St.3d 163, 920 N.E.2d 949 (2009).

25. Arizona v. Gant, 129 S.Ct. 1710 (2009).

26. See e.g., United States v. Finley, 477 F.3d 250 (5th Cir. 2007); Wurie, 612 F.Supp.2d at 109–110; United States v. Cole, 2010 WL 3210963 (N.D.Ga. Aug. 11, 2010) (unpublished); United States v. McCray, 2009 WL 29607 (S.D.Ga. Jan. 5, 2009) (unpublished).

27. United States v. Flores-Montano, 541 United States 149 (2004); United States v. Ickes, 393 F.3d 501 (4th Cir. 2005).

28. Almeida-Sanchez v. United States, 413 United States 266, 273 (1973); United States v. Arnold, 533 F.3d 1003 (9th Cir. 2008); United States v. Romm, 455 F.3d 990 (9th Cir. 2006); United States v. Roberts, 274 F.3d 1007 (5th Cir. 2001).

29. United States v. Cotterman, 637 F.3d 1068 (9th Cir. 2011).

Critical Thinking

1. Of the questions answered at the site, which answer surprised you the most?

2. Of the questions answered at the site, did you disagree with any of the rights currently in force? If so, which ones and why?

From *Electronic Frontier Foundation*, June 27, 2011. https://www.eff.org/files/EFF_Know_Your_Rights_2011.pdf. Copyright © 2011 by Electronic Frontier Foundation. Reprinted under the Creative Commons Attribution License. http://creativecommons.org/licenses/by/3.0/us/

The Yin and Yang of Copyright and Technology

Examining the recurring conflicts between copyright and technology from piano rolls to domain-name filtering.

RANDAL C. PICKER

The emergence of the Internet has put enormous pressure on the rights model of United States copyright law. That model is premised on the notion that copyright holders are entitled to control the making of copies of their works, but technology has made that control somewhere between fragile and nonexistent. Content creators have struggled to restore the control assumed by copyright law. Two recent developments, one pending federal legislation and the second an industry wide agreement between Internet service providers and content distributors, provide new looks at this ongoing issue.

Technology and copyright have a complex relationship. New waves of technology have created novel expressive opportunities and dramatic improvements in the ability to distribute copyrighted works. But new technology rarely asks permission, and with each technical advance, we have seen new opportunities and new clashes. Perforated rolls for player pianos in the early 1900s came from sheet music and roll producers were not eager to write checks to copyright holders. Radio saw recorded music as a way to fill the airways even though disks came with a legend stating that the music was not licensed for radio broadcast. And the VCR introduced a new vocabulary time shifting and the chance to watch TV on your schedule, not broadcasters schedules. It did so without offering any compensation to broadcasters or show producers and even created the risk that the financing model for free broadcast TV would be put at risk by viewers with nimble fingers who fast-forwarded through commercials.

> **The rights model of the law has not changed—authors are entitled to control copying—but the practical ability to enforce that right has shrunk.**

Since at least the advent of Napster, the music industry has struggled to find a strategy to control illegal downloads of music. Technology made it very easy to rip CDs and share the results with the world. The music industry responded with lawsuits, first against Napster, Aimster, and Grokster, and then against individual consumers, leading to prominent examples such as the ongoing saga of Jammie Thomas-Rasset. The suits have been on the whole quite successful, at least as measured by the standards that lawyers use. Grokster lost 9-0 on the question of whether it might be liable for inducing copyright infringement (there was much more division on the question of how the U.S. Supreme Courts prior Sony case should apply to this situation). Thomas-Rasset has faced juries multiple times and each time jurors have come back with damage awards the first time $1.92 million and second time $1.5 million that judges found too high.

Notwithstanding all of that, the music industry sees these as paper victories, as file sharing has continued largely unabated. In some basic sense, law has failed the music industry. Technology has changed the integrity associated with distributing copies of copyrighted works by making copying easy and worldwide distribution instantaneous. To distribute a copy of the work is to put the means of production into the hands of consumers.

The rights model of the law has not changed authors are entitled to control copying but the practical ability to enforce that right has shrunk. The music industry started by chasing firms that were facilitating peer-to-peer file swapping. But this was like chasing quicksilver: even if you got your hands on one version, another would quickly reappear and the hive-mind of the P2P networks would reorganize around the new version.

The litigation clock is wildly out of sync with the speed of P2P organization. Ordinary law enforcement scales poorly and it is easy to see why the content industry would like a scalable way to enforce the key right to control whether copies are made of copyrighted works.

The Rojadirecta Case

In late 2008, Congress passed the Prioritizing Resources and Organization for Intellectual Property Act of 2008. The sole virtue of such a clumsy name is that it shortens to the PRO IP Act. The new act made it possible for the federal government to seize domain names associated with Web sites where allegedly infringing behavior was taking place or being facilitated. And seize it has. On June 30, 2010, the U.S. Immigration and Customs Enforcement bureau launched Operation in Our Sites and seized nine domain names and physical assets connected to commercial movie and television piracy Web sites. The program has expanded with additional domain name seizures for 77 sites in November, 2010 and with three additional sets of seizures of domain names through mid-2011.

Take a closer look at one of these cases. On February 1, 2011, the U.S. government seized the rojadirecta.com and rojadirecta.org domain names. Before the seizures, rojadirecta.com and rojadirecta.org offered up a guide to Internet TV focusing on sports (a lot of what the U.S. calls soccer but the rest of the world calls football). Like the early Napster, Rojadirecta offers links, not direct hosting, to facilitate what it calls P2P TV.

But if you go to those domain names today, when you type the .com or .org sites into a browser after the seizure, you are not offered links to the beautiful game. The URL bar for your browser will indicate you have indeed reached your intended destination, but when you look at your screen you see three U.S. governmental enforcement seals. The rest of the page briefly sets out the basis for the seizure a search warrant under two federal statutes and states that copyright infringement can be a federal crime.

Search rojadirecta.org on the whois database. The current registrant for the domain name is the U.S. Department of Homeland Security with corresponding physical addresses, email addresses, and phone numbers. This is what a domain name seizure looks like. Prior to the seizure, the registrar Go Daddy dealt with Rojadirecta as its customer, but now the federal government has been substituted as its customer and the feds exercise control over the domain name.

But there is more to the story, of course. You do not have to type in a domain name to reach a Web site. That is just a convenience for us humans. You can type in an IP address directly and the seizure of rojadirecta.org means nothing for direct connection to the Rojadirecta Web site through the IP address. And, if that is too clumsy, Rojadirecta solved that problem by setting up new domain names offshore, including relocating to Spain at rojadirecta.es. Rojadirecta immediately announced its new domain names through its accounts on Facebook and Twitter and was back up and running. That is not to say that Rojadirecta does not want its original domain names back it does and is in litigation over that but the move to offshore domain names makes clear why the Pro IP Act is not the be-all and end-all for protecting copyrights.

The litigation over the Rojadirecta domain names is at a very early stage. In August, 2011, a federal court rejected Rojadirecta s preliminary efforts to get back its domain names. Part of this analysis turned on the injury that Rojadirecta was suffering from not having access to the old domain names and the court found that that injury was minimal. Why? Because Rojadirecta had been able to set up new domain names outside of the

reach of U.S. officials and Rojadirecta could easily inform its users about its new locations. So, to be a tad cynical, the complete ineffectiveness of the seizure meant it did not matter in the short run that Rojadirecta could not use its original domain names. Rojadirecta sought to press a First Amendment claim, but the court left that for subsequent litigation, again on the view that the speech was not blocked but was instead just displaced to a new location.

New Enforcement Tools

The Rojadirecta saga should make clear why the content industry is looking for new enforcement tools. New legislation passed in 2008 in the form of the Pro IP Act, domain names seized and yet the activity continues elsewhere outside of the country. What might a solution look like? A technological approach by companies with the market position and financial stakes to make something work, companies with something to lose if they fail to comply with their obligations. Digital rights management was a technical response, but one that embedded the technical protection in the digital object itself, and not in the Internet s infrastructure. Something based in the U.S., so the firms can' t just exit overseas. The natural target might be big firms with bottlenecks. This sounds like Internet service providers, search engines, and the like. It sounds like, in fact, S.968, the draft act on Preventing Real Online Threats to Economic Creativity and Theft of Intellectual Property Act of 2011 the Protect IP Act for those of you quick with abbreviations and the industry wide memorandum of understanding implemented in July, 2011. (And the House of Representatives has put its own dog in the fight with H.R. 3261, the Stop Online Piracy Act.)

The Rojadirecta saga should make clear why the content industry is looking for new enforcement tools.

Start with the latter and call it the ISP Memorandum. This is an agreement between key players in the content industry the Recording Industry Association of America, the Motion Picture Association of America, and a number of the corporate members of the RIAA and the MPPA and the leading Internet service providers, including corporate entities for Verizon, Comcast, and Time Warner Cable (but without consumers at the bargaining table). The core of the agreement is a graduated six-step protocol for Internet service providers to respond to customers thought to be engaging in IP infringement. The protocol calls for education of offending consumers through steps such as temporary landing pages before consumers are able to access the Internet generally. Education is backed by a variety of mitigation measures directed at degrading the quality of the service delivered by the Internet service provider such as reduction in download and upload speeds.

The Protect IP Act would impose obligations on intermediaries and infrastructure providers to make it more difficult to find and get to sites that are, in the language of the bill, "dedicated to infringing activities." The idea behind this is simple: if technology has created the problem of easy file sharing, technology also should provide the solution. This would include, after action by the federal government in court, blocking domain names from resolving to the matching IP address DNS filtering and not serving up links to infringing Web sites. And there is no shortage of criticism of these provisions: many law professors are up in arms about the First Amendment, while a white paper by leading technologists suggests the act would accomplish little while interfering with efforts to roll out the new DNS Security Extensions.

Conclusion

The ISP Memorandum and the draft acts represent the current bleeding edge in the ongoing struggle between copyright and technology. We have moved from piano rolls to DNSSEC, but the conflicts recur. The legal regime gives copyright holders the right to control the making of copies, but no one told that to technology. Technological engineering is frequently easier to do than institutional engineering and yet these systems need to coevolve and to do that we need to talk across the disciplines in a coherent way. If we fail to do that, we will produce a sloppy result that will not accomplish anything for law or for technology.

Critical Thinking

1. Time-shifting is recording television broadcasts to play them back at a different time of the viewer's own choosing. Courts have ruled that time-shifting does not violate copyright. But many, perhaps most, time-shifters fast-forward through commercials thereby harming the broadcasters ability to make money in the current business model. Should broadcasters have a legal right to force the viewer to step through the commercials at regular speed? Does the viewer have any ethical obligation to cooperate with this process? Is there a different approach broadcaster might use (a new business model, perhaps) that would create a win-win solution?

2. When Picker writes, "To distribute a copy of the work is to put the means of production into the hands of consumers." What does he mean?

3. Picker describes the basic contours of the SOPA and PIPA legislation proposed in 2011. While that legislation did not pass during the 112th Congress (2011–2012), it is likely similar legislation will be proposed again in 2013. Given his description and the commentary about that legislation you can find from this Unit's Internet References, do you favor or oppose these proposals? Why?

4. Research the status of the Rojodirecta.com case since this article was published in January 2012. What is the current status of the case? How does the Rojadirecta case compare to the Megaupload case making its way through the courts in parallel?

RANDAL C. PICKER (r-picker@uchicago.edu) is Paul and Theo Leffmann Professor of Commercial Law at The University of Chicago Law School and Senior Fellow at The Computation Institute of the University of Chicago and Argonne National Laboratory.

From *Communications of the ACM*, vol. 55, no. 1, January 2012, pp. 30–32. Copyright © 2012 by Randal C. Picker. Reprinted by permission.

The Online Copyright War: The Day the Internet Hit Back at Big Media

As the demise of the Sopa anti-piracy act showed, established arguments for protecting the rights of content creators are almost impossible to apply to a digital world.

DOMINIC RUSHE

A casual observer could be forgiven for thinking that major media firms hate technology. They certainly fear it. Since Jack Valenti, the legendary film industry lobbyist, said in 1982 that the VCR was like the Boston Strangler, preparing to murder the innocents of Hollywood, they have viewed such advances as a Godzilla creature rising from the sea to threaten their existence.

In the past 30 years in the US, they have lobbied for 15 pieces of legislation aimed at tightening their grip on their content, as technology has moved ever faster to prise their fingers open.

In this seemingly never-ending battle, 18 January 2012 was a defining date, a day when the internet hit back. Mike Masnick, founder of TechDirt and one of Silicon Valley's most well-connected bloggers, remembers running through the corridors of the Senate in Washington, laptop open, desperately trying to find a Wi-Fi signal.

Around him was chaos. Amid a cacophony of phones, political interns were struggling to keep up with the calls and emails from angry people across the US and the world claiming Hollywood-backed legislation was about to break the internet and end its open culture forever. In an unprecedented day of action, Wikipedia and Reddit, a social news website, had gone offline in a protest organised by their communities of editors, and backed by thousands of other sites, large and small. Google had blacked out its logo in protest. Students around the world were bitching on Twitter that they couldn't get their homework done without Wikipedia. Even Kim Kardashian came out swinging.

One senator's office that Masnick visited calculated they had taken 3,000 calls. Within hours of the unprecedented assault, Sopa, the Stop Online Piracy Act, was dead and a sister act, Pipa, a neat acronym for the tortuously titled Protect IP Act (Preventing Real Online Threats to Economic Creativity and Theft of Intellectual Property Act) was sunk too. In Europe, the action buoyed up opponents of Acta, the US-backed international copyright treaty that has sparked protests across the continent. Countries including Bulgaria, Germany, the Netherlands, Poland and Slovakia have all refused to sign, arguing that Acta endangers freedom of speech and privacy, and the bill has stalled. But for how long? "The industry has this down cold," Masnick says. The Motion Picture Association of America (MPAA), Valenti's old stomping ground and one of the most powerful lobbying bodies in Washington, has emerged bruised from the battle, but few doubt it will rally.

There is widespread anger among leading media companies about the way the Sopa fight played out. The protest had many voices but there was no doubting whom the media executives blamed—Silicon Valley in general and Google in particular. President Barack Obama had "thrown in his lot with Silicon Valley paymasters", according to Rupert Murdoch, whose News Corp empire includes the Fox studios. "Piracy leader is Google who streams movies free, sells advts around them," Murdoch wrote on Twitter. "No wonder pouring millions into lobbying."

But trying to blame Google or even to cast this as a battle between Silicon Valley and Hollywood is to misrepresent a major shift in the media landscape, say those pushing for a more open internet.

Elizabeth Stark, a free culture advocate who has been campaigning for a relaxation of copyright law for years, says the Sopa battle will be seen as a landmark in a much wider debate about the open nature of the internet compared with the closed, copyright-protected world from before the digital age.

"This wasn't Google v Hollywood," says Stark, a visiting fellow at the Yale Information Society Project. "This was 15 million internet users v Hollywood. That's what they don't get. I think they think we can just get a few executives and put them in a room and call those people 'the internet'. Well, now they know that's not going to work." That said, Stark doubts that this battle is over. The losing side is rallying its troops. The media giant Viacom, owner of Paramount Pictures and Comedy Network, has reanimated a $1bn (£630m)suit against Google's YouTube, which it accuses of allowing users to use its copyright material from shows such as South Park and The Colbert Report. No legislation in the US is likely before November's election. But as Wikileaks showed, the US has already pushed for Sopa-style legislation in Spain and in the tech community, few doubt that Sopa will be revived.

After the act was shelved, Cary Sherman, chief executive of the Recording Industry Association of America (RIAA), which represents music labels, wrote a blistering article in the New York Times attacking Wikipedia and Google for spreading misinformation in order to cause a "digital tsunami" that "raised questions about how the democratic process functions in the digital age".

Sherman wrote: "The hyperbolic mistruths, presented on the home pages of some of the world's most popular websites, amounted to an abuse of trust and a misuse of power. When Wikipedia and Google purport to be neutral sources of information, but then exploit their stature to present information that is not only not neutral but affirmatively incomplete and misleading, they are duping their users into accepting as truth what are merely self-serving political declarations." Wikipedia's co-founder Jimmy Wales says the RIAA is missing the point. "They are irrelevant at this point. I don't care what they have to say. Someone is so far out of touch with what is going on in Washington, with the public and with their own industry."

For decades, the media industry has tightened its hold on copyright material. There are valid arguments for protecting the rights of content creators, but it is now clear that applying these rules to the digital age isn't going to work—not least because those now affected by copyright rules are not just other companies but ordinary people. "The public think it's gone too far," said Wales. "It's just possible that we may be at a point where we can stop the march forward of this ridiculousness."

The internet has changed the world so much that current legislation is not adequate, said Wales. "Go back 50 years and copyright was an industrial regulation that most people had no contact with," he said. "It was pretty difficult to find yourself in a position where you had committed a felony." Now the US is trying to extradite Richard O'Dwyer, a 23-year-old UK-based computer science student, on copyright infringement charges. "When, 50 years ago, could a kid sitting in his basement in the UK commit a crime in the US? It's disturbing."

What are the legitimate limits to copyright? What's the ethical norm for copying? "None of that is clear yet. It's going to take time to work that out," said Wales. Until 18 January, the debate within legislatures had been about extension and enforcement of the current rules. Now he hopes there may be time for a bigger debate. "We also need to bring back into discussion serious issues about the length of copyright, which has been extended again and again for no good purpose. We need to talk about what constitutes fair use, what kind of copying can the public do without getting into trouble." If, for example, someone uploads a video of their child's birthday party and then finds it has been deleted because a copyrighted song is playing in the background, "that's not piracy. That's how we use our music these days," says Wales. "A lot of what people want to do now is not legal but should be legal. We can say that and still be against full-scale piracy."

Wales said he had never heard of Megaupload, the online file sharing site at the centre of an international criminal investigation, before it was shut down, but had friends who used it. "It was people who lived outside the US who said they would have bought such and such but they don't sell it here," he says. "If there's some great show that they are not showing over here, they are very tempted. We can morally disapprove, but that's the way people are." Megaupload was charging a subscription to people who wanted a lot of content. "Why should you pay these assholes money when you could pay the people who actually made it some money?" said Wales. If the media industry addressed the needs of its audience, there would be less piracy, he believes.

Stark points to a study by Musiksverige (Music Sweden), an industry association, that found music piracy in Sweden fell significantly after the introduction of Spotify, a streaming music service. "It shows what we have said all along: people want to reward artists for their work."

Alexis Ohanian, Reddit's co-founder, agrees. "I'm hopeful right now. These are not soundbite issues, they are complicated. If you look at the work that Reddit's community did investigating Sopa, you can see that there is a lot of thought going into these issues in the community. Like a lot of rights, I think we took our right to a life online for granted until it was challenged. I think we are on guard now."

Media execs are on guard too. Many look to the music industry and fear they may be next. Since the peer-to-peer filesharing site Napster emerged in 1999, music sales in the US have dropped 53%, from $14.6bn to $6.9bn in 2010. The digital world is a lot less lucrative than selling DVDs.

Last year the movie industry made $30bn at the box office worldwide. Ed Epstein, author of The Hollywood Economist, calculates box office revenue accounts for just 10% of a hit movie's money. The rest comes from cable and satellite channels, pay-per-view TV, video rentals, DVD sales and digital downloads. All that extra cash comes from sources that Hollywood once railed against, and pressed Washington to crack down on.

But this time Epstein believes the industry may be right to be worried.

As the music industry has shown, digital sales are worth a fraction of physical sales. There are already signs that the movie industry is changing.

There was a new player in town at the Sundance film festival this year, one who had financed 17 of the movies on show. That player was you. Kickstarter, a three-year-old website that hosts crowdsourced fundraising for creative projects, had funded 17 films at Sundance, about 10% of the total, and had another 33 films at the South by Southwest festival in March. The company is now a significant player in independent film, allowing cinematic hopefuls to take their case right to the people. It's just the beginning of a major change in the industry, says Kickstarter's co-founder Yancey Strickler.

"I think we are at a point where we are asking whether you really need a film industry for a film to be made or a music industry to make music. People can now speak directly to their audiences," he said. "And the demands of an audience are very different to the demands of an industry. An industry wants to know about merchandising tie-ins with McDonalds—that's not necessarily what the audience is looking for, or what the artist is concerned with."

Strickler was at Sundance this year, where a number of Kickstarter-financed films were offered distribution deals. But many people were also rejecting deals they saw as disadvantageous.

"Going straight to the web, or video on demand, or doing a deal with independent cinemas—these are all viable options now," said Strickler. "Look at the success of that Joseph Kony video. This is just the beginning."

Critical Thinking

1. Rushe asks, "What are the legitimate limits to copyright? What's the ethical norm for copying?" Consider these questions for digital music and digital video. Who should own the copyright of a song released as an MP3? The composer? The performer(s)? The studio producer? The record company? Should it be a copyright violation to sample one artist's music in another artist's song? Or a violation for fans to produce their own versions and publish them on YouTube? Should the copyright holder be paid when these events occur?

2. Read Cary Sherman's op-ed essay in the New York Times http://goo.gl/vCfe2 and consider whether you agree or disagree with him. Then read Mike Masnick's rebuttal to the essay http://goo.gl/Qra52 for the point of view of the opposition.

From *The Guardian*, April 18, 2012. Copyright © 2012 by Guardian News & Media Ltd. Reprinted by permission.

Can Online Piracy Be Stopped by Laws?

Considering the legal responsibilities of Internet intermediaries in the aftermath of the Stop Online Privacy Act controversy.

PAMELA SAMUELSON

While on a scuba diving trip in the Seychelles Islands earlier this year, I found myself worrying about pirates. Real pirates, as in people who attack boats, take hostages, and sometimes kill their prey. This kind of piracy has become unfortunately common in that part of the world.

On board our ship were four former British special forces soldiers who served as security guards. They were armed with semiautomatic weapons and on patrol, 24/7, for the entire trip. The danger was not just hypothetical. The frigate berthed next to us as we boarded had 25 pirates in its brig.

Waking up every morning to the prospect of encountering real pirates added brio to our excursion. It also induced reflections on use of the word "piracy" to describe copyright infringements. Downloading music is really not in the same league as armed attacks on ships.

As we were cruising from Mahe to Aldabra, I expected to be far away from it all. But the ship got a daily fax of the main stories being published in the *New York Times*. Among them were stories about the controversy over the proposed legislation known as the Stop Online Piracy Act (SOPA). SOPA would have given the entertainment industry new legal tools to impede access to foreign "rogue" Web sites that host infringing content and to challenge U.S.-directed Web sites that the industry thought were either indifferent or acquiescent to storage of infringing materials.

For a time, it seemed virtually inevitable that SOPA would become law. Yet because strong opposition emerged from technology companies, computer security experts, civil liberties groups and members of the general public, SOPA has been put on hold. It is unlikely to be enacted in anything like its original form.

This column will explain the key features of SOPA, why the entertainment industry believed SOPA was necessary to combat online piracy, and why SOPA came to be perceived as so flawed that numerous sponsors withdrew their support from the bill.

Blocking Access to "Foreign Rogue Web Sites"

As introduced, SOPA would have empowered the Attorney General (AG) of the U.S. to seek court orders requiring foreign Web sites to cease providing access to infringing copies of U.S. works. Because "rogue" Web sites seemed unlikely to obey a U.S. court order, SOPA further empowered the AG to serve these orders on U.S. Internet intermediaries who would then have been required to take "technically feasible and reasonable measures" to block their users from accessing the foreign Web sites. This included "measures designed to prevent the domain name of the foreign infringing site . . . from resolving to that domain name's Internet protocol address." These measures needed to be undertaken "as expeditiously as possible," but no later than five days after receipt of the orders.

Upon receiving a copy of a rogue-Web site order, search engines would have been required to block access to the sites even if users were searching for items that would otherwise have brought the sites to their attention. Internet service providers would have had to ensure that users who typed certain URLs (for example, http://thepiratebay.se) into their browsers could not reach those sites. Payment providers (such as Visa or Mastercard) would have had to suspend services for completing transactions. Internet advertising services would have had to discontinue serving ads and providing or receiving funds for advertising at these sites.

Those who failed to comply with the DNS blocking obligations could expect the AG to sue them. The AG was also empowered to sue those who provided a service designed to circumvent this DNS blocking (for example, a plug-in or directory that mapped blocked URLs with numerical DNS representations).

Frustrated by the weak enforcement of intellectual property rights (IPRs) abroad, the U.S. entertainment industry urged Congress to adopt SOPA as the best way to impede online infringements. Foreign rogue Web sites might still be out there, but if U.S.-based Internet intermediaries blocked access to the sites, users would not be able to access infringing materials through U.S. intermediaries.

Because ISPs in the U.S. and abroad have no duty to monitor what users do on their sites, it is easy for sites to become hosts of large volumes of infringing materials. Some operators seemingly turn a blind eye to infringement, some encourage posting of infringing content, while other sites may just be misused by infringers. By cutting off sources of transactional and advertising revenues, the hope was to discourage these sites from continuing to operate.

Challenging U.S.-Directed Web Sites

SOPA would also have given holders of U.S. intellectual property rights (IPRs) power to challenge "U.S.-directed sites dedicated to the theft of U.S. property." At first blush, it might seem that reasonable persons should support a law crafted to target such sites. But "dedicated to the theft of U.S. property" was defined in a troublingly ambiguous and overbroad way. It included operators of sites that were taking "deliberate actions to avoid confirming a high probability of the use of [that] site to carry out acts" in violation of copyright or anti-circumvention rules. Also included was any site that was "primarily designed or operated for the purpose of, ha[d] only a limited use other than, or [wa]s marketed by its operator or another acting in concert with that operator in, offering goods or services in a manner that engages in, enables, or facilitates" violations of copyright or anti-circumvention laws.

SOPA would have enabled firms who believed themselves to be harmed by one of these sites to send letters to payment providers and/or to Internet advertising services to demand that they cease providing services to sites alleged to be "dedicated to the theft of U.S. property" shortly after receiving such letters.

Payment providers and Internet advertising services were then tasked with notifying the challenged sites about the "dedicated-to-theft" allegations against them. Challenged sites could contest these allegations by sending counter-notices to the payment providers and Internet advertising services. But without a counter-notice, payment providers and Internet advertising services had to cease further dealings with the challenged Web sites.

Content owners could also sue dedicated-to-theft sites directly to enjoin them from undertaking further actions that evidenced their dedication to theft. SOPA also authorized content owners to sue payment providers or advertising services who failed to comply with demands that they cease dealing with challenged Web sites.

SOPA's Flaws

The main problems with SOPA insofar as it would have employed DNS blocking to impede access to foreign rogue Web sites were, first, that it would undermine the security and stability of the Internet as a platform for communication and commerce and second, that it would be ineffective.

SOPA is fundamentally inconsistent with DNSSEC (DNS Security Extensions), a protocol developed to avoid abusive redirections of Internet traffic, whether by criminals, autocratic

governments, or other wrongdoers. Computer security experts spent more than a decade developing DNSSEC, which is now being implemented all over the world, including by U.S. government agencies.

As the USACM Public Policy Committee observed in a letter sent to members of Congress, DNSSEC Web site operators cannot reliably block offending sites "and so may be faced with the choice of abandoning DNSSEC or being in violation of issued court orders."

This letter explained why DNS blocking would be ineffective. "[I]t is effectively impossible to bar access to alternate DNS servers around the globe because there are millions of them on the Internet." Use of those servers "allows for bypassing of DNS blocking." Circumvention of DNS blocking is, moreover, "technically simple and universally available." Browser add-ons to avoid DNS blocking have already been developed and would be available on servers outside the U.S., even if illegal in the U.S.

The main problems with the dedicated-to-theft provisions of SOPA were, first, that it was too imprecise and second, that it represented a dramatic change in the rules of the road affecting Internet intermediaries.

What does it mean, for instance, for an Internet intermediary to take "deliberate actions to avoid confirming a high probability" of infringement on the site? If Viacom tells YouTube it has found infringing clips of "South Park" shows on its site, does YouTube become a site dedicated to the theft of Viacom's property if it does not investigate these claims? If Universal Music Group objects to the resale of MP3 files of its music on eBay, does eBay become a site dedicated to theft of Universal's property because one or more of its users offer the MP3 files for sale there?

Many Internet companies considered the dedicated-to-theft definition to be fundamentally inconsistent with the safe harbors established by the Digital Millennium Copyright Act (DMCA). Under the DMCA, Internet intermediaries are obliged to take down infringing materials after they are notified about specific infringements at specific parts of their Web sites. They have no obligation to monitor their sites for infringement. The safe harbors have been an important factor in the extraordinary growth of the Internet economy.

The safe harbors have been an important factor in the extraordinary growth of the Internet economy.

It may be apt to characterize sites such as Napster, Aimster, and Grokster as having been dedicated to the theft of U.S. intellectual property, but existing copyright law supplied copyright owners with ample tools with which to shut down those sites.

Had the entertainment industry sought more narrowly targeted rules aimed at inducing payment providers and Internet advertising services to stop the flow of funds to sites that were really dedicated to infringement, such a law might have passed. But that was not SOPA.

Conclusion

The collapse of support for SOPA was principally due to concerted efforts by Internet service providers (including Wikipedia, which went "dark" one day to protest SOPA), computer security experts, civil society groups, and millions of Internet users who contacted their Congressional representatives to voice opposition to the bill.

Because SOPA was a flawed piece of legislation, the collapse was a good thing.

Because SOPA was a flawed piece of legislation, the collapse was a good thing. It would, however, be a mistake to think the battle over Internet intermediary liability for infringing acts of users has been won for good.

The entertainment industry is almost certainly going to make further efforts to place greater legal responsibilities on Internet intermediaries. This industry believes intermediaries are the only actors in the Internet ecosystem who can actually affect the level of online infringements that contributes to entertainment industry panics.

An odd thing about the entertainment industry is its deeply skewed views about piracy. In movies such as *Pirates of the Caribbean,* the industry glamorizes brigands who attack ships by depicting them as romantic heroes who have great adventures and engage in swashbuckling fun. Yet, it demonizes fans who download music and movies as pernicious evildoers who are, in its view, destroying this vital part of the U.S. economy. Something is amiss here, and it is contributing to a profound disconnect in perspectives about how much the law can do to bring about changes in norms about copyright.

Critical Thinking

1. The RIAA likens people who acquire music from "rogue" websites (sites that host torrents or other file sharing applications and are often populated with digital content (music, videos, games, software) acquired outside regular vendor channels and made available without payment. Do you agree?

2. If legislation such as SOPA and PIPA are not the answer to protecting copyright in the digital age, what is? Might different, scaled down, legislation work? Might there be a technological solution? Or might there be a business model solution to this dilemma?

PAMELA SAMUELSON (pam@law.berkeley.edu) is the Richard M. Sherman Distinguished Professor of Law and Information at the University of California, Berkeley.

From *Communications of the ACM*, vol. 55, no. 7, July 2012, pp. 25–27. Copyright © 2012 by Pamela Samuelson. Reprinted by permission.

Aaron Swartz Hacks the Attention Economy

A digital guerrilla fighter explains what's wrong with anti-piracy laws, why the Internet and copyright law don't get along, and how he got into politics.

ANTONIO REGALADO

For Aaron Swartz, sharing files on the Internet isn't just fun and profitable. It's existential.

The 25-year-old programmer faces criminal charges that he hacked into MIT's computer system and downloaded 4.8 million journal articles with the intent of posting them online. He pleaded not guilty, but according to a manifesto he penned in 2008 it is precisely such acts of online civil disobedience that are needed to bring rampant Internet file sharing "into the light" and challenge "unjust laws."

Even before his arrest, Swartz was known for his contributions to the code that runs the Internet—as a teenager, he coauthored the RSS 1.0 specification, which organizes news feeds online. He also helped create the website Reddit, a site for sharing news, ideas, and photos that now logs two billion page views per month.

The hacking case has helped turn Swartz into a political symbol for a generation of young people for whom downloading, re-mixing, and sharing files on the Internet is second nature, even if it sometimes violates copyright laws. While his ideology may seem extreme—he wrote in his manifesto that "we need to take information, wherever it is stored, make our copies and share them with the world"—his point is that such behavior is already widespread and mostly benefits society.

The tension between Internet sharing and copyright law erupted again this January over the Stop Online Piracy Act, also called SOPA, a bill that would have made it easier for Hollywood studios to shut down websites that stream pirated movies, including by preventing search engines from linking to them. The legislation could have affected many Internet sites, including YouTube, news aggregators, and thousands of others where users regularly upload copyrighted text and images.

The bill was shelved after it became the subject of a massive publicity campaign by Internet companies and activists—during one day in January, websites including Wikipedia went dark in protest. Not surprisingly, Swartz had something to do with the Internet protests. During the very week in September 2010 that prosecutors say he was siphoning the JSTOR database into a laptop hidden in a campus network closet, Swartz was also circulating the first online petition to raise awareness of the controversial anti-piracy law.

Technology Review business editor Antonio Regalado interviewed Swartz via telephone. His lawyer, Martin Weinberg, allowed Swartz to be interviewed on the condition that he would not discuss his pending criminal case or his 2008 manifesto.

TR: What role did you play in the fight to stop SOPA?

Swartz: I first heard of the bill shortly after it was introduced in September 2010—back then it was called something else. They kept changing the name. I heard about it and quickly put together a website, which ended up becoming Demand Progress, to try to make people aware of the issues. Their plan was to rush it through a vote before anyone could have a chance to raise any objections.

Very quickly our protest started going viral. Several hundred thousand people signed the petition, and the vote was delayed. And that began this long fight. Since then, my engagement has been on and off. I've had other things to do but have tried to be a catalyst at key moments. The main thing was the incredible community building. That was basically what stopped it in the end.

Why were you opposed to the legislation?

The bill would provide censorship for the Internet, which is something that not only doesn't exist in the U.S. but previously had been seen as kind of crazy. That was the kind of thing you have in China or Iran. In a country with a First Amendment, I never would have expected the government would be going around deciding which websites Americans are allowed to see.

One problem was a due-process issue. If there is a crime, you find the person who's responsible, you bring them to court, you have a trial, and you hear evidence. If they're convicted, then they're convicted. But under SOPA, there was no adversarial

111

trial, just an ex parte hearing before a judge. To shut down a website, you didn't even have to show evidence that they had committed a crime—only that it looked like there was copyrighted material there.

What are the lessons businesspeople should draw from the fight over copyright enforcement?

I think it's often been portrayed as artists versus pirates. That isn't accurate at all. The recording industry and movie industry are infamous for stealing money from artists. I mean, the phrase "Hollywood accounting" is a cliché. And one of the ways that artists have managed to escape that is by going directly to their fans on the Internet. That's very threatening to these middlemen who have been stealing some of the money. I think a big reason the movie studios want to have more control over the Internet is to shut it down as an alternative distribution mechanism, to put it back in the bottle and go back to the old ways where they can take their cut.

Can you think of anyone in the movie industry making the transition to the Internet way of doing things?

The Hollywood unions were in favor of SOPA, but one was against it, and that was the Writer's Guild of America. During the writers' strike a couple of years ago, all these writers took that time off from working on Hollywood films to start making things directly for the Internet. There was this explosion of "I might as well make TV shows" and "I might as well make short films." That raised a lot of writers' profiles and built them an audience independent of the studios. The strike helped them understand the value of the Internet, and I'm hoping that they can explain it to the rest of Hollywood.

Do you think there is a clash of generations on the Internet?

There was this big hearing on SOPA where a whole bunch of members of Congress basically admitted they didn't really understand how this Internet thing works and they didn't personally use the Internet. Their staff had to explain it to them. I think for a lot of young people that was like, you know—that was ridiculous, right?

So there was outrage that the Internet was being regulated by people who didn't even know how to use it. If you use YouTube and Facebook on a regular basis, you realize why it's not okay to require these companies to have people reading every post, every video that goes up. It's totally comprehensible to a young person that there could be a website with a handful of employees that receives 24 hours of video each minute. Whereas I think members of Congress come from an era where . . . well, there's no movie studio that produces 24 hours of footage a minute, right? To them, it's totally reasonable that a studio has to watch every movie that they make and get it approved by certain people.

The Internet is a crucial part of young people's lives; it's the place you hang out with your friends, the place you get your news. What struck a chord was this notion that it could be taken away. That basic Internet companies like YouTube could be taken down and outlawed without even having been found guilty of any crime.

That sounds a bit exaggerated. Is "Save the Internet" becoming like abortion or gun control—a way to rally people on an emotional, irrational level?

To back up the specific point, the way the bill was written originally, any site with a significant amount of infringing content would be subject to a takedown order. The government was always like, "We'd never go after YouTube." And that's probably right. YouTube is probably too big and powerful a company at this point. But it's very easy to believe that when YouTube was just starting, they could have gotten shut down and it would never have grown to the point where it is now. It would have been snuffed out as an infant.

The movie studios complained it wasn't a fair fight, because companies that control Internet sites actually used those media to fight the bill. Any thoughts?

This is what used to be called public relations, right? Propaganda. The difference now is that groups of everyday citizens can do it. I think that's a big part of what we saw with the fight over SOPA. It was not about legal strategy or lobbyists. It was about how do we use these techniques to get people's attention? Wikipedia went dark for a day, Tumblr asked all their bloggers to phone Congress—I think they had over 86,000 calls that one day. There was a guy who built a tool that would automatically dial each member of Congress and the head of the Motion Picture Association of America (MPAA). If you wanted to inform everybody of your position, he could do it with a couple of clicks. What's different about this fight is that a whole community took up the banner and tried to raise attention, and that it's all organized over the Internet.

What can you tell me about your upbringing?

I grew up in a Chicago suburb—you know, pretty lonely. There wasn't a city. There weren't a lot of people around, and so I ended up making a lot of friends on the Internet and getting involved. I learned to program and when I was in sixth or seventh grade got involved in building Web standards and began working with Tim Berners-Lee, creator of the Web.

I really got to see the thing from the inside and understand how the technology works. After that I went on to found Reddit, which is an online news website that would have been threatened by these bills. It was clear to me that no one else was going to be able to see or explain these issues the way I was—to understand how it affected technology, how it would affect business, and also to have some idea of a way to stop it politically.

Are your beliefs shaped by the Internet itself, by things you read there? What were the strongest influences?

It's a little hard to put a finger on what one's influences were. My parents aren't particularly political. I would say they're slightly left of center. My dad was a software entrepreneur, so that's why we had the Internet very early on. I had a computer since the day I was born. It was a part of my life growing up. Over the dinner table we had a culture discussion and debate. I came from a family that prided itself on talking and taking different positions because it forces people to think.

When I surfed on the Internet, and even to this day, the technology community has a very techno-libertarian view: "If we just get the government out of the way and let everyone write software, everything will be fine." I read a lot of that, but I was never persuaded by it. I'm pretty far from being a libertarian. More than anything, it's a personality quirk of mine of just having an incredible sense of empathy for people. I knew I needed to help people. I think the technology community often lacks a sense of empathy.

Do you feel any empathy toward the Hollywood middlemen the Internet is putting out of business?

I know it's got to be hard, and I'm totally empathetic for them as people. But empathy has to be tempered with a sense of perspective about doing the most good for the most people. It's a logic that says, okay, yes, there is a handful of rich people who are going to be hurt, and that's unfortunate. I think the Internet is the thing that is going to change their industry, and it's a little too late to stop the Internet now.

What are your goals for 2012 and beyond?

We've seen this enormous sense among people that they are capable of making a difference over the Internet. I think that feeling of collective efficacy is incredibly powerful. What I am doing now is I'm exploring different ways to capitalize on that with social structures and technological tools to help people organize.

The rest of my life is to figure out what can be built to give people ways to change the way their lives are structured. I think there's a consensus for most people everywhere in the world about the way they want things to be. They want climate change to end, they want people lifted out of poverty, and they want to stop corruption. And I think the Internet provides a way to make this happen.

Critical Thinking

1. Recall back to the Article 10 reflection about Steve Jobs. In what ways does Swartz remind you of Jobs? In what ways is he different?

2. Take a look at reddit.com. Compare the structure of this website to more conventional web news sites such as Slate, Huffington Post, and the Drudge Report. What are the key aspects that differentiate reddit? And what conclusions can you draw from this about the future of copyright?

3. Search and read about Swartz's download of 4.8 million copyrighted JStor articles. Why do you think he chose to do this? Do you think he is right?

4. Why do you think Technology Review titled this article "Aaron Swartz Hacks the Attention Economy?" What is the attention economy? Why is it important?

From *Technology Review*, February 10, 2012. Copyright © 2012 by MIT Press. Reprinted by permission via Copyright Clearance Center.

UNIT 7

International Issues and Perspectives

Unit Selections

Learning Outcomes

After reading this Unit, you will be able to:

- Understand the complexity of both writing and enforcing international law to police criminal behavior and civil disagreements on the Internet.

- Understand how the Internet is governed and the controversies over changing the nature of that governance structure.

- Have read about Internet censorship across the nations of the world; understand how to compare censorship by nation; know where to look to research updated censorship information.

- Have read about some unlikely governmental censors.

- Have learned that other countries take privacy more seriously than does our own.

- Have learned about the process the Chinese government uses to censor Internet discussion, and how the discussants combat that censorship.

- Become familiar with several current international Internet issues.

- Model current international issues against a problem-solving rubric.

Student Website

www.mhhe.com/cls

Internet References

Global Censorship ChokePoints
  https://globalchokepoints.org/
OpenNet Initiative
  http://opennet.net/
Oxford Internet Institute
  www.oii.ox.ac.uk
Wikileaks
  http://wikileaks.org/

When Tom Friedman wrote of the flat word of the 21st century in Article 3, he was speaking of globalization and the increase of interdependent trade we have witnessed over the past 20 years, facilitated by the global availability of the Internet and related information and communication technologies. Without these new technologies, the global marketplace would not be possible. Today, we can withdraw money from our bank accounts using ATMs in Central Turkey, check our e-mail from a terminal located in an Internet café in Florence or Katmandu, and make cell or VoIP phones calls to and from nearly anywhere on the planet. These technologies also make it possible for businesses to transfer funds around the world and, if you happen to be a software developer, to employ talented—and inexpensive—software engineers in growing tech centers like Bangalore, India. But these changes, as Postman would note, have both positive and negative aspects. National borders have become more permeable to financial, digital product (such as digital media), information transfer.

These technologies also enable citizens of countries with a tradition of totalitarian governments to communicate, commiserate, and collaborate in political protest (to assemble, as the U.S. Constitution calls it.) They enable individuals and organizations to host and share internationally controversial information from safe heavens. And such permeability has been exercised by file sharing pirates, terrorist organizations, freedom fighters, and whistleblowers such as Wikileaks.[1]

For all of these reasons international issues around the transfer and use of computing and communication technologies remains controversial and at the forefront of diplomatic and trade negotiations. We have already explored some of the commercial controversies around ACTA and TPP in the last Unit. In this Unit we will explore issues of free speech and censorship (and see how tightly coupled these issues are with commercial speech).

While you may not be surprised by some countries that censor Internet use, you may be surprised by other countries that do. Censorship can take many forms including: filtering of political content; filtering of social content; filtering of security content; and the use of tools to monitor or track Internet use. The OpenNet Initiative is a collaboration of Canadian and American groups tracking levels of national censorship. For a recent report about their work (and listing of censorship levels by nation) read "Internet Censorship Listed: How Does Each Country Compare?"

Not all governments that censor new media are what we generally think of as repressive regimes. In August 2011, transit officials in San Francisco shut down underground cell phone service to thwart protestors angry over police behavior. Australia, France, India, Argentina, and South Korea have all set up Internet firewalls, to combat child pornography, to eliminate file sharing, or to tamp down political radicalism. Each government, including transit officials in San Francisco, can cite perfectly good reasons for its actions. One important lesson is that all media, no matter how apparently decentralized, rely upon an infrastructure that is vulnerable to central disruption.

© Zubin Ii/Getty Images

While censorship actions in the United States and other western nations often makes headlines, such government censorship is already all too common in other parts of the world. In "Watch Your Language," Mark McDonald describes the use of colorful and sometimes circumspect idiom used on Chinese discussion boards to evade, and occasionally taunt the vast array of censors in their midst.

We finish this Unit with "Global Trends to Watch," the summary of a panel discussion of Internet experts on the global erosion of privacy and anonymity on the Internet at the Annual meeting of the Internet Governance Forum.[2] The panel discusses a variety of issues that Internet policy makers and engineers are currently working through. At least four dimensions exist for each issue:

- The problem that needs to be addressed: in what way that problem impacts individuals from a functional, privacy, security, safety, cost, reliability (or multiple from this list) point of view;

- What the policy solution ought to be (and often different stakeholders have different priorities toward a policy);

- How to engineer and implement the policy solution;

- What international complexities arise based on local laws; local culture; determination of jurisdiction; or single point of failure.

As you read through the five issues discussed by the panel, try to map their discussion against this model.

The global interconnectedness that Marshall McLuhan observed 40 years ago has only increased in complexity with developments in computer technology.[3] Now instead of merely receiving one-way satellite feeds, as in McLuhan's day, we can talk back through e-mail, websites, blogs, and Facebook pages. It is not surprising that all of this communication is having unanticipated effects across the planet. Who, for instance, during the Tiananmen Square uprising of 1989, could have predicted that a newly market-centered China would become the world's second largest economy? Or who would have predicted international enthusiasm for a technology that resembles an American high school yearbook circa 1965? Or its acceptance among those for whom high school is a distant memory? No one, in fact, which is why the study of computing is so fascinating (and why so few visionaries continue to get so rich).

Notes

1. Not everyone would see these four categories as mutually exclusive.
2. A complete unofficial transcript of the session is at http://goo.gl/dFSng
3. Marshal McLuhan, *Understanding Media,* MIT Press, 1994.

Internet Censorship Listed: How Does Each Country Compare?

Where is the internet the most open? Where is it the most restricted? Debate the ranking here.

ANDREW RININSL

ONI principal investigator and Citizen Lab director Ronald Deibert says:

"Originally and probably still to a large extent, pornography is both the most widely targeted content and also the one that's justified the most by countries. Most countries, if they're going to engage in internet censorship, start by talking about a broad category of inappropriate content. But what we've found over the last decade is the spectrum of content that's targeted for filtering has grown to include political content and security-related content, especially in authoritarian regimes. The scope and scale of content targeted for filtering has grown.

For each country, the ONI looks at the following four categories of filtering and gives each a rank ranging from "No evidence of filtering" to "Pervasive filtering":

- **Political**–content opposing the current government or its policies; can also relate to human rights, freedom of expression, minority rights or religious movements
- **Social**–content that might be perceived as offensive by the general population such as sexuality, gambling, illegal drugs, etc
- **Conflict/security**–Content related to armed conflicts, border disputes, militant groups and separatist movements
- **Internet tools**–Tools enabling users to communicate with others, circumvent filtering or that otherwise provide a service. Each country is then classified in terms of consistency–how consistently these topics are filtered across internet service providers–and transparency–how visible the process is by which sites are blocked and whether users are able to view what's on the blacklist.

According to the ONI data, Iran was the worst ranked, with "pervasive" filtering in the political, social and internet tools categories and "substantial" for conflict/security filtering. Tested in 2011, Iran's filtering was rated as being "highly" consistent and had "medium" transparency. Even the country's president isn't immune to the blacklist–it was reported in February this year that censors had blocked access to several news sites supporting Ahmadinejad ahead of the parliamentary elections in March. Worse yet, Iran has proposed a national internet, which would both increase the government's grip over individual connections but also restrict foreign users from accessing Iranian websites. Additionally, individuals are also required to provide personal details to even use a cybercafe.

After Iran was China, which had "pervasive" political and conflict/security filtering, along with "substantial" internet tools and social filtering. In addition to highly consistent filtering, China also had a lower transparency score than Iran. On April 12, Chinese users were cut off from all foreign websites, possibly due to a reconfiguration of the so-called "great firewall."

Meanwhile, authorities have shut down 42 websites since March this year. "The market for filtering technologies has grown worldwide; what started out as a market primarily oriented to corporate environments in the west has now become a major growing business for government," said Deibert.

Our research identified many corporations–mostly Silicon Valley corporations–that have provided products and services to regimes that have violated human rights. The market for these types of technologies that are used to implement control is growing more sophisticated.

However, Deibert feels governments are moving away from widespread blacklists of websites to filter and towards what the ONI calls "next-generation filtering," which includes targeted surveillance and "just in time" filtering, or temporarily filtering content only when it's valuable–for instance, during an election. "We're seeing a trend away from traditional internet censorship and towards next-generation controls," he said. "The future is not in the great firewall but in the way countries like Iran have come to filter content."

Data Summary   ONI Ranking of Each Country for Internet Censorship

Country	Political filtering	Social filtering	Internet tools filtering	Conflict/security filtering
United Arab Emirates	substantial	pervasive	pervasive	selective
Afghanistan	no evidence	no evidence	no evidence	no evidence
Armenia	substantial	selective	selective	selective
Australia	no evidence	no evidence	no evidence	no evidence
Azerbaijan	selective	selective	no evidence	no evidence
Bangladesh	no evidence	no evidence	no evidence	no evidence
Bahrain	pervasive	pervasive	substantial	selective
Belarus	selective	selective	selective	selective
Canada	no evidence	no evidence	no evidence	no evidence
China	pervasive	substantial	substantial	pervasive
Colombia	no evidence	selective	no evidence	no evidence
Germany	no evidence	no evidence	no evidence	no evidence
Denmark	no evidence	no evidence	no evidence	no evidence
Algeria	no evidence	no evidence	no evidence	no evidence
Egypt	no evidence	no evidence	no evidence	no evidence
Ethiopia	substantial	selective	selective	selective
Finland	no evidence	no evidence	no evidence	no evidence
France	no evidence	no evidence	no evidence	no evidence
United Kingdom	no evidence	no evidence	no evidence	no evidence
Georgia	selective	no evidence	no evidence	selective
Guatemala	no evidence	no evidence	no evidence	no evidence
Croatia	no evidence	no evidence	no evidence	no evidence
Hungary	no evidence	no evidence	no evidence	no evidence
Indonesia	selective	substantial	selective	no evidence
Israel	no evidence	no evidence	no evidence	no evidence
India	selective	selective	selective	selective
Iraq	no evidence	no evidence	no evidence	no evidence
Iran	pervasive	pervasive	pervasive	substantial
Italy	no evidence	selective	no evidence	no evidence
Jordan	selective	no evidence	no evidence	no evidence
Kyrgyzstan	selective	selective	no evidence	no evidence
South Korea	no evidence	selective	no evidence	pervasive
Kuwait	selective	pervasive	pervasive	selective
Kazakhstan	selective	selective	no evidence	no evidence
Laos	no evidence	no evidence	no evidence	no evidence
Lebanon	no evidence	no evidence	no evidence	no evidence
Sri Lanka	no evidence	no evidence	no evidence	no evidence
Latvia	no evidence	no evidence	no evidence	no evidence
Libya	selective	no evidence	no evidence	no evidence
Morocco	no evidence	selective	selective	selective
Moldova	selective	no evidence	no evidence	no evidence
Burma (Myanmar)	pervasive	substantial	substantial	substantial
Mauritania	selective	no evidence	no evidence	no evidence
Mexico	no evidence	no evidence	no evidence	selective
Malaysia	no evidence	no evidence	no evidence	no evidence
Nigeria	no evidence	no evidence	no evidence	no evidence
Norway	no evidence	no evidence	no evidence	no evidence
Nepal	no evidence	no evidence	no evidence	no evidence
Oman	selective	pervasive	substantial	no evidence
Peru	no evidence	no evidence	no evidence	no evidence
Philippines	no evidence	no evidence	no evidence	no evidence
Pakistan	selective	selective	selective	substantial
Gaza and the West Bank	no evidence	substantial	no evidence	no evidence
Qatar	selective	pervasive	pervasive	selective
Romania	no evidence	no evidence	no evidence	no evidence
Russia	selective	selective	no evidence	no evidence
Saudi Arabia	substantial	pervasive	pervasive	selective
Sudan	selective	substantial	substantial	no evidence
Sweden	no evidence	no evidence	no evidence	no evidence
Singapore	no evidence	selective	no evidence	no evidence

Data Summary   ONI Ranking of Each Country for Internet Censorship

Syria	pervasive	selective	pervasive	selective
Thailand	selective	selective	selective	no evidence
Tajikistan	selective	no evidence	no evidence	no evidence
Turkmenistan	pervasive	selective	selective	selective
Tunisia	no evidence	selective	selective	no evidence
Turkey	selective	selective	selective	no evidence
Ukraine	no evidence	no evidence	no evidence	no evidence
Uganda	no evidence	no evidence	no evidence	no evidence
United States	no evidence	no evidence	no evidence	no evidence
Uzbekistan	pervasive	selective	selective	selective
Venezuela	no evidence	selective	no evidence	no evidence
Vietnam	pervasive	selective	substantial	selective
Yemen	substantial	pervasive	pervasive	selective
Zimbabwe	no evidence	no evidence	no evidence	no evidence

Source: ONI

Critical Thinking

1. Find this article on the Web and open the Interactive Map of national censorship data.

2. Use the buttons below the map to see how countries load by type of censorship. Do you see any patterns emerge?

3. Click on the United States and at least one country from each region of the world. Open and read the country profiles. Why do you think the countries you selected load high or low on particular types of censorship?

4. Do you agree with the ONI assessment? Do you agree with the methods they used to characterize countries?

From *The Guardian*, April 16, 2012. Copyright © 2012 by Guardian News & Media Ltd. Reprinted by permission.

Watch Your Language! (In China, They Really Do)

These words—mild, silly, inoffensive—are part of the subversive lexicon being used by Chinese bloggers to ridicule the government, poke fun at Communist Party leaders and circumvent the heavily censored Internet in China. A popular blog that tracks online political vocabulary, China Digital Times, calls them part of the "resistance discourse" on the mainland.

MARK MCDONALD

Internet usage in China, of course, is massive. A single microblogging site, Sina Weibo, has more than 300 million users. Nationwide there are some 460 million users of the Internet, and more than 300 million Chinese can access it on their cellphones. No need to mention the numbers on Twitter and Facebook: They're blocked by the Chinese government.

Internet traffic is examined with a thoroughness and ruthlessness that is almost admirable in its scope. The term "Great Firewall" is appropriate and descriptive—and also banned by the censors. The government prefers its own name for its Internet surveillance program—the Golden Shield Project.

The system ferrets out pornography and commercial scams, but it also blocks certain search terms. Its algorithms sniff out words or names it considers politically odorous. It sometimes deletes offending messages altogether.

More than 16 percent of all messages in China get deleted, according to a study by the Language Technologies Institute at Carnegie Mellon University in Pittsburgh. The survey, published in the online journal First Monday, analyzed 70 million messages sent last summer, mostly on Sina Weibo.

"Weibo users—whose numbers recently surpassed 300 million—realize the days of unfettered, anonymous criticism may be drawing to a close," writes Andrew Jacobs, a colleague in the Beijing bureau of The New York Times. "Beginning on March 16, new government regulations will require real-name registration."

In short, no more anonymity.

"Another rule will require Sina Weibo to review the posts of those who have more than 100,000 followers," Mr. Jacobs says. "Those 'harmful' to national interests, according to the rules, must be summarily deleted within five minutes."

The Carnegie Mellon team found "295 terms with a high probability of being censored." China Digital Space has compiled its own impressive dictionary of political slang and terminology, along with etymologies and back stories.

So good luck searching for terms like *Tibet, immolation, the Dalai Lama, Falun Gong, democracy movement, Sheng Xue* (dissident writer), *Ai Weiwei* (outspoken artist), *Liu Xiaobo* (imprisoned Nobel laureate), *June 4* (date of the Tiananmen Square massacre in 1989), and *Playboy* (the magazine).

From time to time over the past year, the words *jasmine, Egypt, Jon Huntsman* (the former American ambassador) and *Occupy Beijing* also have been banned.

And after the Fukushima nuclear disaster last March, online searches for the term "iodized salt" were blocked, presumably to quash the rumor racing across China that eating large quantities of salt would prevent radiation poisoning.

Two of the most pointed online jabs are "grass-mud horse" and "river crab."

Another colleague in Beijing, Michael Wines, has explicated the origin of grass-mud horse, describing the horse as "a mythical creature whose name, in Chinese, sounds very much like an especially vile obscenity."

(Interested readers can scale our own well-mannered firewall and find a fuller description of the terminology here.)

"Conceived as an impish protest against censorship," Mr. Wines writes, "the foul-named little horse has not merely made government censors look ridiculous, although it has surely done that. It has also raised real questions about China's ability to stanch the flow of information over the Internet—a project on which the Chinese government already has expended untold riches, and written countless software algorithms to weed deviant thought from the world's largest cyber-community."

A subtitled video of the gamboling horse is here—they're actually alpacas—and Ai Weiwei singing the equine anthem in Chinese is here.

Perry Link, the author of "Liu Xiaobo's Empty Chair," described the use of code words and Aesopian allegory by Mr. Liu and other popular bloggers like Han Han: "Harmony, for example, is a key word used in the government's rhetoric, and Internet writers use hexie, or river crab, which is a near-homonym of the Chinese word for harmony, to mean repression."

To be harmonized, these days, is to be censored.

"Officials are aware, of course, of its barbed meaning on the Internet," said the Chinese writer Yu Ha in an essay in the IHT Magazine, "but they can hardly ban it, because to do so would outlaw the 'harmonious society' they are plugging. Harmony has been hijacked by the public."

A handful of the underground terms we mentioned earlier, with characters from China Digital Times:

- Getting soy sauce. "A humorous way for netizens to distance themselves from a sensitive or political topic." The etymology derives from an on-the-street TV interview about a celebrity scandal. A man interviewed at random, according to China Digital Times, issues a profanity and says he has no connection to the matter, proclaiming, "I was just out buying some soy sauce."

- Scale the wall. Bo Xilai, the powerful head of the Communist Party in the megacity of Chongqing, has been entangled in a mysterious political scandal in recent weeks. So his temporary absence from a session of the National People's Congress last week sent rumors flying online. Many bloggers reported that they were gathering information "over the wall" or were "scaling the wall"—that is, going beyond the Internet firewall, using a tunnel or proxy. At one point, there were mentions of big doings in "the tomato," which in Mandarin sounds like "western red city," a new online euphemism for Chongqing. To scale the wall.

- Mayor Lymph. China Digital Times calls this "a code word for its near homophone, Charter 08," the democracy manifesto that enraged the government and turned up its paranoia dial to 11. Mr. Liu, the principal author of Charter 08, remains in prison.

- Mild collision. A subway crash in Shanghai last fall injured hundreds of passengers, and the accident occurred shortly after a high-speed rail crash that killed dozens and injured nearly 200. The rail incident outraged many Chinese, and the authorities were on alert for mass protests.

"The evening after the accident, CCTV, Xinhua and a Shanghai television station all reported that 'a mild collision' occurred on Shanghai's Metro Line 10,'" according to China Digital Times. "The claim that this was a mild accident elicited the derision of netizens who felt that the reporting was more intended to dampen fears about China's train system than report what actually occurred. The phrase 'mild collision' instantly became an Internet buzzword."

- Fifty cents. "Netizens first coined the term 'Fifty Cent Party' to refer to undercover Internet commentators who were paid by the government to sway public opinion" by posting pro-Beijing statements, reputedly for 50 cents a shot, according to China Digital Times.

"Now, however, the term is used to describe anyone who actively and publicly posts opinions online that defend or support government policy. As such, the so-called Fifty Cent Party has become the object of much scorn for many netizens."

- May 35. In other words, June 4. Also on the censors' blacklist are any consecutive combinations of the numbers 6, 4 and 89.

Critical Thinking

1. Construct an argument in favor of government censorship of social networking discussions. Construct an argument opposing such censorship. After constructing both arguments, consider: Why do you think the Chinese government chooses to censor social networking discussions?

2. Is censorship appropriate if it ferrets out pornography and commercial scams?

3. Do you think censorship exists on American social networks? What evidence can you present to defend your point of view? Do you think any form of censorship should be appropriate on American social networks?

From *The New York Times*, March 13, 2012. Copyright © 2012 by The New York Times Company. All rights reserved. Used by permission via PARS International and protected by the Copyright Laws of the United States. The printing, copying, redistribution or retransmission of this Content without express written permission is prohibited.

Global Trends to Watch:
The Erosion of Privacy and Anonymity
and the Need of Transparency
of Government Access Requests

A report from workshop 160 written by *Katitza Rodriguez,* International Rights Director, Electronic Frontier Foundation and *Katarzyna Szymielewicz,* Executive Director, Panoptykon Foundation.

KATITZA RODRIGUEZ AND KATARZYNA SZYMIELEWICZ

A Brief Substantive Summary: General Remarks

This panel discussion at the Internet Governance Forum in Kenya offered a snapshot of existing and proposed regulatory frameworks for Internet privacy. It looked at potential risks, global trends, best and worst practices. Panelists examined the Cybercrime Convention, mutual legal assistance treaties for gathering and exchanging information among countries, and the need for transparency in government requests for access to personal data.

At a time when individuals regularly turn to search engines, social networks and other Internet intermediaries to find information online, blog their most private thoughts, share personal data with friends, store sensitive information and share their location through mobile devices via GPS tracking, digital privacy is of paramount importance. Yet research by social scientists has found that few Internet users fully understand how much information they are revealing about themselves and the potential impact this disclosure can have.

Moreover, the ongoing move towards cloud computing means that more and more of our information will be stored online. Millions of people are trusting web-based email services such as Google Gmail to store years worth of private correspondence. Cloud services such as Dropbox or Google Docs store your most private documents. At the same time, the cloud is changing the economics

and dynamics of surveillance. The mere flow and storage of traffic data can reveal our online routines; social networks, interests and/or believes. As panelists noted, this information is not adequately protected against misuse or abuse by both corporate entities and governments.

As consumers have embraced cloud computing and mobile technologies, law enforcement agencies have followed. Presenters on this panel noted that governments are seeking broader powers to surveil their own citizens. India RIM was forced to provide intercept capabilities to their Blackberry services. The Iranian government hacked into the Dutch certificate authority Diginotar in order to obtain the credentials necessary to intercept the communications of 300,000 Iranian Gmail sessions. Panelist Christopher Soghoian, a research fellow at Indiana University, noted that cloud computing has made surveillance and the seizure of personal documents much easier and less expansive for United States law enforcement. "Google charges $25 to hand over your inbox," says Soghoian who added that the wireless carrier Sprint has 100 employees working full time on surveillance requests. "Yahoo! charges $20 plus the cost of a stamp. Facebook and Microsoft don't even bother charging because they say it's too difficult to get compensated for this."

Presenters on the panel observed that existing laws and treaties do not respond to various privacy risks that arise in digital environment. The Budapest Cybercrime Convention is a decade old, while the European Data

Protection Directive and the US Electronic Communications Privacy Act date back to 1980s, predating the modern Internet ecosystem.

Profiling and Behavioral Advertising

Information about users' behavior on-line is often utilized for profiling and targeting purposes. This is not only beyond users' control but also frequently without their awareness. The entire online behavioral advertising ecosystem is based on uncontrolled data processing, which operates smoothly without the need to obtain users' informed consent.

One particular topic that surfaced in this context was the promise of privacy enhancing technologies and the way these technologies conflict with the business models of companies that provide services for free via ads. Soghoian pointed out that it is very difficult to deploy privacy protective policies at companies with ad-supported services. If data stored in Google docs or on Amazon's servers was encrypted, those companies will not be able to monetize the data. "They are analyzing the content of your e-mail to show you ads, and there's not really a privacy preserving way for them to target those ads to you without seeing your data," says Soghoian. "When you give your data to a third party, you lose your control over it and the government can come in whenever it likes, with a valid court order, but they are relatively easy to obtain, and get your data."

Vint Cerf, the father of the Internet who is now the vice president and chief Internet evangelist for Google noted during the panel that Google encrypts access to its services,—such as HTTPS access to its search engines. But Cerf acknowledged that implementing encryption with cloud-based systems is difficult, especially if all the crypto must happen in the browser. "We couldn't run our system if everything in it were encrypted because then we wouldn't know which ads to show you," said Cerf. "So this is a system that was designed around a particular business model."

Cerf says the biggest problem is that cryptography is not very convenient or easy to use. He said companies should work hard to make it simpler and give users more tools to limit what happens to their information. Cerf said Google has designed its system to control personal data.

"At Google, anyway, we don't share any of the information that's in the system with any third parties except under the legal constraints that we're required to abide by," Cerf. "It's true that we use a lot of information to generate, select and display ads, but we don't share that information with third parties. Some people misunderstand the way the system works. The information stays in the environment."

A person participating in the discussion noted that Google Analytics on his web site allows him to see user's personal data such as what key words were searched to get to that site and what browser is being used. But participants agreed that Google is taking firm steps to help preserve privacy by promoting SSL by default. Participants noted that most users do not have an effective legal regime that would protect their privacy in this context. Only some of the leading Internet companies offer their users the possibility to opt-out from cookie-based behavioral targeting. It was noted that European Commission is currently considering a revision of its legal framework regarding e-commerce and online privacy.

Access to Data Stored in the Cloud by Law Enforcement Agencies

Governmental access to data stored in the cloud is particularly worrying given the globalization of web based services and the fact that data is often stored in a different country than the user's country of origin. If the data is stored in a country with doubtful human rights record or very lax regulation on the access to data for public security reasons, a number of privacy risks will arise.

Cerf insisted that Google only responds to valid requests that are accompanied by court orders or subpoenas. However, it was noted that even international corporations will struggle while confronted with a perfectly valid subpoena issued by the authority representing authoritarian or totalitarian regime.

"As far as governments go it's pretty clear that if the information is available and public and the government feels the need to protect the citizens that they are going to take advantage of whatever they can find in public," said Cerf. "So we have little choice; if things are shared in that way, governments are going to go after and use that information."

Participants discussed the unique surveillance capabilities available to the US government, due to the fact that so many widely used cloud computing and communications services are located in the US. Although European countries may have strong laws that protect the data of their citizens, the US government and its powers issued under the Patriot Act and FISA have a long reach—thus putting companies in a very difficult position, where they are in conflict between the laws of the US and other countries. As European, Asian and African governments consider placing their own citizens' data in the cloud, they will have to evaluate the cost savings against the legitimate desire to keep such data safe from foreign political surveillance.

Soghoian noted that Google's use of SSL encryption by default for Google's Gmail service helps to both protect against computer crime and enhance privacy. But he notes that Facebook and Twitter and Microsoft and Yahoo! have not followed Google's lead and some governments are also unhappy with SSL by default. Soghoian noted that Google was the target of a sophisticated man-in-the-middle attack performed in August by the Iranian government in which 300,000 Iranian users' e-mail communications were intercepted to get around Google's encryption.

If CoE, law enforcement agencies and governments were really concerned about protecting against cybercrime, Soghoian argued, they should push for default SSL, timely security updates and OS hard disk encryption. "So if we do care about cybersecurity and cybercrime, we would be seeing governments pushing for real security instead of just expanding their powers," said Soghoian.

Mandatory Data Retention

Another issue that was given substantial attention during the panel and open discussion is mandatory data retention. It was noted that government agencies throughout the world are pushing for laws that force online third party providers to collect and store more personal information that they need for the purposes of their business. Moreover, data retention's legal obligations to log users' Internet use are usually paired with provisions that allow the government to obtain those records, ultimately expanding governments' ability to surveil their citizens.

Citizens groups and civil society organizations find these controversial laws invasive and overbroad. Some countries' courts and tribunals have struck down data retention laws unconstitutional. This is the case with mandatory data retention regime existing in the EU, which forces all Internet Service Providers to store traffic data for the period up to 2 years so that it can be easily accessed by law enforcement entities. It was noted that Data Retention Directive is currently under review.

Panelist Katarzyna, director of the Panoptykon Foundation, noted that her home country of Poland has one of the worst data retention law in Europe with more than 1,000,400 requests for information per year and many cases of abuse. She noted that privacy activists in the EU are discussing how to fight data profiling and whether user consent should be needed to place cookies. Szymielewicz observed that the EU is pushing data retention proposals that go beyond the current requirements for telecommunications companies and Internet service providers to any entity that provides an online service.

"Data stored by telecommunication companies says a lot about your routines, a lot about your social network, a lot about where you go, what is your location," says Szymielewicz. "So law enforcement can not only trace you back, but can also predict your future behavior.

Security vs. Privacy

Another significant theme of the discussion was an alleged conflict between security and privacy. It was suggested that these two values can be reconciled if sound security policy is pursued. Neither privacy nor general freedom must be the price for increase in public security. At the same time it was noted with concern that some governments justify their notorious attempts to pierce the veil of anonymity and waive the protection of personal data through by pointing to a need to protect national security and engage in lawful investigations.

The Cybercrime Treaty

In recent years the CoE has prioritized ratification of the Cybercrime Convention by non-European countries, and has provided extensive technical assistance to countries that are implementing its provisions in their national law. Even for countries that have not chosen to ratify it, the Convention has become a "guideline" for those interested in developing national legislation against the perceived increased threats of cybercrime.

EFF remains concerned about the potential impact of the Convention, and overbroad national implementations of it, on citizens' fundamental rights. We have several concerns.

The Treaty provides detail on the types and character of surveillance powers it grants law enforcement agencies. While it mentions the need for privacy protections in a general sense, it fails to encode specific privacy protections necessary to limit the new powers it grants. As a model, then, the treaty is more likely (and has proven more likely) to encourage overbroad surveillance and less likely to ensure adequate privacy protection.

The flaws inherent in the Convention itself are exacerbated by the fact that it was drafted over ten years ago and much has changed since then. The Convention was premised on the notion that 'traffic data' (data generated by computers as a by-product of online interactions) is 'less sensitive', and so should be more readily accessible to law enforcement. But today's 'traffic data' can include such sensitive information as your otherwise anonymous online identity or your social network of interactions. Mobile companies and our Internet services providers are now recording our whereabouts at every moment, and we are leaving far more detailed footprints that reveal sensitive information of our daily lives. Sensitive data of this nature warrants stronger protection, not an all-access pass.

Panelist Alexander Seger, the head of Economic Crime Division at the Council of Europe, told the gathering that cybercrime is a greater threat to privacy than governments and that the European Court of Human Rights has ruled that governments have an obligation to protect the privacy of citizens against criminal intrusion. Seger believes that references to human rights language in Article 15 of the Convention promotes human rights and the rule of law and allows the treaty to comply with the European Convention of Human Rights and other agreements. He said that the Convention offers safeguards to prevent over-criminalization by supporting the principle that the legal measures are proportional to the offense and by requiring judges to authorize more invasive measures. "It clearly says that interception should be limited to serious offenses, not just to—not be applied to any offense," said Seger. "Service providers are not asked under the Budapest Convention to preemptively retain data. It's data expedited preservation. It's for specific specified traffic or content data, but it's specific."

Panel moderator Katitza Rodriguez noted in response to these comments that, the convention is specific on new powers, but vague on protections. Rodriguez was especially concerned that the Convention provides itemizes specific new powers while fails to encode human rights protections with equal specificity. This lack of specific allows countries to implement provisions that can criminalize legal efforts, such as security research activities. Also, while the Treaty does state in general terms that human rights must be respected, it does not clearly set out specific legal standards countries should use to ensure the extensive powers it grants law enforcement are not abused. This is particularly an issue in non-European countries with weak civil liberties. "There are many countries—and just my country, I am from Peru, from Latin America—we have an ex President, currently in jail, for massive illegal interception of communications." In many countries law enforcement agencies may not need increased surveillance powers and their judicial system might lack independence.

Seger pointed out that the Convention helps countries around the world establish proper codes of criminal conduct. "We can engage in a dialogue, and that's what we are trying to do in order to help countries take measures against cybercrime, but also improve human rights and the rule of law in any country."

But panelist Amr Gharbeia, a technology and freedom program officer from the Egyptian Initiative for Personal Rights, countered that in transitional countries like Egypt, ensuring privacy requires that policy makers address questions about rule of law, transparency, national security definitions, and investigative procedures that treat the Internet as a special domain. This is particularly a potential issue where 'cybercrime' is already defined very broadly. Gharbeia noted that, in Egypt, "[i]t's actually illegal for you to use any encrypted transmission. So basically everyone who is logging on the Facebook or Twitter account (...) are actually violating the law in Egypt."

Gharbeia added that in Egypt, developing privacy safeguards that respect the rule of law would require the reinvention of enforcement agencies. He says transparency is also very difficult and companies are required to keep logs for indefinite periods and then hand them over without any clear process. "Trojan horses like Finfisher, by the U.K. based company Gamma, and other systems that live in the center of the network have been found out," said Gharbia. "The only way to find out what the surveillance operations are going on in a security apparatus is if you actually break that. There is no transparency."

Conclusion and Further Comments

The architecture and development of the Internet have caused individuals to lose control over the collection, use and transfer of their personal data online. The fundamental value exchange underlying the Internet economy is that services are provided free of charge in return for pervasive use of individuals' information. This business model remains opaque to many users, who willingly or unwillingly share massive amounts of personal online data with a myriad of parties.

Users should not be alone in their struggle to maintain privacy in digital environment. Sound legal regulation is needed to ensure that fundamental rights of the users are respected. Users should be offered real choices whether to share their data with corporate entities and trade certain services for their privacy. This choice should not be limited to a formal right of consent. The notion of "informed consent" has eroded in the digital environment because of lack of education and awareness of how popular services work. There are also too few viable alternatives for equivalent services that do not require that users provide personal data.

"If you are paying a company for a service, then maybe they will deploy some more privacy enhancing technologies," observed Soghoian. "But when the company is monetizing your data, to provide you with a free and useful service, it's going to be really difficult for them to justify not saving any data by default or deleting IP addresses the minute they come in the door. Those are going to be tough decisions to get past the marketing team and other teams within the company."

Ensuring transparency and education should be the very first step in empowering users in online environment. The next step is to make fundamental principles of data protection—such as data minimization, proportionality and accountability of data processors—internationally binding. One way to work towards this ambitious goal is through the revision of the Convention 108 under the auspices of the Council of Europe. A second important forum for creating new standards can be offered by the EU through a pending revision of the Data Protection Directive that can reshape the whole data protection framework. Another possibility, which should be explored in parallel (never as an alternative) is putting further pressure on international corporations to adopt binding corporate rules with regard to privacy.

Binding privacy standards should also be enforceable against national states. While existing international conventions do contain sound principles with regard to the right to privacy, such principles are notoriously violated by both authoritarian and democratic states under the label of national security. Gharbeia pointed out that in 2006, according to Amnesty U.K., Microsoft handed over the details of the Hotmail account belonging to antinuclear activist Mordechai Vanunu's before a court order had been obtained by alluding that he was being investigated for espionage.

The challenge of mandatory data retention and the use of commercial data stored in the cloud by law enforcement agencies is increasingly relevant across the globe. One of the most striking examples of this tendency is a US law that allows for political surveillance of foreigners' data stored by US-based companies (FISA).

There is clearly an urgent need to adopt international standards for data protection in vertical relationships such as the citizens vs. state authorities. In order to do so, we need to consider the following questions:

- What limitations should apply to the scope of data being collected by various types of commercial entities, Internet access providers, search engines, on-line shops, social networks or web mail services?
- Should there be a legal obligation to store any data generated for commercial purposes and if so, for how long and for what purposes?
- Finally, what should be the conditions for law enforcements agencies to obtain access to personal data, regardless of whether it is stored for commercial or public security purposes?

Data protection should be seen in a broader context. The principles we adopt today will become more and more relevant in the future. They must be robust and adapt to the development of new web-based services, such as Internet of things, the smart grid or increasingly popular geolocation services. Policy makers have an obligation to protect basic human rights and develop strategies that work.

Workshop 160: Global Trends to Watch: The Erosion of Privacy and Anonymity and The Need of Transparency of Government Access Requests

Speakers:

- Vinton G. Cerf, vice president and chief Internet evangelist for Google, USA.
- Amr Gharbeia, Egyptian blogger, technology and freedom program officer from the Egyptian Initiative for Personal Rights, EGYPT.
- Alexander Seger, Head of Economic Crime Division of the Council of Europe, EUROPE.
- Christopher Soghoian, Ph.D. Candidate in the School of Informatics and Computing at Indiana University, USA.
- Katarzyna Szymielewicz, human rights lawyer and activist. Co-founder and executive director of the Panoptykon Foundation—a Polish NGO member of European Digital Rights, EUROPE.

Moderator:

- Katitza Rodriguez, Electronic Frontier Foundation's international rights director, PERU, USA.

Remote Moderator:

- Joana Varon, Researcher on Development and Intellectual Property at the Centre for Technology and Society (CTS/FGV) from Fundação Getúlio Vargas (FGV) School of Law in Rio de Janeiro.

Organizers:

- **Electronic Frontier Foundation (EFF):** From the Internet to the iPod, technologies are transforming our society and empowering us as speakers, citizens, creators, and consumers. When our freedoms in the networked world come under attack, the Electronic Frontier Foundation (EFF) is the first line of defense. EFF broke new ground when it was founded in 1990—well before the Internet was on most people's radar— and continues to confront cutting-edge issues defending free speech, privacy, innovation, and consumer rights today. From the beginning, EFF has championed the public interest in every critical battle affecting digital rights. EFF fights for freedom primarily in the courts, bringing and defending lawsuits even when that means taking on the US government or large corporations. By mobilizing more than 61,000 concerned citizens through our Action Center, EFF beats back bad legislation. In addition to advising policymakers, EFF educates the press and public.

- **Panoptykon Foundation:** Its mission is to protect human rights, in particular the right to privacy, in the clash with modern technology used for surveillance purposes. We want to analyze the risks associated with the operation of modern surveillance systems, monitor the actions of both public and private entities in this and intervene when human rights or democratic values are threatened. We are not opposed to the use of modern technology. However, what we do care about is the preparation of legal solutions that will strike a balance between competing values, such as security and freedom. We do believe that aspirations to increase public security or broadly conceived

efficiency should not be pursued at the cost of the right to privacy and individual freedom. Our aim is to provoke social discussion on the reasons, signs and consequences of this phenomenon.

Critical Thinking

1. Which of the five issues discussed by the panel do you believe to be the most serious or risky to the future of the Internet? Why?

2. Apply the bullet point model presented in the Introduction to Unit 7 against the five issues discussed by the 160 panel. For each issue, is there a significant international component to the problem? That is: are their cross-national or cross-cultural barriers to achieving a workable solution?

3. When national law or national culture differences impede a solution to an Internet problem, how should an appropriate international solution be negotiated?

From *Electronic Frontier Foundation*, November 11, 2011, pp. 1–9. https://www.eff.org/sites/default/files/filenode/IGF-privacy-surveillance-160.pdf Copyright © 2011 by Electronic Frontier Foundation. Reprinted under the Creative Commons Attribution License. http://creativecommons.org/licenses/by/3.0/us/

UNIT 8
Projecting the Future

Unit Selections

Learning Outcomes

After reading this Unit, you will be able to:

- Have applied a model for evaluating potential future technologies, and further applied Postman's model for evaluating future technologies.

- Have learned about Watson, the IBM heavyweight that recently defeated two *Jeopardy!* champions.

- Understanding of Moore's Law and exponential growth of computing technologies, with consideration for its business model and behavior adaption implications.

- Understand the concept of augmented reality, and how augmented reality is being productized.

- Have learned about mobile technology for gene sequencing; explored the business model implications and potential societal impact of this technology.

Student Website
www.mhhe.com/cls

Internet References

Freakonomics
www.freakonomicsradio.com/hour-long-special-the-folly-of-predicition.html
IBM Watson: Ushering in a New Era of Computing
www.ibm.com/watson
Institute for Ethics & Emerging Technologies
www.ieet.org
Institute for the Future
www.iftf.org
International Society for Augmentative and Alternative Communication
www.isaac-online.org/english/home
The World Information Institute
www.world-information.org
World Future Society
www.wfs.org

In "Five Things We Need to Know about Technological Change" Postman jokes that "to a person with a computer, everything looks like data." And indeed it does. Famously, Thomas Watson Jr., then the Chairman of IBM, predicted in 1953 a market for IBM of "maybe five computers."[1] (That is not a typo and I am not making it up; although to his credit, at the time each computer was the size of a living room, required more air conditioning than a commercial freezer, needed a staff of people to support it, and rented for over $11,000 a month.[2]) Twenty four years later, Ken Olson, President of Digital Equipment Corporation (DEC) then one of the largest computer companies in the world, looked at the newly released Apple II computer by an unknown start up in California and surmised, "There is no reason anyone would want a computer in their home." Today, of course, Apple is, by measure of stock value, the largest company in the world. DEC ceased to exist as an independent company in 1998, subsumed by Compaq Computers, which was later subsumed by Hewlett-Packard in 2002.

Clearly, predicting the future is risky business.

We tend to view the future through the lens of the present day, thinking the future will simply be a variation of the now. Sometimes this thinking works, but historically we have found that as computer capabilities rise and computer size and price drop, every decade or so we break through to a new epoch. And each new epoch brings new markets, new business rules, and new business and consumer behaviors. We experienced this change in the early 1980s with the introduction of the Apple II and the IBM PC. We experienced it again in the mid 1990s with the commercialization of the Internet and the introduction of the World Wide Web. Most recently, we are experiencing a new mobile computing epoch brought about by faster 3G and 4G connectivity, Web 2.0 programming technologies, and device miniaturization (think: iPhone, iPad, Android) enabling smart mobile interactivity. We are still in the middle of the hardware, software, network technology introductions, as well as business model and use behavior modifications from this most recent epochal change. We live in a very exciting time.

When I teach my own social issues and technology course my favorite week each semester is when I get to come in to the classroom and show my students what new technology tools and toys are coming to market in the near future. In that same vein, this last Unit of the Annual Edition is my favorite as we are able to peek each year at a slice of new offerings from IT inventors. Space limitations permit us to select only a few areas to focus on, but more—and more recent—visions of IT's future are available online.

If the future is so hard to predict that CEOs of major computer companies have erred in embarrassing ways, is there a model we might apply to do better? In "How to Spot the Future," Thomas Goetz lays out the seven rules used at Wired Magazine. What do these rules predict for the technologies described in subsequent articles in this Unit? Using these rules, can you spot any trends that are not readily apparent to others?

Praised by some as a leap forward in language processing and machine intelligence, Watson (named after Thomas Watson Sr.), a 2880 processor machine from IBM programmed

© Colin Anderson/Blend Images LLC

with unique artificial intelligence capabilities, roundly defeated two *Jeopardy!* champions. Some readers will recall IBM's Deep Blue that beat chess world champion Garry Kasparov in a hard-fought match back in 1997. Though critics remain skeptical about both accomplishments, much to the dismay of AI researchers, watching Watson at work in fall 2010 was impressive. Read "Weighing Watson's Impact" to see for yourself.

While one group of inventors tinkers with Internet-enabling household objects, another group of inventors is looking at blending the real world with the virtual world by augmenting our abilities to perceive the reality though smart, integrated interface devices. In "Augmented Reality Is Finally Getting Real," Kiji McCafferty describes a Yelp iPhone app that lets you view your immediate surroundings through the iPhone camera and screen, but overlays on top of that reality additional content to enhance your vision. Augmented reality has existed for a while, but has been applied largely in high end devices such as fighter planes. The iPhone/Yelp app experiment suggests it may soon go mobile. And in fact, augmented reality may quickly become even more mobile than an iPhone. Manjoo mentions that "You Will Want Google Goggles" as soon as Google's prototype becomes a commercial product. While the prototype lacks style, except for the most nerd-like among us, commercial versions should embed the technology more fashionably. The goggles bypass the iPhone/Android handheld and, perhaps, will permit you to augment your eyesight by projecting useful data about whatever you are looking through your glasses to appear in front of you. Imagine never forgetting a name because the glasses run the image of the person in front of you through your contact database and project both name and interesting conversational topics right before your eyes. For a look at the Google Goggles prototype, see Farhad Manjoo's article.

Our final article explores a very different computing device that might impact your future. This device does not do something no other machine can do, rather it does it faster and cheaper (and is smaller to be more mobile.) Just as making computers smaller, faster, and cheaper has been the catalyst for the last three epochs of computing advances—each time the changes in form and price enabled behaviors and uses never before possible, this small gene sequencing device may lead to whole new industries, different approaches to treating disease, and a new sort of relationship between doctor and patient. Read "Gene Machine" to explore these possibilities for yourself.

The Personal Genome Machine is a great place to end this year's Annual Edition as it evidences so many of the concepts Postman wrote about in the first article. It is an evolutionary advancement of an existing, albeit still novel, technology of gene sequencing. But the advances from this device contain very powerful, potentially world changing ideas.

Notes

1. This quote is often attributed to his father, Thomas Watson Sr., as saying he predicted a world market of maybe five computers. But there is no evidence Watson Sr. ever said any such thing. Watson Jr. did say something to this effect as IBM began marketing their first commercial computer, the 701, in 1953. While he predicted they would sell five of them, they actually sold 18 during their first pitch.

2. The UNIVAC, the first commercial computer, weighed 29,000 pounds, and took up 382 square feet of floor space, and used about as much electricity as 250 modern refrigerators.

How to Spot the Future

THOMAS GOETZ

Thirty years ago, when John Naisbitt was writing Megatrends, his prescient vision of America's future, he used a simple yet powerful tool to spot new ideas that were bubbling in the zeitgeist: the newspaper. He didn't just read it, though. He took out a ruler and measured it. The more column inches a particular topic earned over time, the more likely it represented an emerging trend. "The collective news hole," Naisbitt wrote, "becomes a mechanical representation of society sorting out its priorities"—and he used that mechanism to predict the information society, globalism, decentralization, and the rise of networks.

As clever as Naisbitt's method was, it would never work today. There's an infinite amount of ink and pixels spilled on most any topic. These days, spotting the future requires a different set of tools. That's why at Wired, where we constantly endeavor to pinpoint the inventions and trends that will define the future, we have developed our own set of rules. They allow us to size up ideas and separate the truly world-changing from the merely interesting. After 20 years of watching how technology creates a bold and better tomorrow, we have seen some common themes emerge, patterns that have fostered the most profound innovations of our age.

This may sound like a paradox. Surely technology always promises something radically new, wholly unexpected, and unlike anything anybody has seen before. But in fact even when a product or service breaks new ground, it's usually following a familiar trajectory. After all, the factors governing thermodynamics, economics, and human interaction don't change that much. And they provide an intellectual platform that has allowed technology to succeed on a massive scale, to organize, to accelerate, to connect.

So how do we spot the future—and how might you? The seven rules that follow are not a bad place to start. They are the principles that underlie many of our contemporary innovations. Odds are that any story in our pages, any idea we deem potentially transformative, any trend we think has legs, draws on one or more of these core principles. They have played a major part in creating the world we see today. And they'll be the forces behind the world we'll be living in tomorrow.

Look for Cross-Pollinators

It's no secret that the best ideas—the ones with the most impact and longevity—are transferable; an innovation in one industry can be exported to transform another. But even more resonant are those ideas that are cross-disciplinary not just in their application but in their origin.

This notion goes way back. When the mathematician John von Neumann applied mathematics to human strategy, he created game theory—and when he crossed physics and engineering, he helped hatch both the Manhattan Project and computer science. His contemporary Buckminster Fuller drew freely from engineering, economics, and biology to tackle problems in transportation, architecture, and urban design.

Sometimes the cross-pollination is potent enough to create entirely new disciplines. This is what happened when Daniel Kahneman and Amos Tversky started to fuse psychology and economics in the 1970s. They were trying to understand why people didn't behave rationally, despite the assumption by economists that they would do so. It was a question that economists had failed to answer for decades, but by cross-breeding economics with their own training as psychologists, Kahneman and Tversky were able to shed light on what motivates people. The field they created—behavioral economics—is still growing today, informing everything from US economic policy to the produce displays at Whole Foods.

More recently, the commonalities between biology and digital technology—code is code, after all—have inspired a new generation to reach across specialties and create a range of new cross-bred disciplines: bioinformatics, computational genomics, synthetic biology, systems biology. All these fields view biology as a technology that

131

can be manipulated and industrialized. As Rob Carlson, founder of Biodesic and a pioneer in this arena, puts it, "The technology we use to manipulate biological systems is now experiencing the same rapid improvement that has produced today's computers, cars, and airplanes." These similarities and common toolsets can accelerate the pace of innovation.

The same goes for old industries, as well. The vitality we see in today's car industry resulted from the recognition that auto manufacturing isn't a singular industry siloed in Detroit. In the past decade, car companies have gone from occasionally dispatching ambassadors to Silicon Valley to opening lab space there—and eagerly incorporating ideas from information technology and robotics into their products. When Ford CEO Alan Mulally talks about cars as the "all-time mobile application," he's not speaking figuratively—he's trying to reframe the identity of his company and the industry. That's testimony to a wave of cross-pollination that will blur the line between personal electronics and automobiles.

The point here is that by drawing on threads from several areas, interdisciplinary pioneers can weave together a stronger, more robust notion that exceeds the bounds of any one field. (One caveat: Real cross-pollination is literal, not metaphorical. Be wary of flimflam futurists who spin analogies and draw equivalences without actually identifying common structures and complementary systems).

Surf the Exponentials

Some trends are so constant, they verge on cliché. Just mentioning Moore's law can cause eyes to roll, but that overfamiliarity doesn't make Gordon Moore's 1965 insight—that chips will steadily, exponentially get smaller, cheaper, faster—any less remarkable. Not only has it been the engine of the information age, it has also given us good reason to believe in our capacity to invent our future, not just submit to it. After all, Moore's law doesn't know which silicon innovation will take us to the next level. It just says that if the previous 50 years are any indication, something will come along. And so far, it always has.

Moore's law has been joined by—and has itself propelled—exponential progress in other technologies: in networks, sensors, and data storage (the first iPod, in 2001, offered 5 gigabytes for $399, while today's "classic" model offers 160 gigs for $249, a 51-fold improvement). Each of these cyclically improving technologies creates the opportunity to "surf exponentials," in the words of synthetic biologist Drew Endy—to catch the wave of smaller, cheaper, and faster and to channel that steady improvement into business plans and research agendas.

This was the great insight that inspired YouTube, when cofounder Jawed Karim realized (while reading Wired, it so happens) that broadband was becoming so cheap and ubiquitous that it was on the verge of disrupting how people watched videos. And it's what Dropbox did with digital storage. As the cost of disc space was dropping at an exponential rate, Dropbox provided a service capitalizing on that phenomenon, offering to store people's data in the cloud, gratis. In 2007 the two free gigabytes the company offered were really worth something. These days 2 gigs is a pittance, but it remains enough of a lure that people are still signing up in droves—some fraction of whom then upgrade to the paid service and more storage.

And it's what allowed Fitbit to outdo Nike+. As accelerometers dropped in cost and size, Fitbit could use them to measure not just jogging, but any activity where movement matters, from walking to sleep. For all its marketing muscle, Nike didn't recognize that accelerometers were the dynamo of a personal health revolution. The new FuelBand shows that the company has now caught on, but Fitbit recognized the bigger trend first.

Exponentials, it turns out, are everywhere. Just choose one, look where it leads, and take a ride.

Favor the Liberators

Liberation comes in two flavors. First are those who recognize an artificial scarcity and move to eliminate it by creating access to goods. See the MP3 revolutionaries who untethered music from the CD, or the BitTorrent anti-tyrannists who created real video-on-demand.

Sometimes, of course, the revolution takes longer than expected. Back in 1993, George Gilder pointed out in these pages that the cost of bandwidth was plummeting so fast as to be imminently free. Gilder's vision has been proven correct, paving the way for Netflix and Hulu. And yet telcos are today—still!—trying to throttle bandwidth. But this is just biding time on the scaffold. In the words of investor Fred Wilson, "scarcity is a shitty business model."

The second flavor of liberation takes a more subtle approach to turning scarcity into plenty. These liberators use the advent of powerful software to put fallow infrastructure to work. Think of how Netflix piggybacked on a national distribution infrastructure by having the US Postal Service carry its red envelopes. Or how the founders of Airbnb recognized our homes as a massive stock of underutilized beds, ready to be put into the lodging market. Or how Uber turns idling drivers into on-call icons on a Google map, blipping their way to you in mere minutes. Reid Hoffman, the philosopher-investor, describes these companies as bringing liquidity to locked-up assets. He means this in the financial sense of "liquidity," the ability to turn capital into currency, but it also works in a more evocative sense. These companies turn static into flow, bringing motion where there was obstruction.

What's it like to live in the future? Ask an Uber driver—these guys are electrons pulsing through a real-life network, and they're delighted by it. So should we all be.

Give Points for Audacity

When "big hairy audacious goal" entered the lexicon in 1994 (courtesy of Built to Last, the management tome by James Collins and Jerry Porras), it applied to ambitious executives eager to set high targets for annual revenue growth and increased market share. Yawn. But the term—shortened to BHAG—also coincided with the birth of the web, when innovators began to posit a whole new sort of audacity: to make every book, in every language, available in less than a minute; to organize all the world's information; or to make financial transactions frictionless and transparent.

Audacity is easily written off as naïveté, as overshooting your resources or talents. And that's a danger. Plenty of would-be Napoleons have called for revolutions that never found an army. But you can't make the future without imagining what it might look like.

Too much of the technology world is trying to build clever solutions to picayune problems. Better parking apps or restaurant finders might appeal to venture capitalists looking for a niche, but they are not ideas that seed revolutions. Instead, take a lesson from Tesla Motors, which had the pluck to spend $42 million of its precious capital to buy a factory roughly the size of the Pentagon, stock it with state-of-the-art robots, and begin making wholly viable electric cars. Or look to Square, which has pronounced the cash register a counter-cluttering vestige of the 19th century and created an alternative that will not only make buying things easier but will deliver retailers from their sclerotic relationship with credit card companies.

These times especially call for more than mere incrementalism. Let's demand that our leaders get in over their heads, that they remain a little bit naive about what they're getting into. As venture capitalist Peter Thiel told wired two years ago, "Am I right and early, or am I just wrong? You always have to wonder." This kind of willingness to take a chance and be early is what keeps the world moving.

Bank on Openness

In 1997 Wired's founding executive editor, Kevin Kelly, wrote a story called "New Rules for the New Economy"

(it was in many ways the inspiration for this very piece). His focus was on networks, the "thickening web" that was forging connections of catalytic power. Many of his radical rules have become commonalities today, but two of them are just coming into their own: Connected individuals with shared interests and goals, he argued, create "virtuous circles" that can produce remarkable returns for any company that serves their needs. And organizations that "let go at the top"—forsaking proprietary claims and avoiding hierarchy—will be agile, flexible, and poised to leap from opportunity to opportunity, sacrificing short-term payoffs for long-term prosperity. Since Kelly wrote his piece, these forces have flourished. Back then open source software was a programming kibbutz, good for creating a hippy-dippy operating system but nothing that could rival the work of Oracle or Microsoft. Today open source is the default choice for corporations from IBM to Google. Even Microsoft is on board, evangelizing Hadoop and Python and opening the Xbox Kinect controller so it can be a platform for artists and roboticists. Supported by coder clubhouses like SourceForge and GitHub, collaborative circles can emerge with stunning spontaneity, responding elastically to any programming need.

More tellingly, in many organizations openness itself has become a philosophical necessity, the catalyst that turns one employee's lark into a billion-dollar business. Companies from Lego to Twitter have created a product and then called on its users to chart its course, allowing virtuous circles to multiply and flourish. Time after time, the open option has prevailed, as Zipcar has gained on Hertz and users have upvoted Reddit over Digg.

The best example may be nearly invisible, even to a dedicated user of the Internet: blogging platforms. Less than a decade ago there were a multitude of services competing for the emerging legion of bloggers: Movable Type, TypePad, Blogger, WordPress. Today, only the last two remain relevant, and of these, the small, scrappy WordPress is the champ. WordPress prevailed for several reasons. For one, it was free and fantastically easy to install, allowing an aspiring blogger (or blogging company) to get off the ground in hours. Users who wanted a more robust design or additional features could turn to a community of fellow users who had created tools to meet their own needs. And that community didn't just use WordPress—many made money on it by selling their designs and plug-ins. Their investment of time and resources emboldened others, and soon the WordPress community was stronger than any top-down business model forged inside the walls of their competition.

Sure, there are Apples and Facebooks that thrive under the old rules of walled gardens and monocultures. But even they try to tap into openness (albeit on their own terms) by luring developers to the App Store and the Open

Graph. And for all the closed-world success of these companies, the world at large is moving the other way: toward transparency, collaboration, and bottom-up innovation. True openness requires trust, and that's not available as a plug-in. When transparency is just a marketing slogan, people can see right through it.

Demand Deep Design

Too often in technology, design is applied like a veneer after the hard work is done. That approach ignores how essential design is in our lives. Our lives are beset by clutter, not just of physical goods but of ideas and options and instructions—and design, at its best, lets us prioritize. Think of a supremely honed technology: the book. It elegantly organizes information, delivering it in a compact form, easily scanned asynchronously or in one sitting. The ebook is a worthy attempt to reverse-engineer these qualities—a process that has taken decades and chewed up millions in capital. But still, despite the ingenuity and functionality of the Kindle and the Nook, they don't entirely capture the charms of the original technology. Good design is hard.

Indeed, good design is much, much harder than it looks. When Target redesigned its prescription pill bottle in 2005, the improvement was instantly recognizable—an easy-to-read label that plainly explains what the pill is and when to take it. It was a why-didn't-I-think-of-it innovation that begged to be replicated elsewhere. But judging by the profusion of products and labels that continue to baffle consumers, it has been largely ignored. Same with Apple: The company's design imperative is forever cited as intrinsic to its success, but Apple still stands curiously alone as a company where engineers integrate design into the bones of its products.

Thankfully, we are on the verge of a golden age of design, where the necessary tools and skills—once such limited resources—are becoming automated and available to all of us. This timing is critical. "Too much information" has become the chorus of complaint from all quarters, and the cure is not more design but deeper design, design that filters complexity into accessible units of comprehension and utility. Forget Apple's overpraised hardware aesthetic; its greatest contribution to industrial design was to recognize that nobody reads user's manuals. So it pretty much eliminated them. You can build as many stunning features into a product as you like; without a design that makes them easy to use, they may as well be Easter eggs.

No company has managed this better than Facebook, which outstripped MySpace because it offered constraint over chaos and rigor over randomness. Facebook has tweaked its interface half a dozen times over the years, but it has never lost the essential functionality that users expect. Indeed, its redesigns have been consistently purposeful. Each time, the company's goal has been to nudge users to share a little more information, to connect a little more deeply. And so every change has offered tools for users to better manage their information, making it easier to share, organize, and access the detritus of our lives. Privacy concerns aside, Facebook has helped people bring design into their lives as never before, letting us curate our friends, categorize our family photos, and bring (at least the appearance of) continuity to our personal histories. Services like Pinterest only make this more explicit. They promise to let us organize our interests and inspirations into a clear, elegant form. They turn us into designers and our daily experience into a lifelong project of curation. This is deep design commoditized—the expertise of IDEO without the pricey consulting contract. And done right, it is irresistible.

Spend Time with Time Wasters

The classic business plan imposes efficiency on an inefficient market. Where there is waste, there is opportunity. Dispatch the engineers, route around the problem, and boom—opportunity seized.

That's a great way to make money, but it's not necessarily a way to find the future. A better signal, perhaps, is to look at where people—individuals—are being consciously, deliberately, enthusiastically inefficient. In other words, where are they spending their precious time doing something that they don't have to do? Where are they fiddling with tools, coining new lingo, swapping new techniques? That's where culture is created. The classic example, of course, is the Homebrew Computer Club—the group of Silicon Valley hobbyists who traded circuits and advice in the 1970s, long before the actual utility of personal computers was evident. Out of this hacker collective grew the first portable PC and, most famously, Apple itself.

This same phenomenon—people playing—has spurred various industries, from videogames (thank you, game modders) to the social web (thank you, oversharers). Today, inspired dissipation is everywhere. The maker movement is merging bits with atoms, combining new tools (3-D printing) with old ones (soldering irons). The DIY bio crowd is using off-the-shelf techniques and bargain-basement lab equipment, along with a dose of PhD know-how, to put biology into garage lab experiments. And the Quantified Self movement is no longer just Bay Area self-tracking geeks. It has exploded into a worldwide phenomenon, as millions of people turn their daily lives into measurable experiments.

The phenomenon of hackathons, meanwhile, converts free time into a development platform. Hackathons harness the natural enthusiasm of code junkies, aim it at a target, and create a partylike competition atmosphere to make innovation fun. (And increasingly hackathons are drawing folks other than coders.) No doubt there will be more such eruptions of excitement, as the tools become easier, cheaper, and more available.

These rules don't create the future, and they don't guarantee success for those who use them. But they do give us a glimpse around the corner, a way to recognize that in this idea or that person, there might be something big.

Critical Thinking

1. Construct an argument in favor of government censorship of social networking discussions. Construct an argument opposing such censorship. After constructing both arguments, consider: Why do you think the Chinese government chooses to censor social networking discussions?

2. Is censorship appropriate if it ferrets out pornography and commercial scams?

3. Do you think censorship exists on American social networks? What evidence can you present to defend your point of view? Do you think any form of censorship should be appropriate on American social networks?

THOMAS GOETZ (thomas@wired.com) is the executive editor of Wired.

From *Wired*, April 24, 2012. Copyright © 2012 by Conde Nast Publications, Inc. All rights reserved. Reprinted by permission.

Weighing Watson's Impact

Does IBM's Watson represent a distinct breakthrough in machine learning and natural language processing or is the 2,880-core wunderkind merely a solid feat of engineering?

IBM's Watson soundly defeated the two most successful contestants in the history of the game show "Jeopardy!," Ken Jennings and Brad Rutter, in a three-day competition in February.

KIRK L. KROEKER

In the history of speculative fiction, from the golden age of science fiction to the present, there are many examples of artificial intelligences engaging their interlocutors in dialogue that exhibits self-awareness, personality, and even empathy. Several fields in computer science, including machine learning and natural language processing, have been steadily approaching the point at which real-world systems will be able to approximate this kind of interaction. IBM's Watson computer, the latest example in a long series of efforts in this area, made a television appearance earlier this year in a widely promoted human-versus-machine "Jeopardy!" game show contest. To many observers, Watson's appearance on "Jeopardy!" marked a milestone on the path toward achieving the kind of sophisticated, knowledge-based interaction that has traditionally been relegated to the realm of fiction.

The "Jeopardy!" event, in which Watson competed against Ken Jennings and Brad Rutter, the two most successful contestants in the game show's history, created a wave of coverage across mainstream and social media. During the three-day contest in February, hints of what might be called Watson's quirky personality shone through, with the machine wagering oddly precise amounts, guessing at answers after wildly misinterpreting clues, but ultimately prevailing against its formidable human opponents.

Leading up to the million-dollar challenge, Watson played more than 50 practice matches against former "Jeopardy!" contestants, and was required to pass the same tests that humans must take to qualify for the show and compete against Jennings, who broke the "Jeopardy!" record for the most consecutive games played, resulting in winnings of more than $2.5 million, and Rutter, whose total winnings amounted to $3.25 million, the most money ever won by a single "Jeopardy!" player. At the end

of the three-day event, Watson finished with $77,147, beating Jennings, who had $24,000, and Rutter, who had $21,600. The million-dollar prize money awarded to Watson went to charity.

Named after IBM founder Thomas J. Watson, the Watson system was built by a team of IBM scientists whose goal was to create a standalone platform that could rival a human's ability to answer questions posed in natural language. During the "Jeopardy!" challenge, Watson was not connected to the Internet or any external data sources. Instead, Watson operated as an independent system contained in several large floor units housing 90 IBM Power 750 servers with a total of 2,880 processing cores and 15 terabytes of memory. Watson's technology, developed by IBM and several contributing universities, was guided by principles described in the Open Advancement of Question-Answering (OAQA) framework, which is still operating today and facilitating ongoing input from outside institutions.

Judging by the sizeable coverage of the event, Watson piqued the interest of technology enthusiasts and the general public alike, earning "Jeopardy!" the highest viewer numbers it had achieved in several years and leading to analysts and other industry observers speculating about whether Watson represents a fundamental new idea in computer science or merely a solid feat of engineering. Richard Doherty, the research director at Envisioneering Group, a technology consulting firm based in Seaford, NY, was quoted in an Associated Press story as saying that Watson is "the most significant breakthrough of this century."

Doherty was not alone in making such claims, although the researchers on the IBM team responsible for designing Watson have been far more modest in their assessment of the technology they created. "Watson is a novel approach and a powerful architecture," says David Ferrucci, director of the IBM DeepQA research team that created Watson. Ferrucci does characterize

Watson as a breakthrough in artificial intelligence, but he is careful to qualify this assertion by saying that the breakthrough is in the development of artificial-intelligence systems.

"The breakthrough is how we pulled everything together, how we integrated natural language processing, information retrieval, knowledge representation, machine learning, and a general reasoning paradigm," says Ferrucci. "I think this represents a breakthrough. We would have failed had we not invested in a rigorous scientific method and systems engineering. Both were needed to succeed."

Contextual Evidence

The DeepQA team was inspired by several overarching design principles, with the core idea being that no single algorithm or formula would accurately understand or answer all questions, says Ferrucci. Rather, the idea was to build Watson's intelligence from a broad collection of algorithms that would probabilistically and imperfectly interpret language and score evidence from different perspectives. Watson's candidate answers, those answers in which Watson has the most confidence, are produced from hundreds of parallel hypotheses collected and scored from contextual evidence.

Ferrucci says this approach required innovation at the systems level so individual algorithms could be developed independently, then evaluated for their contribution to the system's overall performance. The approach allowed for loosely coupled interaction between algorithm components, which Ferrucci says ultimately reduced the need for team-wide agreement. "If every algorithm developer had to agree with every other or reach some sort of consensus, progress would have been slowed," he says. "The key was to let different members of the team develop diverse algorithms independently, but regularly perform rigorous integration testing to evaluate relative impact in the context of the whole system."

Ferrucci and the DeepQA team are expected to release more details later this year in a series of papers that will outline how they dealt with specific aspects of the Watson design. For now, only bits and pieces of the complete picture are being disclosed. Ferrucci says that, looking ahead, his team's research agenda is to focus on how Watson can understand, learn, and interact more effectively. "Natural language understanding remains a tremendously difficult challenge, and while Watson demonstrated a powerful approach, we have only scratched the surface," he says. "The challenge continues to be about how you build systems to accurately connect language to some representation, so the system can automatically learn from text and then reason to discover evidence and answers."

Lillian Lee, a professor in the computer science department at Cornell University, says the reactions about Watson's victory echo the reactions following Deep Blue's 1997 victory over chess champion Garry Kasparov, but with several important differences. Lee, whose research focus is natural language processing, points out that some observers were dismissive about Deep Blue's victory, suggesting that the system's capability was due largely to brute-force reasoning rather than machine learning.

The same criticism, she says, cannot be leveled at Watson because the overall system needed to determine how to assess and integrate diverse responses.

"Watson incorporates machine learning in several crucial stages of its processing pipeline," Lee says. "For example, reinforcement learning was used to enable Watson to engage in strategic game play, and the key problem of determining how confident to be in an answer was approached using machine-learning techniques, too."

Lee says that while there has been substantial research on the particular problems the "Jeopardy!" challenge involved for Watson, that prior work should not diminish the team's accomplishment in advancing the state of the art to Watson's championship performance. "The contest really showcased real-time, broad-domain question-answering, and provided as comparison points two extremely formidable contestants," she says. "Watson represents an absolutely extraordinary achievement."

Lee suggests that with language processing technologies now maturing, with the most recent example of such maturation being Watson, the field appears to have passed through an important early stage. It now faces an unprecedented opportunity in helping sift through the massive amounts of user-generated content online, such as opinion-oriented information in product reviews or political analysis, according to Lee.

While natural-language processing is already used, with varying degrees of success, in search engines and other applications, it might be some time before Watson's unique question-answering capabilities will help sift through online reviews and other user-generated content. Even so, that day might not be too far off, as IBM has already begun work with Nuance Communications to commercialize the technology for medical applications. The idea is for Watson to assist physicians and nurses in finding information buried in medical tomes, prior cases, and the latest science journals. The first commercial offerings from the collaboration are expected to be available within two years.

Beyond medicine, likely application areas for Watson's technology would be in law, education, or the financial industry. Of course, as with any technology, glitches and inconsistencies will have to be worked out for each new domain. Glitches notwithstanding, technology analysts say that Watsonlike technologies will have a significant impact on computing in particular and human life in general. Ferrucci, for his part, says these new technologies likely will mean a demand for higher-density hardware and for tools to help developers understand and debug machine-learning systems more effectively. Ferrucci also says it's likely that user expectations will be raised, leading to systems that do a better job at interacting in natural language and sifting through unstructured content.

To this end, explains Ferrucci, the DeepQA team is moving away from attempting to squeeze ever-diminishing performance improvements out of Watson in terms of parsers and local components. Instead, they are focusing on how to use context and information to evaluate competing interpretations more effectively. "What we learned is that, for this approach to extend beyond one domain, you need to implement a positive feedback loop of extracting basic syntax and local semantics from language, learning from context, and then interacting with users and a broader community to acquire knowledge that is otherwise difficult to extract," he says. "The system must be able to bootstrap and learn from its own failing with the help of this loop."

In an ideal future, says Ferrucci, Watson will operate much like the ship computer on "Star Trek," where the input can be expressed in human terms and the output is accurate and understandable. Of course, the "Star Trek" ship computer was largely humorless and devoid of personality, responding to queries and commands with a consistently even tone. If the "Jeopardy!" challenge serves as a small glimpse of things to come for Watson—in particular, Watson's precise wagers, which produced laughter in the audience, and Watson's visualization component, which appeared to express the state of a contemplative mind through moving lines and colors—the DeepQA team's focus on active learning might also include a personality loop so Watson can accommodate subtle emotional cues and engage in dialogue with the kind of good humor reminiscent of the most personable artificial intelligences in fiction.

Further Readings

Baker, S. *Final Jeopardy: Man vs. Machine and the Quest to Know Everything.* Houghton Mifflin Harcourt, New York, NY, 2011.

Ferrucci, D., Brown, E., Chu-Carroll, J., Fan, J., Gondek, D., Kalyanpur, A.A., Lally, A., Murdock, J.W., Nyberg, E., Prager, J., Schlaefer, N., and Welty, C. Building Watson: An overview of the DeepQA project, *AI Magazine 59*, Fall 2010.

Ferrucci, D., et al. Towards the Open Advancement of Question Answering Systems. *IBM Research Report RC24789 (W0904-093)*, April 2009.

Simmons, R.F. Natural language question-answering systems, *Communications of the ACM 13*, 1, Jan. 1970.

Strzalkowski, T., and Harabagiu, S. (Eds.) *Advances in Open Domain Question Answering.* Springer-Verlag, Secaucus, NJ, 2006.

Critical Thinking

1. IBM maintains a website about the Watson project: www-03.ibm.com/innovation/us/watson. Watch a few of the videos. IBM thinks that "this technology will impact the way humans communicate with computers." Do you agree?

2. Can you think of a downside to a Watson-like machine handing your health-care and finance questions? What about a Watson descendent teaching your classes?

3. What imperative is driving the computer industry to produce question-answering software? Who/what performs these tasks right now?

4. David Ferucci, the manager of the Watson project, is proud but modest about its accomplishments. Do they fall under the heading of science or engineering or both?

5. Watson defeated its opponents much more easily than Deep Blue did Gary Kasparov fifteen years ago. Use the Internet to see if anyone has commented on the two matches. Is chess harder or Watson smarter?

Based in Los Angeles, **KIRK L. KROEKER** is a freelance editor and writer specializing in science and technology.

From *Communications of the ACM*, July 2011. Copyright © 2011 by Association for Computing Machinery. Reprinted by permission.

Augmented Reality Is Finally Getting Real

As smartphones explode in popularity, augmented reality is starting to move from novelty to utility.

KIJI MCCAFFERTY

In the summer of 2009, Yelp quietly added a feature to its iPhone app that blurred the line between the real and the virtual. If you held your handset up and looked at the world through its screen, you'd see little floating tags containing the names, user ratings, and other details of businesses around you.

The feature, called Monocle, was an experiment with augmented reality—one of many that appeared around this time, as companies tossed around various ways to mesh digital content with the real world, hoping to catch consumers' eyes.

Several years later, augmented reality is still mostly used by early tech adopters, but it's starting to graze the mainstream, helped by the massive popularity of smartphones and tablets, and their constantly improving processors and sensors, along with the growth of high-speed wireless data networks. Apps featuring augmented reality are available for everything from gaming to driving to furniture arrangement. Slowly but surely, augmented reality is becoming less of a novelty and more of a utility.

While the term is only just becoming common parlance among consumers, augmented reality's history stretches back years: it has long been an area of academic research. Boeing used it with head-mounted displays in the 1990s to aid in aircraft wiring.

Early augmented-reality smartphone apps used a device's GPS and digital compass to determine your location and direction. More recently, app makers have begun incorporating computer vision and increasingly powerful processors to provide greater accuracy.

Jon Fisher, CEO and cofounder of San Francisco-based CrowdOptic, is one entrepreneur trying to take augmented reality mainstream. His startup's software can recognize the direction in which a crowd of people have their phones pointed while taking photos or videos at events, and invite the group to communicate, share content, or get more information about the object of their attention, via an app.

The software uses a smartphone's GPS, accelerometer, and compass to determine a user's position and line of site; but also to triangulate with other phones using the same software to determine specifically what everyone in a cluster is looking at. The company's technology has been used in a number of apps, including one for a recent NASCAR race in which fans, who couldn't see the entire 2.5-mile track, could point their phones at distant turns and get photos and videos generated by others who were closer to the action.

Another company, iOnRoad, offers an augmented-reality collision-warning app for drivers using smartphones that run Google's Android software (an iPhone version is in the works).

IOnRoad CEO Alon Atsmon says the app uses the phone's camera stream along with image processing software to identify relevant objects like the lane in which you're driving and the position of the car in front of you. GPS on your phone determines your speed. The app measures the distance between you and the car in front of you, and divides this by your speed to get a time gap. If the gap is perceived as too small, iOnRoad will warn you that you're not keeping enough distance. Among other things, the app can determine what lane you're driving in, and give you a warning if you start to drift, he says.

So far, nearly 500,000 people have downloaded the Android app since it was released late last year. Most of those chose a free version over a premium one that costs $4.99.

Moves by major companies—Google in particular—have helped make augmented reality seem less far-fetched. This spring, Google confirmed it is working on glasses that can show maps, messages, and other data to the wearer. In June, Google started allowing developers to preorder, for $1,500, a prototype called Project Glass that will be available in early 2013. While not strictly focused on augmented reality, Project Glass draws attention to the idea of a digital layer on top of the physical world.

"Definitely, the attention is good," says Pattie Maes, a professor at MIT's Media Lab who has done extensive research on augmented reality. "It will motivate all the other consumer electronics companies and cell-phone companies to look at this a lot more seriously."

For augmented reality to really become popular, however, a widespread number of apps will have to adopt it. Creative

Strategies analyst Ben Bajarin believes the breakthrough could be apps for museums or zoos—while standing cage-side, you might hold up your smartphone to learn more about a bear or a giraffe, for example.

In fact, several zoos and museums already have experimented with the technology. At Toronto's Royal Ontario Museum, for example, visitors can use iPads at a dinosaur exhibit to see how the beasts would have looked in real life. And augmented reality is about to get its biggest mass-market push yet: Swedish furniture maker Ikea's 2013 catalog, 211 million copies of which were shipped out Wednesday, includes additional content that readers can see with an Android or iOS app.

The move could be a good one, Bajarin says, assuming it works well. "You don't want people to try it and hate it, and go, 'Eh, I'm not going to use that again,'" he says.

Critical Thinking

1. How will augmented reality impact using Yelp to select a restaurant?

2. How will augmented reality impact the experience of retail shopping (such as at the grocery or in the shopping mall)?

3. Metz mentions the use of augmented reality at a NASCAR race. How might it be used to enhance the experience of watching a football, basketball, or baseball game? Should athletes be permitted to use augmented reality while playing a sport?

4. How do Wired Magazines seven rules inform the future of augmented reality (including Google Goggles)?

From *Technology Review*, August 2, 2012. Copyright © 2012 by MIT Press. Reprinted by permission via Copyright Clearance Center.

You Will Want Google Goggles

I thought that glasses with "augmented reality" would be hopelessly dorky and could never go mainstream—until I saw the technology in action.

Farhad Manjoo

At first glance, Thad Starner does not look out of place at Google. A pioneering researcher in the field of wearable computing, Starner is a big, charming man with unruly hair. But everyone who meets him does a double take, because mounted over the left lens of his eyeglasses is a small rectangle. It looks like a car's side-view mirror made for a human face. The device is actually a minuscule computer monitor aimed at Starner's eye; he sees its display—pictures, e-mails, anything—superimposed on top of the world, Terminator-style.

Starner's heads-up display is his own system, not a prototype of Project Glass, Google's recently announced effort to build augmented-reality goggles. In April, Google X, the company's special-projects lab, posted a video in which an imaginary user meanders around New York City while maps, text messages, and calendar reminders pop up in front of his eye—a digital wonderland overlaid on the analog world. Google says the project is still in its early phases; Google employees have been testing the technology in public, but the company has declined to show prototypes to most journalists, including myself.

Instead, Google let me speak to Starner, a technical lead for the project, who is one of the world's leading experts on what it's like to live a cyborg's life. He has been wearing various kinds of augmented-reality goggles full time since the early 1990s, which once meant he walked around with video displays that obscured much of his face and required seven pounds of batteries. Even in computer science circles, then, Starner has long been an oddity. I went to Google headquarters not only to find out how he gets by in the world but also to challenge him. Project Glass—and the whole idea of machines that directly augment your senses—seemed to me to be a nerd's fantasy, not a potential mainstream technology.

But as soon as Starner walked into the colorful Google conference room where we met, I began to question my skepticism. I'd come to the meeting laden with gadgets—I'd compiled my questions on an iPad, I was recording audio using a digital smart pen, and in my pocket my phone buzzed with updates. As we chatted, my attention wandered from device to device in the distracted dance of a tech-addled madman.

Starner, meanwhile, was the picture of concentration. His tiny display is connected to a computer he carries in a messenger bag, a machine he controls with a small, one-handed keyboard that he's always gripping in his left hand. He owns an Android phone, too, but he says he never uses it other than for calls (though it would be possible to route calls through his eyeglass system). The spectacles take the place of his desktop computer, his mobile computer, and his all-knowing digital assistant. For all its utility, though, Starner's machine is less distracting than any other computer I've ever seen. This was a revelation. Here was a guy wearing a computer, but because he could use it without becoming lost in it—as we all do when we consult our many devices—he appeared less in thrall to the digital world than you and I are every day. "One of the key points here," Starner says, "is that we're trying to make mobile systems that help the user pay more attention to the real world as opposed to retreating from it."

By the end of my meeting with Starner, I decided that if Google manages to pull off anything like the machine he uses, wearable computers seem certain to conquer the world. It simply will be better to have a machine that's hooked onto your body than one that responds to it relatively slowly and clumsily.

I understand that this might not seem plausible now. When Google unveiled Project Glass, many people shared my early take, criticizing the plan as just too geeky for the masses. But while it will take some time to get used to interactive goggles as a mainstream necessity, we have already gotten used to wearable electronics such as headphones, Bluetooth headsets, and health and sleep monitoring devices. And even though you don't exactly wear your smart phone, it derives its utility from its immediate proximity to your body.

In fact, wearable computers could end up being a fashion statement. They actually fit into a larger history of functional wearable objects—think of glasses, monocles, wristwatches, and whistles. "There's a lot of things we wear today that are just decorative, just jewelry," says Travis -Bogard, vice president of product management and strategy at Jawbone, which makes a line of fashion-conscious Bluetooth headsets. "When we talk about this new stuff, we think about it as 'functional jewelry.'" The trick for makers of wearable machines, Bogard explains, is to add utility to jewelry without negatively affecting aesthetics.

This wasn't possible 20 years ago, when the technology behind Starner's cyborg life was ridiculously awkward. But Starner points out that since he first began wearing his goggles, wearable computing has followed the same path as all digital technology—devices keep getter smaller and better, and as they do, they become ever more difficult to resist. "Back in 1993, the question I would always get was, 'Why would I want a mobile computer?'" he says. "Then the Newton came out and people were still like, 'Why do I want a mobile computer?' But then the Palm Pilot came out, and then when MP3 players and smart phones came out, people started saying, 'Hey, there's something really useful here.'" Today, -Starner's device is as small as a Bluetooth headset, and as researchers figure out ways to miniaturize displays—or even embed them into glasses and contact lenses—they'll get still less obtrusive.

At the moment, the biggest stumbling block may be the input device—Starner's miniature keyboard requires a learning curve that many consumers would find daunting, and keeping a trackpad in your pocket might seem a little creepy. The best input system eventually could be your voice, though it could take a few years to perfect that technology. Still, Starner says, the wearable future is coming into focus. "It's only been recently that these on-body devices have enough power, the networks are good enough, and the prices have gone down enough that it's actually capturing people's imagination," Starner says. "This display I'm wearing costs $3,000—that's not reasonable for most people. But I think you're going to see it happen real soon."

One criticism of Google's demo video of Project Glass is that it paints a picture of a guy lost in his own digital cocoon. But Starner argues that a heads-up display will actually tether you more firmly to real-life social interactions. He says the video's augmented—reality visualizations—images that are tied to real-world sights, like direction bubbles that pop up on the sidewalk, showing you how to get to your friend's house—are all meant to be relevant to what you're doing at any given point and thus won't seem like distracting interruptions.

Much of what I think you'll use goggles for will be the sort of quotidian stuff you do on your smart phone all the time—look up your next appointment on your calendar, check to see whether that last text was important, quickly fire up Shazam to learn the title of a song you heard on the radio. So why not just keep your smart phone? Because the goggles promise speed and invisibility. Imagine that one afternoon at work, you meet your boss in the hall and he asks you how your weekly sales numbers are looking. The truth is, you haven't checked your sales numbers in a few days. You could easily look up the info on your phone, but how obvious would that be? A socially aware heads-up display could someday solve this problem. At Starner's computer science lab at the Georgia Institute of Technology, grad students built a wearable display system that listens for "dual-purpose speech" in conversation—speech that seems natural to humans but is actually meant as a cue to the machine. For instance, when your boss asks you about your sales numbers, you might repeat, "This week's sales numbers?" Your goggles—with Siri-like prowess—would instantly look up the info and present it to you in your display.

You could argue that the glasses would open up all kinds of problems: would people be concerned that you were constantly recording them? And what about the potential for deeper distraction—goofing off by watching YouTube during a meeting, say? But Starner counters that most of these problems exist today. Your cell phone can record video and audio of everything around you, and your iPad is an ever—present invitation to goof off. Starner says we'll create social and design norms for digital goggles the way we have with all new technologies. For instance, you'll probably need to do something obvious—like put your hand to your frames—to take a photo, and perhaps a light will come on to signal that you're recording or that you're watching a video. It seems likely that once we get over the initial shock, goggles could go far in mitigating many of the social annoyances that other gadgets have caused.

I know this because during my hour-long conversation with Starner, he was constantly pulling up notes and conducting Web searches on his glasses, but I didn't notice anything amiss. To an outside observer, he would have seemed far less distracted than I was. "One of the coolest things is that this makes me more socially graceful," he says.

I got to see this firsthand when Starner let me try on his glasses. It took my eye a few seconds to adjust to the display, but after that, things began to look clearer. I could see the room around me, except now, hovering off to the side, was a computer screen. Suddenly I noticed something on the screen: Starner had left open some notes that a Google public-relations rep had sent him. The notes were about me and what Starner should and should not say during the interview, including "Try to steer the conversation away from the specifics of Project Glass." In other words, Starner was being coached, invisibly, right there in his glasses. And you know what? He'd totally won me over.

Critical Thinking

1. Beyond uses suggested in the article, what creative uses (software applications) can you brainstorm for Google Goggles?

2. How might wearing Google Goggles impact our everyday conversations with others? How might it impact ordering at a fast food restaurant? How might it impact driving? How might it impact your classroom experience?

FARHAD MANJOO is the technology columnist at Slate and contributes regularly to Fast Company and the New York Times. He is the author of True Enough: Learning to Live in a Post-Fact Society.

From *Technology Review*, July/August 2, 2012. Copyright © 2012 by MIT Press. Reprinted by permission via Copyright Clearance Center.

Gene Machine

Matthew Herper

The machine that could change your life is a compact device, only 24 inches wide, 20 inches deep and 21 inches high. At a glance you might mistake it for a Playskool toy—or, better yet, the Apple II computer, which sparked a revolution. Indeed, this gizmo, developed in a drab office park overlooking a duck pond in Guilford, Conn., could have as dramatic an impact as any technology since the personal computer and help kick off a market that one day could be worth perhaps as much as $100 billion.

Take a closer look. On the right side is an 8-inch touch-screen, on the left a dock that allows data to be downloaded to an iPhone. Below that is a row of four test tubes, marked with a circle, an X, a square and a plus sign. These symbols represent the four basic chemical letters, or bases, the body uses to form DNA—guanine, cytosine, adenine and thymine.

Audaciously named the Personal Genome Machine (PGM), the silicon-based device is the smallest and cheapest DNA decoder ever to hit the market. It can read 10 million letters of genetic code, with a high degree of accuracy, in just two hours. Unlike existing DNA scanners the size of mainframes and servers, it fits on a tabletop and sells for only $50,000, one-tenth the price of machines already out there. For the first time every scientist, local hospital and college will be able to afford one. If the PGM takes off and regulators let him, your family doctor could buy one—and so could you, if, say, you wanted to see how fast that thing growing in your fridge is mutating.

Invented by engineer and entrepreneur Jonathan Rothberg, such desktop gene machines could transform medicine, agriculture, nanotechnology and the search for alternative fuels. Using DNA sequencing, Rothberg says, doctors in the not-too-distant future will finger genetic weak spots in tumors and treat cancer patients with customized drugs. (This is already happening at some cancer centers.) Kids born with rare diseases will get large portions of their genome decoded to pinpoint the cause, eliminating guesswork and misdiagnoses.

Outside the lab, rescue workers in the Third World might use portable gene machines to trace bacteria or viruses causing waterborne epidemics. Airport officials could take genetic samples from travelers to track infectious bacteria and viruses before they become outbreaks. Engineers can use DNA readers to concoct designer microbes to grow future fuels. DNA sequencing will help farmers breed supercrops that grow faster, resist pests and drought and need less fertilizer. Synthetic biologists might harness bacteria to make laundry detergent, clothes, furniture, even concrete that self-heals cracks.

"Sequencing is going to affect everything," says Rothberg, 47. "This is biology's century—just [as] physics was the foundation of the last century." Citing the $100 billion medical imaging industry, he boasts, "I believe sequencing will be that big."

There's substance behind the bravado. An engineering geek with a flair for marketing, he has founded four genetics companies. His current startup, Ion Torrent, created the PGM just three years after Rothberg dreamed up the idea; a soft launch took place Dec. 14. The device has at least one big believer: Life Technologies, a $3 billion (sales) lab equipment maker, was so impressed that it bought his company for $375 million (plus milestones worth another $350 million or so) this fall, before the machine was done. "He has wonderfully romantic ideas and pulls together dream teams of people and doesn't let anyone get in his way," says Kevin Davies, who has a doctorate in molecular genetics and is author of The $1,000 Genome (Simon & Schuster, 2010).

You think you've heard this before, don't you? Genomics has certainly been overhyped—and so far failed to deliver on its promises. Many intelligent people have relegated the idea to the dusty corner shared by hopes for cold fusion, world peace and World Series rings for the Chicago Cubs. When scientists first mapped the human genome a decade ago, they bragged it would lead to cures for Alzheimer's, heart disease, schizophrenia and more. It hasn't happened. Drug approvals have gone down. The search for the genetic roots of heart disease, diabetes and other common ills has yielded surprisingly little useful information for the average person. Even 23andMe, the high-profile consumer gene-testing company cofounded by Anne Wojcicki, the wife of Google's Sergey Brin, had to lay off people last year.

The problem, Rothberg says, is that technology simply hasn't been powerful enough to decode the genetic secrets lurking behind diseases like cancer, lupus and autism. As you may or may not remember from high-school biology, there are 6 billion chemical letters that make up the DNA double helix at the center of every cell. Some of it is probably genetic gibberish; a lot of functions are waiting to be discovered. But scattered throughout that DNA are 20,000 genes, the recipe books that tell the body how to make proteins such as insulin, muscle, hemoglobin, brain tissue, bone, clotting factor—virtually everything in our bodies. A single wrong letter hidden deep inside a gene can boost the risk of colon cancer or diabetes.

Finding the errors that cause disease and distinguishing them from numerous harmless genetic variants is turning out to be an immense data-crunching challenge. But the technology to meet that challenge is also improving at an extraordinary rate. It took government researchers a decade to decode the first human genome at a cost of $3 billion to taxpayers. In a virtual tie with private efforts by gene maverick Craig Venter, the race was finally finished in 2001. Now you can get an accurate reading of a person's entire DNA sequence for only $10,000 in a few weeks. Nearly 3,000 people have gotten such scans, mostly as part of research studies. The number could soar to hundreds of thousands by 2012, say sequencing experts. "What is possible now . . . even a few years ago would have been unthinkable," National Institutes of Health director Francis Collins said in a recent speech.

Despite the steady drone of genetics studies in top medical journals, most scientists still don't have access to DNA-decoding technology. Existing sequencers are like computer mainframes in the 1960s. They cost $600,000, take a week to yield results and need scads of technicians to run them. Half of the 1,400 DNA-sequencing machines in the world reside at just 20 big academic and government research centers, according to Goldman Sachs.

Rothberg's machine could change all that through speed of analysis and wider dissemination of tools. He says that only 400 labs are currently doing this sort of genomics, and he wants the PGM to open the field to 4,000 research groups that are not participating. That will multiply the number of minds working on genetics problems and unleash lots of experiments that now languish on the sidelines. "I can create a fanatical user base, and people will start coming up with more and more applications for the technology," says Rothberg. "The demand is going to be enormous," predicts UC, Davis researcher Jonathan Eisen. "You're going to see a huge number of people buying it." George Church—a Harvard gene researcher, sequencing pioneer and Ion Torrent adviser—predicts the PGM will be "like an iPad" for geneticists. Everyone will want it "big-time, even if there are warts."

But as of now it's still a small-time business. Right now the market for DNA sequencing hardware is $1.5 billion, mostly through sales to scientists. Medical gene tests and other molecular diagnostics generate another $2.6 billion, according to PricewaterhouseCoopers.

How do you get from a $4 billion business to a $100 billion one? Rothberg's answer is that, like radiology, there will be armies of trained physicians using specialized machines, as gene scanning hits the medical mainstream; that gets expensive very quickly. Here are the assumptions—admittedly very speculative—for what could happen in 20 years:

- Cancer is the biggest near-term market. Today treating a cancer patient costs hundreds of thousands, sometimes millions, of dollars. Some breast cancer patients already get a specialized gene test to help determine what treatment is right for them. If similar gene tests become routine for all 4 million cancer patients in the United States and Europe, as many oncologists expect, this alone could be a $20 billion market. Some patients might be sequenced multiple times as a tumor spreads and mutates. Total so far: $40 billion.

- Another $10 billion market could come in scanning kids and adults with unexplained symptoms for rare inherited diseases or other genetic risk factors. A whole new medical specialty may sprout up to interpret the complicated data produced by gene scans and tell patients what it all means, another $10 billion. Now you're up to $60 billion.

- Tracking the movement of infections in hospitals, airports and public places like shopping malls to identify microbes and prevent them from becoming epidemics—that has to be a $10 billion industry. Running tab: $70 billion.

- If costs drop low enough, affluent people may start getting their genomes—or those of their newborn children—on a thumb drive as a precautionary measure. If 50 million people a year do this at a cost of $2,000 per test, that would bring the tally to $80 billion.

- The market for sequencing genes in agriculture, resulting in better mate selection in the livestock industry and for optimal seed selection to get maximum yields is, perhaps, a $5 billion market. Total thus far: $85 billion.

- Numerous other industrial applications, such as searching for designer biofuels, designing new enzymes for laundry detergent—and doing other things that haven't even been imagined yet could easily add another $15 billion over time. Et voilà: $100 billion.

Have we mentioned the ifs? Like all potentially disruptive innovations, gene sequencers could fizzle. Their success depends on unpredictable events: how fast the technology improves, how quickly researchers can make medical discoveries based on the new machines and—most critically—whether drugs can be developed to treat diseases. Gene test prices could drop, becoming a low-margin commodity like medical blood tests (cholesterol, blood sugar and so on), which, at a few bucks a pop, are a $40 billion business. Ultimately Rothberg's machine may not win. Like the Commodore 64 home computer that dominated in the 1980s and disappeared soon after, the PGM could be quickly eclipsed.

Rothberg faces three formidable hurdles. First, the market for sequencing is dominated by Illumina of San Diego, whose big machines have helped make most of the major discoveries so far—and competing won't be easy. Next, a novel (and faster) approach could leapfrog the Ion Torrent device. Finally, sequencing could ultimately be a bust if it proves tough to find genes linked to disease, or improved cancer diagnoses and hoped-for improvements in manufacturing drugs.

At least a dozen venture-backed companies are competing for the title. Pacific Biosciences in Menlo Park, Calif. raised $200 million in an October initial offering on top of $370 million of venture funding. Its machine is due in early 2011 and will be the first to scan a single DNA molecule. Nearby, in Mountain View, Complete Genomics (whose November IPO raised $90 million) is betting that DNA scanning will become a service industry like pathology where everything is sent to giant centralized labs.

Like early PCs, Rothberg's gizmo has limitations. It won't compete immediately with the monster machines from Illumina because it can decode only a tiny fraction of the human genome at a time. The first version of the PGM can read a modest 20 genes at once. This may be enough for many smaller jobs, as when a doctor wants to test a tumor for a small number of disease-causing genes and whether a certain drug is likely to work on a particular tumor, or if an infectious-disease researcher wants to verify which strain of microbe is present in a saliva sample or water source.

Race to the Future   New, Powerful DNA Decoders Are a Fast-Growing Market, According to Goldman Sachs. Here Is a Rundown of the Players.

Company	Position/Battle Plan
ILLUMINA San Diego, Calif.	The leader. Lowered cost of sequencing a human genome below $10,000. It has 63% market share of next-gen sequencers and is betting on new technologies to maintain its lead. Annual sequencing sales: $450 million.
LIFE TECHNOLOGIES Carlsbad, Calif.	The comeback? Once the only maker of DNA sequencers it now has only a 17% share of next-gen machines, though it still sells older models. Can devices like the Ion Torrent Personal Gene Machine help it grap back the cutting edge?
COMPLETE GENOMICS Mountain View, Calif.	The factory. The company sells DNA sequencing at a bulk rate from a single, giant complex. It counts Pfizer and Eli Lilly as customers and says it can sequence 400 genomes per month.
PACIFIC BIOSCIENCES Menlo Park, Calif.	Speed reader. PacBio is the first sequencer to read single molecules of DNA. It is fast and potentially useful for infections and cancer, but some experts worry the error rate is too high. PacBio says the errors average out.
OXFORD NANOPORE Oxford, U.K.	The next wave. Its device reads a single molecule of DNA in a way that could become very cheap. It is still at least three years away, but its alliance with Illumina could be a powerful marketing advantage.
ROCHE AND IBM Basel, Switzerland and Armonk, N.Y.	The giants. Roche has the first of the new sequencers (the one invited by Rothberg): this 454 sequencer has 18% market share. Its next bet is on "DNA transistor" technology from IBM that could be fast and cheap.

Sources: Goldman Sachs Analyst Isaac Ro; Company Statements; Forbes Reporting.

Illumina Chief Executive Jay Flatley claims the PGM poses no threat. "We've gone faster than anybody thought we could," he says. Indeed, his machines can crunch a thousand times as much data as the PGM. "That has relegated everybody else to niche markets." More proof: Illumina's shares are up 700% over five years. His team is working on many next-generation technologies that could render Ion Torrent obsolete, including one that will read a single DNA molecule. That's huge. Right now detection isn't able to do this and instead requires thousands of copies of molecules to be made.

But Rothberg's secret sauce is rapid scalability. Because his gene machine is the first DNA decoder to rely on silicon transistors, it should improve performance very quickly; he says an upgrade, due out in the first half of 2011, will be ten times as powerful as the original. He explains he is building on the $1 trillion already spent on microchip R&D and manufacturing. "Once you move to a semiconductor device, obviously taking advantage of Moore's Law"—that you can double the number of transistors on a chip every 18 months—"things get cheaper and they become ubiquitous," he says.

He vows to have a machine by 2012 that will decode in two hours all 20,000 human genes that code for proteins. (This is roughly 3% of all DNA and will still be far behind Illumina, which can do all the DNA twice.) Eventually, he hopes to create a machine the size of an iPad. "There isn't a technology that we will not pass in a very short period of time," he says. "It doesn't matter how far ahead they are."

Behind the swagger lies a serious mission. Rothberg's 14-year-old daughter, the oldest of his five kids, has a mild form of an inherited disease called tuberous sclerosis complex, a relatively rare disorder (50,000 or so Americans have it) that can cause benign tumors in the heart, kidney, skin, lungs, eyes and brain, where seizures can occur. Gene scanning might help nail the causes so that drugmakers can find a cure. "All motivation forever has been personal," Rothberg says, "because we all want to affect the people we love," adding: "If it [were] just intellectual, I would have a company now doing artificial life . . . making non-DNA."

Rothberg grew up in New Haven, Conn. in a family of science-oriented entrepreneurs. His father, a chemical engineer, owns a company that makes high-performance adhesive for tiles. As a kid Jonathan went on sales calls with his dad. In college at Carnegie Mellon, where he majored in chemical engineering, he idolized Steve Jobs and went to hear him speak. He still has a 1982 Time magazine cover story on the Apple founder.

He founded his first company, Curagen, in his basement in 1991 soon after getting a doctorate in biochemistry from Yale. It was one of the first biotech firms to automate the search for new genes with robots and easy-to-repeat experiments.

The timing was great. Just a few years later Craig Venter started making headlines for his gene-sequencing work—giving biotechnology a lofty place alongside the dot-com boom. Curagen went public in 1999. By the next year it had a market cap of $5 billion, bigger than American Airlines. In 2001 Curagen notched one of the biggest biotech deals of its time, a $1.5 billion agreement with Bayer to develop drugs for obesity and diabetes.

Like most of its high-flying genomics peers, Curagen was soon in Icarus free fall. Its lead drug to treat chemotherapy side effects failed, and the Bayer deal yielded nothing fast. Investors started to bail. Rothberg got pushed out in 2004. In 2009 drug developer Celldex Therapeutics of Needham, Mass. bought the remnants of Curagen for just $95 million.

While still at Curagen Rothberg realized that better technology was needed to make genetic medicine a reality. When Noah, his second child, was born in 1999, he had to be sent to the neonatal intensive care unit because of breathing troubles. Noah turned out to be fine, but Rothberg was frustrated that doctors didn't have a rapid test to ensure his son didn't have an inherited disease. Sitting in the hospital waiting room, he thought about the similarities between gene sequencing and microelectronics. Existing DNA sequencers, he reasoned, used clunky technology akin to computers based on vacuum tubes. He thought he could do better. He infuriated his wife by spending most of his paternity leave working on the new technology that used firefly enzymes to read DNA with light.

The idea evolved into 454 Life Sciences, a Curagen subsidiary Rothberg created to commercialize the new machine. He clung to 454, even after he left Curagen, announcing with dramatic flair in 2005 that he would use the machine to decipher the genome of DNA codiscoverer James Watson for only $1 million, far lower than anything before. The project finished on budget in 2007. By that time Rothberg had lost control of 454. Curagen sold it to Roche for $140 million in 2007 to raise cash; Rothberg's creation is still on the market but has been crushed by machines from rival Illumina.

Rothberg himself is indestructible. It's a little hard to tell whether the 8-foot-high slabs, made of 700 tons of Norwegian granite, he recently installed in his back yard is a monument to Stonehenge—or to his own obstinacy. His neighbors in Guilford hate "The Circle of Life," as the sculpture is known. "I don't do anything out of spite," says Rothberg.

A conversation with his son Noah in 2007 led to the founding of Ion Torrent. Acting the precocious 8-year-old he was, Noah asked his dad to invent a machine to read minds. Rothberg, addressing the boy as he would a peer, told him the best way to do that would be to create a tiny chemical sensor that could read electrical signals passing between brain cells. It slowly dawned on Rothberg that a sensor like that could be used for DNA sequencing.

Most existing DNA sequencers (including the 454 machine) do their reading by attaching light-producing molecules to DNA, taking pictures and analyzing the resulting image. This optical technology requires all sorts of complicated cameras and robotics, along with huge data files to handle the images.

Rothberg's elegant contribution was to come up with a sensor that directly reads telltale electrical signals produced as DNA copies itself. This vastly simplifies the process and allows engineers to make machines for far less. He founded Ion Torrent with an undisclosed amount of his own money in 2007 and later took in $23 million in venture capital. Still smarting from the loss of 454, he made sure this time to retain a supervoting share majority so he couldn't be forced out.

At the heart of the personal genome machine is a silicon chip with 21 million transistors on it—the equivalent of a desktop computer circa 1995. On top of the chip is a tiny channel the width of two human hairs into which DNA is fed. Each DNA molecule in the body contains two long strands of chemical letters, or bases—A,T, C and G—that come together like a twisted ladder (a.k.a. the double helix). The machine takes a single DNA strand and uses an enzyme to attach bases to it. Every time the enzyme connects two bases—an A to a T or a C to a G—an electrically charged ion is released and detected by sensors on the machine. By exposing the DNA sample to only one letter at the time, the machine can reconstruct the entire sequence.

"It is an absolutely beautiful machine," says Randy Scott, chairman of the cancer-gene tester Genomic Health. He adds that his company may switch to the Ion Torrent machines if they live up to their potential. "Jonathan has done a great job at staying ahead of the curve."

That curve is arcing toward guiding cancer treatment. Illumina's Flatley has had his own genome sequenced and learned that he has a gene for a condition that causes people to get a rash when they are cold. His company is seeing "a stream of infants and cancer patients" who want their genomes sequenced. Life Technologies has signed up a network of cancer centers to probe tumors with its current mainframe system. If a DNA scan of a tumor can predict which treatment will work best, insurers will likely pay up, even though treating cancer patients can be hugely expensive.

But existing machines from Illumina and Life Technologies can take up to eight days to return any data—an

eternity for cancer patients who need treatment right away. Moreover, the current technology forces cancer pathologists to wait that entire time, even if they just want to analyze a few genes. It's almost like the difference between waiting for a letter and a text message.

Right now all DNA sequencers are only approved for research use, but scientists are trying to move them into clinical practice anyway. Gordon Mills, chairman of the department of molecular therapeutics at MD Anderson Cancer Center in Houston, says such use is "imminent." He is starting a project to sequence 1,000 genes that might serve as targets for cancer drugs in 10,000 patients. He hopes to figure out if this improves the odds for sick patients, as well as to find ways to get and store tumor samples, save data afterward—and leap over barriers set up by Medicare and the Food & Drug Administration.

Rothberg sees potential health care applications for the PGM. Doctors already use genetic mutations in HIV to predict which drugs a patient's virus will be able to fight off. They are always looking for better ways to do this, and the PGM could help, he says.

He says his next machine, due within six months, will data mine 200 or more genes at a time, and that's what oncologists need right now to make diagnoses and pick drugs. That's just what Massachusetts General Hospital pathologist John Iafrate, who received a free sequencer as part of a contest Ion Torrent held to drum up interest in the technology, is hoping to prove.

There are plenty of uses beyond cancer treatment. Because Rothberg and his wife are both Ashkenazi Jews, they were advised to get 15 genetic tests (for such things as Tay-Sachs disease) before they had children. This, too, he says, represents a perfect niche for the PGM. As new disease genes are discovered by sequencing hundreds of thousands of people, a swelling population will undergo specific panels of tests of 15 genes or more.

Another free-machine recipient, Mitchell Sogin of the Marine Biology Laboratory in Woods Hole, has developed a way to use DNA sequencing to track down sources of fecal contamination in drinking water in developing countries and elsewhere. He is currently using 454 machines for the project but hopes the PGM will be fast enough to pinpoint the source of microbes in real time. Ion Torrent has competition here. In December Pacific Biosciences used its DNA reader to identify the lethal cholera germ in Haiti. The data proved that the microbes did not travel across the ocean, as some feared, and were instead carried by human hosts who might have been caught by better screening.

Ironically, perhaps, the first iteration of Rothberg's genome machine is poorly suited to the one market closest to his heart: rare inherited diseases. These are "at the core of everything I do," he says. There are roughly 6,000 such diseases, including Charcot-Marie-Tooth, a neurological disorder, and Miller Syndrome, characterized by severe facial and limb deformities. Their causes are being identified using DNA scanning. And a few kids had their treatment changed as well. Some diseases may not be so rare. Autism could turn out to be a collection of unusual genetic defects that produce similar symptoms.

Rothberg won't openly discuss his daughter, who was diagnosed with tuberous sclerosis complex (TSC) in 1997 when she was an infant. And yet, during conversations, he constantly steers the subject back to the disease, even though it makes him emotional.

In 2001 Rothberg and his wife, Bonnie, a medical epidemiologist, started the Rothberg Institute for Childhood Diseases in Guilford, near his 11-acre home, to speed the hunt for rare disease cures. Two genes that cause most cases of TSC are already known. Rothberg's Institute is sponsoring a search for a third. In 2003 a small clinical trial sponsored by the Institute showed that the generic transplant drug rapamycin targeted the two bad genes and helped tuberous sclerosis symptoms, making some skin lesions go away. In the wake of the results Novartis decided to test its similar medicine, Afinitor, in kids with the condition. It worked and is now approved for preventing brain tumors in kids with the disease.

Rothberg says a few years ago he would have snapped at anyone who told him that TSC might be curable. "I would have said you're naive, the kidney's damaged, the skin's damaged," he says. Now he is much more optimistic.

There are still respected scientists who think genomic sequencing is doomed to stay forever in the labs, absorbing funds in absurd proportion to the benefits they provide. Cynics are advised to recall what Kenneth Olsen, founder of minicomputer maker Digital Equipment Corp., once told the World Future Society: "There is no reason for any individual to have a computer in his home."

Critical Thinking

1. How do Wired Magazines seven rules inform the future of gene sequencing?

2. Apply Postman's five ideas to the Personal Genome Machine.

From *Forbes*, January 2011, pp. 68–77. Copyright © 2011 by Forbes Inc. Reprinted by permission of Forbes Media LLC.

Test-Your-Knowledge Form

We encourage you to photocopy and use this page as a tool to assess how the articles in *Annual Editions* expand on the information in your textbook. By reflecting on the articles you will gain enhanced text information. You can also access this useful form on a product's book support website at www.mhhe.com/cls.

NAME: _____ DATE: _____

TITLE AND NUMBER OF ARTICLE:
_____

BRIEFLY STATE THE MAIN IDEA OF THIS ARTICLE:
_____

LIST THREE IMPORTANT FACTS THAT THE AUTHOR USES TO SUPPORT THE MAIN IDEA:

_____

WHAT INFORMATION OR IDEAS DISCUSSED IN THIS ARTICLE ARE ALSO DISCUSSED IN YOUR TEXTBOOK OR OTHER READINGS THAT YOU HAVE DONE? LIST THE TEXTBOOK CHAPTERS AND PAGE NUMBERS:

_____

LIST ANY EXAMPLES OF BIAS OR FAULTY REASONING THAT YOU FOUND IN THE ARTICLE:

_____

LIST ANY NEW TERMS/CONCEPTS THAT WERE DISCUSSED IN THE ARTICLE, AND WRITE A SHORT DEFINITION:

NOTES

NOTES

NOTES

NOTES

NOTES

NOTES

NOTES

NOTES